THE HOME ON GORHAM STREET

and the Voices of Its Children

THE HOME ON GORHAM STREET

and the Voices of Its Children

Howard Goldstein

THE UNIVERSITY OF ALABAMA PRESS

Tuscaloosa and London

THE UNIVERSITY OF ALABAMA PRESS

Tuscaloosa, Alabama 35487-0380

All rights reserved

Manufactured in the

United States of America

DESIGNED BY ERIN T. BRADLEY

The photograph on the title page shows residents of the Rochester Jewish Children's Home, wearing crepe-paper hats for a celebration, circa 1923. (Courtesy Jewish Family Service of Rochester, New York, Inc.)

∞

The paper on which this book is printed

meets the minimum requirements

of American National Standard

for Information Science-Permanence of Paper

for Printed Library Materials,

ANSI Z39.48-1984.

Library of Congress Cataloging-in-Publication Data

Goldstein, Howard, 1922–

The home on Gorham Street and the voices of its children / Howard Goldstein.

p.   cm.

Includes bibliographical references (p.   ) and index.

ISBN 0-8173-0781-8 (acid-free paper)

1.   Jewish Children's Home (Rochester, N.Y.)—History. 2.   Jewish orphanages—New York (State)—Rochester—History. 3.   Orphans—New York (State)—Rochester—Social conditions.

HV995.R62J494   1995

362.7′ 32′ 0974789—dc20   95-1934

British Library Cataloguing-in-Publication Data available

Will and Mim Greenberg
Phil and Iris Nusbaum

and all the
"kids" of the old
Home on Gorham Street

CONTENTS

Contents

ILLUSTRATIONS

PREFACE

Gorham Street and the Rochester Jewish Children's Home were gone. That was the first discovery. The second immediately followed: the extinction of Gorham Street meant that my old pile of a home also was gone. A fragment of the old street remained, only now it was St. Bridget's Place, just a curved stub bearing the name of its one dreary survivor, the red brick Catholic church that once served a succession of immigrants—the Germans, the Irish, the Italians. In my time, you could stand at Weber's barber shop at the corner of Clinton Avenue and look straight down the three blocks—my house was right there in the middle—to the workingman's bar at the corner of St. Paul Street. Now, as your eye follows the short curve, there is only the corner of a factory parking lot to be seen where our home once stood. No historical markers remain to give witness to the fact that at one time No. 27 housed a multitude of energetic and restless youngsters while, for all of my youth, my family occupied No. 36 across the street.

In the sixties and seventies, the old neighborhood was scraped away to make space for public housing for the black and Hispanic families who replaced, as was the case in many northern cities, the previous residents, the Jews and Italians. Acres of what the public housing people euphemistically call "garden apartments" spread over the crisscrossed pattern of streets that shaped the neighborhood.

Like incisions, the main thoroughfares that slice through the area open to view the decay and ruin typical of northern industrial towns. Joseph Avenue, for one, never pretended to be a charming parkway or boulevard; now there remains only a shadow of its former robust, coarse, and lively ethnic commerce. It's been a long time since Joseph Avenue sent up its bouquet of Yiddish delights; the sweet-acrid smell of the pickle or herring barrels sitting in front of the old delicatessens, the rich buttery fragrances flowing out of the creameries, or the redolence of fresh-baked rye or pumpernickel.

Although it was a poor neighborhood then, it was alive with people who were joined by kinship and their Old Country identities and values. It is an even poorer neighborhood now, bereft even of the bright hopes that once inspired ardor and ambition. But this is not a story of two ghettos, one old, the other aging too quickly, places where poverty and the struggle to get by literally go with the territory. It is the study of a place, its people, and their lives—specifically, an institution and its children once firmly planted (we thought, forever) at the center of this community with its own culture and faith.

The thought of "going home again" holds a kind of morbid lure. Among its promises is physical proof of the reality of one's earlier existence and its memories. This thought occurred to me many times over the years. But now, after fifty years, I had a solid and estimable reason and the credentials to return—namely, to reconstruct the social history of the Jewish Children's Home and to recapture as an ethnographer the lives of "the kids" who had been the young wards of that institution.

By returning, I hoped first to use the Children's Home as a representative example of institutional services that antedated current practices in child care. More than just a historical account, I saw the opportunity to bring this study to life by making it possible for some of the dwindling number of aging graduates of the Home to offer their first-hand reminiscences and impressions about what it was like to live and grow up in—by present standards—such an archaic institution. I anticipated that their narratives might offer fresh insights on what it takes for a child to survive, overcome, and succeed. Not the least was the possibility that the results of this study might be instructive for contemporary child-care practices and policies.

My intent, methods, and procedures were disciplined by a high order of scholarship: still, I was not hoodwinking myself into believing that this was a purely impersonal investigation. That I shared a common history with many of my respondents necessarily affected the research process. At the same time, this sharing enriched this inquiry. We, the former residents and myself, were part of the same idiom, culture, and history. We knew, almost naturally, what to begin to ask about and where to look in these, our later years, to make sense of what our earlier years had been all about.

For over three decades, the children of the Home came and went, many not knowing any other home. But the Home itself persisted within its own cultural and physical world until its doors finally shut in 1947. Folks in the neighborhood and the surrounding Jewish community casually referred to it as "the orphanage," though it held very few parentless children. To the kids, then and now, it always was and still is "The Home," a designation that has as much to do with identity and belonging, with important relationships, with a sense of security, as it does with the physical institution as a structure.

"Institution" is a harsh word both as sound and symbol, evoking stony images of coldness and isolation. The structure of the Home on Gorham Street did not itself help soften that image by much. The collection of flat yellow, brown-trimmed, slate-roofed brick buildings dominating its part of the block was, like some of the houses on the street, faintly Victorian in style. The little gray-white stuccoed synagogue with its few stained glass windows, erected in the center of the grounds during the Home's midlife, did its bit to relieve the starkness of the rest of the architecture. A gravel driveway flanked by scraggly lawns separated the Girls House from the main buildings that housed the boys' dormitories, the long open washroom, the superintendent's office, the dining room, and small library.

Paradoxically, the discovery that every marker of my youth—the street, the

Children's Home, my home—had been erased led me to broaden the original scope and motif of the project. The strong sense of loss of the anchor for my memories compelled me to re-create in words and pictures at least a rough likeness of that neighborhood and community. More important, it seemed that to make vital sense of the children's lives, it would be essential to include the communal as well as the individual, the tribal as well as the personal. This intuition was soundly affirmed when I was welcomed into narratives of the former residents' lives.

Their stories were, of course, personal, often intimately so. But each individual's recollections were typically wrapped in the bundle of others' lives and experiences: in their stories, the *I* was always part of the *We*, and *We* was firmly bound by community and culture. In any text, including the personal narrative, context is basic to meaning. And so, to understand these lives and the existence of the institution itself, they needed to be viewed against their horizon of community, neighborhood, group, culture, and faith.

It is this principle, *context informs meaning*, that determines the logic and structure of this book. It is context that lends substance to the stories of lives so generously and openly imparted. Context also comprises the historical, philosophical, theological, social, and situational influences that permit the institution to be known not just as an austere edifice but also as a mortal being in its own right.

Chapter 1 accounts as it should for the beginnings—commencing, after almost a half century, with a renewal of my ties with two of the Home's alumni, Will and Phil. Both retired social workers, they proved to be my sources of wisdom, my guides, my mentors, over the long course of this study. Here and in the subsequent chapters, the stories told to me by one or another of thirty other alumni of the Home are called on to animate a point, to give life to a concept or impression. In all but two instances, the actual first names of the Home's former residents are used in this narrative for various reasons. First, no one had any hesitation about being identified; many, in fact, wanted their names to accompany their recollections and thoughts. Second, since I shared a common background with all of them and familiarity with most—conditions not generally prevalent in formal research—it would have been clumsy and inappropriate for me to step out of this role. Many remembered and referred to me as "Howie," and would have no doubt guffawed had I tried to assume the researcher pose. Third, I will make the point many times that every conversation was marked by two voices: one is that of the elder who recounts and reviews a life span; the other, the voice of the child who endured those early institutional years. Each was still one of the "kids." Only first names capture this dual identity, but full names will be found in the index. Finally, as I will later note, the inspiration and model for this book is Barbara Myerhoff's study, *Number Our Days*, a gentle and moving account of elderly Jewish men and women. The strength of her work is its flowing, narrative quality, unencumbered by certain formalities of social science research. Research methods—ethnography and social history—and their rationales are elucidated. A sketch of the old immigrant community, embracing its physical, tribal, cultural, and religious character begins to set the context. The broader purposes of this study and its implications for current issues in child care are noted.

Chapter 2 surveys historical origins of philosophies and schemes of group child care that influenced and provided the foundations for the doctrines and arrangements of the Children's Home. Early views of childhood, behavioral and moral expectations, institutional regulations, and the orphanage as an unusual setting for women's involvement are discussed. We move forward to the changes in child care in the Progressive Era of the early twentieth century. The contributions of such leaders as Drs. Reeder and Bernstein are noted. A comparison of Reform and Orthodox Jewish orphanages shows why the first was responsive to progress and development in child care while the Orthodox held fast to its traditions.

Chapter 3 covers the nature of the catastrophes that wrecked immigrant families and the community's response that led to the conception and organization of the Jewish Children's Home in 1914. Its mission: to shelter and provide for dependent children and to build citizenship, virtue, and self-reliance under Orthodox training. The first children admitted are shown to represent the special ordeals of the wards of the Home's first era. The vital and caring auxiliaries are created.

Chapter 4 includes facts and figures. Facts take in: admissions and procedures; data from the Home's records of families and children; population shifts indicating that the first children, victims of family catastrophes of death and illness, are later replaced by problem children of divorce and conflict. Figures literally refer to significant men and women, community leaders and philanthropists, whose brief biographies show their commitments and contributions to the Home. The routines, procedures, and ironies of life in the Home are sketched.

Chapter 5 considers a paradox: although the Children's Home was plainly perceived as a harsh and, in many ways, unpleasant asylum by its former residents, it was also plainly confirmed that it was also *their home.* That the stern patriarchal control and regimentation coexisted with a benevolent "extended family," the generosities of the community auxiliaries, is carefully examined. Here it is done "objectively," from an "outside" perspective and the Home's newsletters and other archival sources. A year in the midlife of the Home is selected to represent the regimentation, rituals, procedures, holidays, entertainments, work of auxiliaries, gifts and endowments, achievements, and other events that suggest the order as well as the opportunities of life in the institution.

Chapter 6 balances the objective view with the subjective recollections of the graduates about "how it really was for us." Definitive themes personify such issues as coping with discipline, routines, and demands for piety and devotion; the positive consequences of group identity and comradeship; stigma and its meaning; the centrality of play in the achievement of mastery and self-reli-ance—and typically, avoidance of the victim role.

Chapter 7 focuses on the specific lives of some of the Home's children over time. Their accounts and meanings reveal the importance of ingrained pro-cesses: caring and trust, the ironies typical of institutional life, the adaptive functions of play that encourage and nurture resilience and mastery. Three groups are considered. First, the odd, disabled, or "deviant" kids who were protected and helped by the "big kids." Second, three lives that individually portray overcoming, victory, and inexplicable tragedy. Third, the lives of the respondents—from institutional childhood onto maturity and adulthood and now, life in their later years. Their themes include not losing the fight, making what you can out of what little there is, and, above all, the unrelenting drive to become a "mensch."

Before its focus on conclusions and implications, chapter 8 first presents two instructive views of how and why the Home closed its doors in 1947—the offi-cial view contained in the minutes of the Board and the contrasting and dra-matic recollections of an insider, an alumnus and social worker. A brief review of the research methods and their implications takes account of their limits and strengths. An overview of the Children's Home recommends that institutions should not be judged by structure and program alone but also by the inner processes and opportunities for learning and change. Resilience as an interac-tional theory provides a more instructive alternative to pathological assump-tions to explain how maturation and success can and do evolve out of hardship and deprivation. The matter of the role of virtue, self-reliance, and morality growth and development is reconsidered. Based on the findings and discussion, I plead for the reappraisal of the merit of group child care as a response to the seemingly insoluble problems of children in the present. Recommendations are offered relative to the dynamics, expectations, learnings, and other conditions that help shape effective and responsive group care.

ACKNOWLEDGMENTS

Over the many years spent in the research for and the writing of this book, colleagues, family, and institutions have offered encouragement and support for this project. But it could not have been attempted and accomplished without the generous involvement and the rich memories of the former residents of the Jewish Children's Home.

This study was launched with the support of the Charles Rieley Armington Research Program on Values in Children at Case Western Reserve University. In the next years, support from the School of Applied Social Sciences, Case Western Reserve University, and the Jeanne and M. Larry Lawrence Foundation, Coronado, California, enabled me to engage in the travel, interviewing, archival searches, and other activities required to accomplish this study. The Board of Directors of the Rochester Jewish Children's Home, still active and providing scholarships for descendants of former wards, funded the final stage of the integration and writing of this work.

Two institutions were of incalculable help in locating archival material. Staff of Jewish Family Service of Rochester, New York, Inc., located virtual treasures including records of the former residents of the Home and directed me to Mrs. Sylvia Itkin, the caretaker of all the issues of the *Home Review*, the newsletter published monthly from 1927 to 1948. Mrs. Itkin graciously shared this chronology of the Home with me. The Archives of the University of Rochester Library made available to me their compiled assortment of records, ledgers, and miscellany that offered details and facts about the operations of the Home. Archivist Karl Kabelac was especially helpful.

I am grateful to the daughters and sons of the philanthropists and community leaders who shared special insights about the lives and incentives of their parents. Hazel Hart Beckerman offered grand accounts of her father and mother, Alfred and Ida Hart, the principal benefactors of the Children's Home. I am thankful to Mort and Sam Kolko and Ruth Vinney, to Henry Rubens, Nathan Robfogel, and Morton Hollander for their anecdotes about their fathers. And Adeline Rubenstein's stories about her mother, Mrs. Brudno, enriched my understanding of her role as leader in the Mothers Club.

My brother, Herbert Goldstein, does what big brothers do best. Distance notwithstanding, he was and is always by my side as a mentor, supporter, friend, and exacting critic. His reviews of my chapters and his reflections on his experiences with the Home and its children served both to discover and to keep me on the right trail. I appreciate the suggestions and ideas of other readers including Dr. Max Siporin, Dr. Edmund Sherman, and a recent friend whose scholarship has afforded me fresh ideas about group care, Dr. Jerome Beker. And as the text will reveal, Will Greenberg and Phil Nusbaum, who read each chapter as it was produced, were my constant beacons.

The foundations—intellectual, critical, inspirational, and loving—of this work were set by my dear wife, Linda, a fine scholar and author in her own right. She consistently urged me to find my voice and, in so doing, helped me temper it. And always, she was there as companion and friend.

Finally, tribute needs to be given to old "Rose" and her successor, "Sadie," devoted and loyal pals.

THE HOME ON GORHAM STREET

and the Voices of Its Children

ONE

Home and Community

Ah, the neighborhood and the women who lived there . . . you know why I got this far? Because every time I saw Mrs. Kolko she blessed me, "A gezunt auf dein keppel."

—Will, 1988

The dinner that Iris had prepared was as gracious as the manner in which this visitor from former times was so generously received. The elegant dessert and coffee that she set before us didn't interrupt Phil and Will one bit: like two old war veterans, they pressed on as they had all during the meal, matching stories about the old days, the 1920s and 1930s, when they were children in the old "Orphans Home." Although they squabbled now and then or reminded one another about a forgotten person or incident, together they rendered a lively melodrama about what it really meant growing up in the old Jewish Children's Home—what it was really like, what really happened. There was no shortage of hilarious anecdotes—about teasing exasperated cooks, pilfering extra food, sneaking out of religious services. But like the many stories later told to me by other former wards of the Home, they were edged with the wry pathos, the subtle irony, the caustic humor of traditional Jewish comedy: laughter tempered by a touching sadness. Iris and Mim, their wives, had heard these tales many times before; still, they were visibly moved by the deeper meanings their husbands gave to the old stories. I sat quietly, captivated by the exchange, drawn into the intensity of their nostalgic feelings. My tape recorder, there amid the uncollected dishes of the finished meal, captured their words.

Both men, robust, full of vitality and good humor, were now comfortably retired and rightly proud of their thriving careers as social workers. And they remained as active and involved as before. Phil continued his part-time counseling practice with children and families; Will, who had administered a substantial home for the aging for many years, now volunteered his many talents to the agency's board.

Sixty years had not blunted their memories and recollections of their young lives in the Children's Home that had closed its doors in 1947. Phil frequently exploited his seniority to contradict some of Will's recollections, playfully reminding Will that "You were still in the Baby Cottage!" Their reminiscences were both personal and professional: they not only recalled the times and the people that made a difference in their lives but, drawing from accumulated wisdom and experience, they could also conjecture on how life in the Home might have impressed their own and their comrades' lives.

Their respective images of growing up in the Home on Gorham Street varied, say, about matters of stigma, what they were fed, or who got punished and when. Yet, the warmth and closeness they shared melted the rhetoric of disagreement: although certain fractions of their lives were interpreted differently, they held in common special meanings unknown to outsiders about what it meant to be an "orphan," a child in an institution. In his droll manner, Will stirred laughter when he described the chain of prayers, rituals, and rites that were crammed into every day, sardonically concluding that "If I got nothing else from the Home, I learned how to daven (pray)." The meaning of that ambiguous remark was not lost on Phil. After a moment's pause he tried to figure out "what it was that *was* so different for us that we all had this feeling that is still there. Comradeship. Maybe it had something to do with our Jewishness—that we learned how to "daven." There was a lot of protectiveness, too."

The occasion was a May evening in 1987, my first return to Rochester after forty-five years. The formal purpose of my visit was to set in motion, after many months of preparation, an ethnographic study of the lives of people who, as children, spent most of their early years as wards of the Rochester Jewish Children's Home. I wanted to discover in conversations with some remaining graduates of the Home what institutional life had been like for them in those former years and what those early years signified as adulthood unfolded. Thanks to experts in the field of child development, theories and opinions about the implications of separation and institutionalization are plentiful. This study, in contrast, intended to search out the "real experts," the elders, the former wards, who might share their sentiments and impressions about their lives. To complement the ethnography, a limited historical study planned to capture the character of that era when placement of children (in this instance, sons and daughters of Eastern European Jewish immigrants) in an institution was a customary practice when even one parent died or living parents were, because of illness or other reasons, no longer able to care for them.

The formal purpose of my trip was surely realized on that warmhearted evening in May. My study was well launched. What I did not anticipate was the goodwill, generosity, and genuine openness that was tendered to me by Will and Phil and their wives and subsequently by the many other alumni with whom I was privileged to talk. Although they acknowledged my research goals, to many I remained an older version of the "Howie" they remembered.

The rekindling of fellowship and affinity more than fulfilled the informal and personal motives that inspired my study in the first place.

There were many times in the past half century that I might have returned to my beginnings in Rochester. Time, distance, or cost was never a serious obstacle to my going back to what had been my home for the first twenty years of my life. I left Rochester during World War II for the Armed Services, as did almost all my friends. But unlike my many friends, I did not retrace my steps and settle back into the community to continue on as a homegrown Rochesterian.

With the passing of time, we may discover in our later years that the story of our lives and our selves remains firmly anchored in the old relationships and places. Even as an outsider who grew up across the street from the Jewish Children's Home, I had been drawn into the peculiar patterns of institutional life since many of the kids were my closest friends and companions. I was fortunate as a child to reap some of the benefits that were occasionally bestowed upon these "orphans" by benevolent community groups—free movies, picnics, boat trips, and parties, for example. But as a child and outsider, I could not know less about the darker side of their asylum lives. Some imprint was undoubtedly felt, perhaps strong enough in my mind to put off chancing a trip back to the old neighborhood: you can't revisit the phantom world that the child once created, especially when even the relics of that world no longer remain.

Yet my curiosity could not be undone. The lives of those young people who, like myself, grew up on Gorham Street were and are as undeniable as my own. The one major difference, however, was that they grew up in a home that was capitalized—*The Home*, an institution. My home was not. Over time and in talks with my older brother, who had his own memories, I wondered: Did that difference really make a difference? What happened to the "kids?" How did they fare? Did they make out OK in their post-institutional years?

In my professional career as a social worker and educator I was, in effect, an audience to the kaleidoscopic stories of other persons' lives. This excited other complex and penetrating questions. I learned early that why peoples' lives turn in one direction or another cannot be explained by alluring but simple cause-effect equations: too many psychological maxims about childhood traumas, separation, and the like turn out, in the end, to be overgeneralized and undependable. Each of us it seems is the author of the singular story and explanation of our own life, as Will and Phil revealed in their dialogue. Naturally, and for our respective purposes, we cull through our histories to create our own persuasive tales about what was meaningful and why it was so. Out of a random assortment of memories we invent what we believe is a coherent rendition of our existence and worth—and often, an affirmation of our resilience and courage.

In this view, the urgency to bring these personal stories and accounts to light became even more heightened. In shaping this inquiry I was not sure about what questions should be asked since I could not anticipate what their life stories were like, what sorts of recollections they were based on, or if there were any common themes and threads among them.

One doesn't get very far with such intentions and ideas unless, according to the dictates and conventions of the institution of scholarship, they are formally transformed into something called *The Research Project*. Such a project brings about several benefits: academic respectability; possible access to financial support; a justifiable reason for asking people personal questions that one would not otherwise risk asking; and, not least, the obligation that such an inquiry will be carried out in an ethical and responsible fashion that respects the rights and privacy of its respondents. The research project also served a purpose closer to my heart. Finally, it became the compelling reason for me to return to my heritage, my neighborhood now gone, literally scraped away.

Such a project poses certain challenges: where and how does one begin; to what specifically should one return after so much time? To be sure, there was much preliminary research to be done, involving a search for archival material—papers, ledgers, and records from the Home that were fortunately lodged at the University of Rochester. That was the easy part. But beyond the artifacts, how do you begin to locate these men and women and, if good fortune is on your side, how do you reintroduce yourself after such a long and unexplained absence? There also were many ethical quandaries to consider: did I have the right to intrude myself into the lives of these folks—to ask them to dredge up memories of times and events that, by definition, were likely to be vexing and discomfiting?

Happenstance, an attribute of ethnography (my brother became reacquainted with Phil at a recent professional conference), led me to Phil, who eased many of these concerns. My letter to him elicited an immediate response of genuine interest in the project. It also revealed how enduring were the relationships that had been shaped in the Home so many years ago. After more than half a lifetime, and without the benefit of a formal organization, it was still important that the graduates of the Home kept in touch with, or at least were aware of the whereabouts of, their former comrades.

Phil's promise that I would have easy access to other alumni was quickly realized. Very soon I received a phone call with the query: "Are you the Howie Goldstein whose father had a shoe store on Gorham Street and who had a dog named Mitzi who understood Yiddish?" Oddly, I recognized the voice of my old friend, Stan, who had left Rochester many years ago; even more astonishing was that he resided just a few blocks from my Cleveland home. Stan's sister in Rochester had talked with Phil and the news quickly spread. Soon after, a Rochester newspaper published a story about my project that generated many letters and phone calls. They came not from Rochester alone but from other parts of the country, from other former graduates, and from the children and widows of those who were deceased. Most of these messages were encouraging, expressing a willingness to participate in the project. Some were pleased that the

Children's Home, that era of Jewish life, or the experiences of the Home's residents would at last be documented. A few letters were clearly skeptical and even suspicious about the intent of the study. The writers, also former residents, feared that I might paint a distorted picture of life in the Home—one that would be bright and glowing and that did not conform with harsh memories of their experiences.

It was now possible to move forward. Having crystallized the questions and design of the study to the point where I could enter the lives of these people with at least a modicum of wisdom and a considerable measure of open receptivity and humility, I could now return to the old neighborhood. Over a two-year period I was gracefully and warmly welcomed into the homes of over thirty former residents of the Children's Home—in Rochester and Fort Lauderdale—including the few who were skeptical about the intent of the study. Usually, I met with the former resident alone or with a mate present who joined in the lengthy and rich conversation. A few alumni arranged a social evening in their homes and invited three or four other graduates for a marvelous long evening of exchanging memories.

NEIGHBORHOOD

We must begin on Gorham Street since, as we will see, the lives and the histories would lack meaning without an appreciation of the enveloping importance of community.

"Neighborhood" can be a sentimental term that arouses something stronger than merely mental snapshots of its streets, buildings, stores, and playgrounds. "Neighborhood" for us was where we prevailed and where we belonged—and by definition that everywhere outside *our* neighborhood was where we didn't belong. Nowadays, we dignify this quality of belonging with the social science jargon that has edged its way into our language, calling it "identity" or "reference group," for example. But insiders don't need these terms. In my conversations with any of the former kids of the Home, a word about Baden Street or Naditz's Bakery or the Lyric Theater evoked a knowing nod that silently acknowledged, "Yes, I know. We were all part of it." The Jewish Children's Home was a conspicuous element of this immigrant neighborhood and community; conversely, the spirit of this community spread into the lives and operations of the Home. Each gave the other meaning and value.

It is already evident that although this brief social history includes certain facts concerned with the locales and events of Gorham Street, the neighborhood, the immigrant community, we will see that the significance of life as it was known and now remembered is more reliably shaped by the cultural symbols, metaphors, and idioms—even the myths—that denizens and neighbors share.

Settlement of the Jewish community to which the Children's Home belonged began in the last quarter of the nineteenth century. The many German

Jews who had arrived earlier were well established by this time. Many of the first Eastern European Jews to arrive in Rochester had no special destination in America. Aboard ship, they learned that Rochester was a thriving city and with others who had arrived in New York City, decided to move upstate.[1] By 1870, the handful of Jews increased enough to permit the first "minyan" (the ten male Jews required for religious services). And their numbers grew.

For the most part, the immigrants who settled on Gorham and other surrounding streets were a poor lot, unschooled and without a trade. Some had come to find the *goldene medina,* the vision of the golden land that had also enticed other immigrant groups. Many others were refugees from the violent pogroms and persecution of Russia or escapees from service in the Czar's army. That they shared the simple Orthodoxy and traditions of Jewishness, as well as privation and suffering, allowed for some sense of unity. However, that some had come from Russia and others from Lithuania, Poland, and Galicia, that some had known only life in the small *shtetls* whereas others had lived in cities, also made for differences in dialects, habits, and customs. The consequence, as occurred in other urban areas, was a considerable spread of synagogues, each created to sustain the rituals of each group's Old Country origins.

There was much more to which these "greenhorns" had to adjust without losing their cherished Old Country traditions and identities. Allowing for their many variations, the bond that united these newcomers was their shared sense of "Yiddishkeit," the blend of history, suffering, language, moral law, and other ingrained beliefs that decided what it meant to be a Jew.[2]

Maintaining their Yiddishkeit and simultaneously striving for a degree of acculturation in the outer community required the development of a common Jewish culture that could accommodate their internal differences. It meant sharing the neighborhood with "goyim" or gentiles, the Italian Catholics, for example, whose God and language were entirely foreign. It meant finding a home, a refuge of some kind, in some small corner of a city governed by and belonging to the real Americans. Another dilemma was how to coexist with others who also called themselves Jews, but whose secular and already Americanized way of life disavowed the traditions of Orthodox Judaism, not to mention Yiddishkeit itself. These were the Reformed German Jews, the second and third generations of families that had come over from Western Europe in the previous century, some of whom were, in fact, the owners of the clothing factories that employed, and in many instances exploited, the newcomers.

The German Jews lived across town in far more pleasant neighborhoods. By this time the Reform movement in Judaism had taken hold in America and, accordingly, this group had erected temples rather than synagogues in which services were no longer conducted in Hebrew but in English. Casting off many restrictive conventions of Orthodoxy, they maintained their own social life that was as integrated with the Christian community to the extent that prevailing anti-Semitic attitudes allowed. Many German Jews entered politics and the professions and became prominent members of the community.

The gap that separated the new and old communities was bridged at least by their shared dedication to an essence of Judaism—*tzedakah*. More of a commitment to social justice than to simple charity, *tzedakah* is the obligation and requirement to care and provide for your less fortunate comrades. And so, the German Jews willingly opened their social services and means of assistance to their immigrant brethren. However grateful the latter were, they quickly chose to create their own philanthropy from within their own community. The Associated Hebrew Charities was founded in 1908 and five years later opened its own building on Baden Street. Along with other beneficent organizations their stated purpose was to relieve "the necessities and suffering of the Jewish poor . . . to furnish temporary care and nursing for deserving Jewish poor; to furnish temporary assistance to those in distress . . . to become self supporting; to provide free Hebrew education to poor Jewish children . . . aid and assistance will be voluntarily given."[3]

The founding of the Rochester Jewish Children's Home in 1914 (originally called the Jewish Sheltering Home), as we will see in chapter 4, was still another example of the recent Jewish immigrants' compulsion to care for their own. The fact was that a reputable Jewish orphanage had been doing its good works since 1877. Some years later, Alfred Hart explained: "Now the question is continually raised why we should have two orphan's homes. Again and again we are obliged to answer: Our Orthodox Jews have tried with every effort but failed to convince our respected Jews of the Reformed Orphan's Home that our little ones are from Orthodox parents, and although we respect them for their good work, why not raise them as their parents would have done if they lived, with all the sacred customs that were so dear to them."[4]

Although the drive to retain independence and identity was important, it did not stand in the way of a special kinship that from the moment of the opening of the Children's Home continued to grow between the Home and its surrounding community and the German-Jewish community as well. Let me touch on these relationships for a moment in anticipation of later discussion.

The Board of Directors of the Home and the dues-paying members represented the many professions, businesses, and strata of the Rochester Jewish community. The Mothers Club, formed soon after the founding of the Home, was made up of women of the neighborhood and surrounding areas. In addition to the individual care and attention they lavished on the children, they sponsored Purim parties, bar mitzvahs, and wedding showers for the graduates. The Big Brothers and Sisters, a club formed by the local young adults, visited the children regularly, and scheduled weekly entertainments and annual picnics for the children. Other local clubs, the Aleph Eien and the True Pal, also sponsored many forms of recreation.

Equally significant was the variety of ways in which ordinary Jewish folk would, without being asked, share what they had with the children. Some would send over a quarter or a dollar, others would contribute a few dollars to the Camp Fund, and a few would leave bequests of two or three hundred dollars. Food and clothing were contributed regularly—a bag of oranges, a box of candy, a crate of fruit, a few new dresses for the girls, complete attire for the boys at Passover, weekly supplies of bread from the bakery.

Many of the community's families were eager to share their moments of joy and celebration with the Home's children. Someone's recovery from an illness, the bar mitzvah of a son, or the engagement of a daughter would be commemorated by the family's sending over ice cream and cake for a party for all the children. Regularly, the monthly newsletter, the *Home Review,* would post announcements such as, "Mr. & Mrs. Amdursky gave a party in honor of the 2nd birthday of their daughter," or "ice cream and cake in honor of the 40th Anniversary of Mr. & Mrs. Frankel," or "party by Sarah Rubin in honor of marriage of daughter. Each child received three pretty handkerchiefs." In addition, children often were invited to the homes of families for special events.

The children gave back what they could to their community. Performances of the annual Purim or Chanukah plays were often repeated for the benefit of the residents of the Home for the Aged. Or children would offer recitations, songs, and dances for the annual meetings of the Mothers Club or other organizations.

In later chapters we will consider what these planned and programmed activities meant to the children—particularly during the barren days of the Depression when few families, including my own, could offer their children much in the way of entertainment. For now, let me say that considering the cost of the loss of family, we will see that the opportunity to remain part of their own community, to continue to partake of and grow within the culture of Yiddishkeit, was vital for many of the youngsters. The Children's Home, after all, was neither a child's wonderland nor a paradise of childhood delights as will be borne out by the recollections of some of its graduates. Sue, for example, looks back some sixty years and recalls: "We didn't have time to play. We were washing. We were cleaning. We were sewing. I didn't have time to do anything. Who could play? I don't remember ever having a doll. So that's why maybe when my daughter was three years old, I had twenty-five dolls in her bedroom. Maybe in the back of my mind, because I didn't have one."

There was no question that the children (or as they still refer to themselves, "the kids") were, by court order or the will of their parents or relatives, firmly bound to the Home as wards. Because the Home lacked walls or fences, the neighborhood and community were open to them and, reciprocally, the youngsters of the neighborhood had free access to the Home's grounds. That the Home's inhabitants had a limited freedom to come and go, to attend the public schools, and partake of the activities of local clubs and organizations should not be interpreted as a sign of planned or progressive thinking of any kind. In every other way, control of the children's lives and actions—and, if possible, their thoughts and values—was the first order of business. Since the Home sat comfortably within a largely Jewish neighborhood, there was perhaps less fear of undesirable outside influences or risks. Artificial barriers weren't necessary.

For those of us on Gorham Street and thereabouts, Rochester was this two- or three-square-mile splinter of the oldest section of the city bordering the towering rocky escarpment that is the east bank of the Genesee River. A few miles farther south, the river tranquilly flowed past gracious estates, golf courses, and the campus of the University of Rochester. Where we resided, the Genesee's thundering falls and turbid waters cut a deep gorge, a scar, across a begrimed spread of factories, gas works, breweries, and warehouses before resuming its more placid course northward through pleasant neighborhoods and on into Lake Ontario. This was our part of town.

Now this tract is called the "inner city," where shells of old houses and empty storefronts surround block after block of public housing of the "garden apartment" variety that supports only weeds and spare patches of yellowed grass. What little is left of Gorham Street itself is now called St. Bridget's Place, named after the only survivor of urban renewal—the homely, old, square-steepled, red brick Roman Catholic Church, built in the 1850s by the former Irish residents of the area. No trace remains of my old dilapidated dwelling or the Children's Home, which once dominated the midpoint of the street. Asylums usually don't earn historical markers.

Our part of town was far more a stew pot than a melting pot, a hodgepodge of distinct nationalities whose simple homes or flats squatted among a scattering of factories and mills. Randomly, the immigrant Eastern European Jews lived side by side with the immigrant Italian families from southern Italy and Sicily—the Goldsteins next to the DeMarcos, the Rinis next to the Friedmans, the Schreibers next to the Tartaglios. And sprinkled among this mixture of swarthier Semitic and Mediterranean types were the occasional fair-haired Slavs and Poles, the Kubarychs and Dombrowskis.

Earlier, this slice of the city had been peopled with Germans and Irish, themselves the immigrants of another time. The Jews who had immigrated from Germany also settled in the area; they were as poor and unskilled as their brethren from Eastern Europe who arrived later. Those who had an aptitude for the needle trades set up their small shops. By the time the Eastern and Southern Europeans began to filter in, these small tailor shops had consolidated and had blossomed into a large and prosperous clothing industry—Bonds Clothiers, Levy-Adler, and Hickey-Freeman to name a few. Their owners, now well-to-do, abandoned the lowly working-class neighborhood to build their elegant homes in the southern reaches of the city. Their places were filled by the newly arrived Jewish and Italian immigrants who were willing to work as tailors, cutters, or pressers in the huge factories.

Even by the 1900s, the small frame and brick houses that the newcomers took over were already timeworn and decrepit. The two larger houses that dominated Gorham Street were occupied by the religious leaders of this Jewish community. Rabbi Sadowsky, who took part in the founding of the Home and was the moving spirit of the Orthodox community until his death in 1946,[5] occupied the ample but plain frame house directly across the street from the

Home. A few doors east, Chazzin (Cantor) Jassin lived in the other pre-Civil War Victorian mansion, its begrimed limestone walls even in the 1920s showing that its more gracious moments were already long past.

The Jews and Italians lived close enough to one another to be able to smell whatever national dish was cooking on their neighbor's stove or to hear the commotions that sometimes exploded in Yiddish or Italian. But only the odors and sounds mixed. Amid an aura of propriety, there was neither animosity nor amity nor even any particular curiosity about the other's very different way of life, religion, or rituals. There were many exceptions, of course: some of the former residents recall close ties between their Jewish families and their Italian neighbors. Phil remembers that Mr. and Mrs. Corella, next door, gave up their bed and slept on the floor while Mrs. Corella nursed his mother, who was seriously ill. But to many Jews, the Italian families, or for that matter, anyone outside the faith, were just goyim, gentiles. Having come over from lands where they had lived as outsiders in ghettos of cities or the isolation of the *shtetl*, the Jews were well adapted to the realities of being segregated, both by choice and demand. At least in the larger immigrant community, separateness in America was by choice in the attempt to preserve the Jewish ethos. It also silently expressed the Eleventh Commandment: "Thou Shall Not Intermarry." If not broken, a few other Commandments might be bent a bit, but marriage to a non-Jew? Never. And so, as it went, if you're not too friendly with the goyim, then you won't think of ever dating one, and if you don't date. . . .

Very practical economic reasons also explain why the two cultures could or had to live side-by-side in a somewhat cautious harmony. The Jewish and Italian workers together had to survive the hazards and instabilities of their employment in the clothing industry. Having been exploited, both groups supported the formation and growth to power of the labor union, the Amalgamated Clothing Workers of America, and banded together at the noisy meetings and affairs at the Amalgamated Hall nearby on Clinton Avenue. When the "slack season" hit, when there was no work at the factories, both the Italian and the Jewish worker suffered. And the Depression itself did not discriminate among the different nationalities.

Paradoxically, our differences made us the same. To the dominant Protestants of greater Rochester, it made no difference whether these immigrants were Catholic or Jewish: we were the foreigners and they were the natives. Whether the Jewish *lontzmon* or the Italian *paisan*, both were of another land. They may have come over to America on different ships but they were now together in the same boat.

Privacy or solitude was not of much importance among this bustling society of Jewish neighbors. Just as the image of the front porch lingers as a metaphor for the age of neighborliness and chatter, so does the memory of the invariably unlocked back door. The kids from the Home across the street also felt welcome in our house. They would come over to play, perhaps to get a piece of my mother's homemade pie, or, sometimes, just to be with a real family.

Yes, it was a neighborhood, a community of families, self-contained, hemmed in by other nationalities and, in turn, surrounded by a white, Protestant society that was as foreign to us as we were to them. Like other neighborhood streets, Gorham Street was also the site of some meager ventures in private enterprise by the few who did not work at the local factories. Who even thought about zoning regulations? If it was possible to scrape out a living in some way, then Gorham Street was as good as anyplace else to do it. A variety of little businesses and shops—a printer, a burlap bag company, a garage—could be found tucked within, between, or behind the old homes. My father's shoe store, located in what would ordinarily have been the dining room and parlor of our second-story flat, was identified only by the sign out front, its fading letters telling you that this was the "Gorham St. Sample Shoe Store." At the corner, Mr. Berger, a cheerless and silent man, and his wife ran his candy store from early morning to almost midnight where transactions usually involved pennies—for a piece of candy or one cigarette. Next to him was the Italian tailor, a kosher poultry store stacked with wooden coops of loudly squawking fowl, and the dark storefront that hid some kind of Italian men's club.

Given the devotion of these immigrants to their fundamental pieties, the spirit, the dogma, and the burdens of religion abundantly affected the neighborhood's patterns of living. As young people, we didn't question our religiosity. Jewish is what *we* were; *they* were Catholic. Similarly, two institutions symbolically dominated our street, each materializing one of the two classic and distinct religious cultures. Both represented the seamless weave of culture, religion, tradition, and ritual of each of the two groups. St. Bridget's Roman Catholic Church was clearly the spiritual center of this Italian community. Here resided the priest and a covey of nuns, all attired in their traditional habits. In our Semitic minds they were strange, awe-stirring, otherworldly figures. Seeing them on occasion in the shoe store in my own home, involved in something as earthly as trying on a pair of black, ankle-high shoes, did little to soften their mystique or my imagination.

The neighborhood Jewish kids kept clear of the church and its grounds: to us it was mysterious, occult, not connected to anything familiar. Sure, they prayed there but we could hear an organ's voice from inside the dark chapel; the sound of any musical instrument in *our* place of worship would be an unthinkable sacrilege. All we knew about Catholicism came from farfetched rumors about what, in our gullible minds, we suspected went on in the rectory and from what we heard and observed on Sundays and at times of festivals and weddings. There was no adult among our people who would even acknowledge the existence of that religion, never mind tell us anything informative about it.

Just as St. Bridget's served as an icon for this Italian-Catholic neighborhood, the Jewish Children's Home, just a few doors west of the church, represented the folkways and traditions of the local Orthodox Jews. It was no less a spiritual center, because daily and Sabbath religious services that were compulsory for the kids of the Home were also open to anyone in the neighborhood who wished to attend. The Home was not only a hub for religious ritual and prayer for the community, it was also the site of our Hebraic rites of passage: here the kids of the Home and other welcomed children of the neighborhood, including my brother and myself, performed the religiously sanctioned rite of manhood, the bar mitzvah. In the Home's earlier years, services were held in the small, unadorned, all-purpose auditorium of the main building. In 1934, a small synagogue was built on the grounds by, and named for, a special benefactor of the Home, Alfred Hart, whom we will have the occasion to meet at many points in this book. The chapel, certainly elegant in its simplicity, was of course far less pretentious than the somewhat medieval ecclesiology of St. Bridget's. But it stood grandly as the visible emblem of the Home's religious Orthodoxy.

The Home was not only a formal religious center; it also mirrored the culture and character of this immigrant Jewish neighborhood. In appearance it had the same somberness of the other homes and structures around it, though the main building was newer by perhaps fifty years (built in 1914) than its neighbors. It not only blended into the general drabness of the neighborhood, but also seemed to reflect the general indifference to design and aesthetics that was often typical of traditional Orthodox Jews.

The interior of the institution was equally uninspiring. At one end of the grounds was the two-story frame house that became the residence of the Home's superintendent, Mr. Hollander, and his family. The rambling three-story brick main building adjoining the superintendent's home was typical of the barracks-type orphanages common to the nineteenth century. It contained the boys' dormitories and smaller sleeping rooms, the superintendent's office, the kitchen and the large dining room where all the children ate, the auditorium, and the recreation room-library. A stark symbol of institutional life was the long tier of washbasins on one side of the tiled corridor that was the common passageway. No one except formal visitors and officials used the front door that led to the main office, the superintendent's domain. Except for the decorations that were tacked up during the joyful holidays of Purim and Chanukah, the walls were mostly bare.

Across the graveled driveway, the other end of the Home, was the Girls House. For myself and all the boys, this was forbidden territory since the unwritten law—although grossly unsuccessful in its intent—suppressed even the thought about putting a foot into that officially segregated female colony. Needless to say, our repressed little-boyish minds overflowed with quizzical and carnal thoughts about life in that more homey-looking building.

Altogether, these structures covered what was equivalent to three or four typical city lots. At the rear of the main building, separated by a driveway, sat a long row of garages topped by a second-story loft that served a variety of unofficial and sometimes covert purposes for boys of the Home and the neighborhood. For a brief period, one of the kids and I raised a small flock of common pigeons in the dark, grimy loft—that is, until the pigeon droppings leaked

Main Building, Rochester Jewish Children's Home and Alfred Hart Synagogue, 1939 (Silver Anniversary Publication, 1939)

through the cracks of the rough wooden floor and spattered the superintendent's automobile. At other times the loft was our indoor basketball court where certain athletic skills, both practical and survival, had to be learned. One set of skills involved the mastery of the technique necessary to sink a basket by looping your shot through the dark maze of beams and rafters. The survival skill required the development of operative hindsight. To stay in the game—that is, physically—one had to learn to dribble the ball while edging backward and simultaneously avoid disappearing out of the open second-story loft door that was our only source of light.

The playground, a rugged square of dirt and stones, spread out behind the garage building. Along with whatever games we might invent, there was always some made-up version of baseball that would accommodate any number of players that we played in spring and summer. In the fall the game was football. In both sports, the equipment was usually makeshift: the well-worn baseball was re-covered many times with layers of electricians tape which meant that the ball stuck firmly to your hand; the football had lost its bladder long ago and was, instead, stuffed with old rags. There wasn't much distance on the kickoff. In the Rochester winters, famous for their abundance of snow, a fair-sized wooden slide was erected at the back end of the playground down which we could bellywhop our sleds.

Except for the high cyclone fence that separated the playground from the backyards of the houses on Hand Street, there was nothing, either materially or by rule or regulation, that would set the Home apart from its neighborhood and Jewish community.

There, Yiddishkeit was a way of life that seeped into every corner of one's way of being. It embodied not merely prayer, ritual, or rule (for many, the overbearing regimentation of Orthodoxy made it an anathema), but also a felt sense of belonging—a quality of being part of an ancient history and a shared life story. The difference it made, for better or worse, swayed not only the lives that unfolded in the Home itself but in the family patterns and careers of adult lives that followed.

Patterns of Yiddish life were nourished not only by the daily patterns of neighborhood goings-on but also by its centers of activity in the little shops, markets, schools, and the like where people mingled and carried out the business of living. The core of these activities was Joseph Avenue, the eight- or ten-block ribbon of little stores and businesses that were mostly Jewish and, where food was concerned, kosher. Joseph Avenue was Rochester's modest version of New York's Delancey Street, Chicago's Halstead Street, or Cleveland's 105th Street.

Around the corner on Baden Street was the exacting burden of most pre–bar mitzvah boys: the Hebrew School or Talmud Torah. Excepting the Sabbath and even in summer, we had no choice about the daily hours we had to spend in the dingy, crudely furnished rooms. There, under the menacing eyes of our underpaid and sullen teacher, Mr. Panitz, we monotonously droned through our recitations of portions of the *Chumash*, the first five books of the Bible, ever watchful of the stick that would crack our knuckles should we stumble over a word. We sure learned how to read Hebrew fluently while our reflexes alertly avoided the parry and thrust of our "rebbe's" rod. Apart from a few obscenities I learned elsewhere, I never understood a word of Hebrew.

Joseph Avenue itself was our own "Main Street," quite different from the genuine Main Street a mile or so south—what we called "downtown"—where the staid, old department stores like Sibleys and McCurdys dominated the main corners and huge, rococo movie palaces bedizened the gray streets.

Joseph Avenue was "ours." It started at Central Avenue, the edge of the downtown area, and dipped under the sooty bridge bearing the New York Central railroad tracks; its strip of small stores provided everything we needed for our plain, ordinary, kosher lives. The merchants were much like our own parents, Yiddish immigrants who were scratching out a meager living as purveyors to the families of the tailors, cutters, and pressers. We knew most everybody and most everybody knew us.

Ruth Kolko Lebovics, who lived on Joseph Avenue until her marriage in 1933, recalls that Nusbaum's department store was the major emporium that even drew non-Jewish clientele from other parts of the city. When it was closed for the Sabbath, people would line up in the Saturday twilight, awaiting its reopening.[6] There were smaller shoe repair shops, Levy's and Cook's, where half-soles could be glued to already well-worn shoes. Auto supply stores such as Wolk's and Joseph Ave. Auto Parts sold gaskets and fuel pumps to the few who were fortunate enough to own an automobile. Since many mothers stitched their own and their children's clothes, they could sort through bolts of cloth at Saperstones, Shoolmans, Orgels, or Tillims Dry Goods or go to Kolko's tailor trimmings store for thread and linings, where old Mr. Kolko would study the Talmud at a desk in the rear of the store until the jangling bell signaled the entry of a customer. A. Brim Caps was nearby, where we would purchase our annual large, pancake-like Passover cap. It was a ready-made children's joke for us: how funny, a cap maker named A. Brim. Other apparel was available at Rose Dress Shop, Brody Women's Clothing, or the Dressey Apparel Shop. There were also watch repairers, furniture stores, dentists, cigar stores, and hardware stores.

Two spots on Joseph Avenue were symbols of our passage into adolescence. One was Kucker's Billiard Parlor, the shady hangout for the local small-time gamblers and pool sharks. Parents always need some ideal evil to warn their children about; the pool room served that need nicely. For a dime or a quarter, one could bet on the ball games or shoot some pool or just rub elbows with some of the real wiseguys.

The other emporium was a bit more legitimate. As the Yiddish counterpart of the American soda fountain or malt shop, Cohen's delicatessen was our so-cial center, our meeting place. The theory of the unity of good friends and good food must have had its start here for, on stopping by, you could usually run into someone you knew and, if nothing else, have a great sandwich without going broke. A root beer was a nickel; if you were better off, you could add a salami sandwich on rye with a dill pickle for fifteen cents more. And if finances were in really great shape, a thick corned beef or hot pastrami sandwich, the "special," would still relieve you of only thirty-five cents.

Food was the real attraction on Joseph Avenue, since Yiddishkeit is as much a gastronomic state of being as it is cultural or spiritual. And so the local stores were the pantheons in which the taste, smell, and other gustatory delights of being Jewish could be celebrated. Amdursky's and Applebaum's sold kosher meats and chickens and, at my mother's request, would give away some odd, unkosher organs for our cat's dining pleasures. The chicken plucker had his place in the middle of the store, ankle deep in feathers. And there was the marvelous aroma of freshly baked pumpernickel—huge, dark, crusty loaves of bread dappled with raisins that sat on the counter of Naditz's Bakery. Or there was the mouth-watering smell of lox and the luscious sight of mounds of fresh butter and cream cheese that stirred cravings even before you got to Simon's Dairy store.

Josef, a lifelong Rochesterian who grew up in the neighborhood and wit-nessed the gradual demolition of what had once been a vital community, recalls Thursday nights on Joseph Avenue when the wives would come out to shop for the Sabbath.

> They would come with their wicker baby carriages, some with the babies, some without, others with their red American Flyer wagons, and others just carrying

Joseph Avenue at Baden Street, Rochester, New York (Courtesy Rochester Museum & Science Center, Rochester, New York)

their groceries in bags. They would dicker with the shop owners to come down on their prices. Sometimes it would work, sometimes it wouldn't. There were barrels of herring and wooden crates of fruits and vegetables out in front of the grocery stores. The women would look at the chickens, pick them up and blow the feathers away from their *taches* to see if there was fat for making "schmaltz" (much desired chicken fat). If there was, that was the perfect chicken. Then on to the bakery for "challah," and black and rye breads and onion rolls. Finished with their shopping, they would head straight for Mr. Vilinsky, the *shochet* (ritual slaughterer) on Herman Street. He would kill the chicken with two strokes—any more than that would not be acceptable to a Jew. Then he would hang it so the blood would run out. The Jewish mother would take it home, pluck the feathers, cut it up and place it on a wooden board, salt it with Kosher salt and let it sit for the night allowing the rest of the blood to drain. If, on opening the chicken, she found needles or pins, she couldn't use it and sold it to the gentile neighbor.

The Jewish community as a whole was marked by involvement, by a ferment of causes, convictions, and caring: Socialists of all stripes and persuasions abounded, seemingly in constant intellectual debate; likewise, there were many Zionist organizations working together or at cross-purposes for a hoped-for Jewish state in Palestine; there were always forums, speeches, and discussions sponsored by the Amalgamated Garment Workers Union and the Workmen's

Circle at the union hall on Clinton Avenue. Women, housewives, belonged to one or more charitable organizations and auxiliaries. The most prominent was the Mothers Club of the Children's Home. In addition to organizations mentioned earlier, there was the Bikur Cholin Society that provided nursing care, the Hadassah, Young Judea, and more. Fund-raising was unceasing: there was always a raffle, picnic, or package party supporting one organization or another. And one was always greeted with the "pushke boxes," metal cans that collected pennies and nickels for The Jewish National Fund and other causes.

The immigrant Jewish neighborhood contained within the few blocks that enclosed Joseph Avenue was itself surrounded by enclaves of yet other nationalities. To the west was, of course, the natural boundary of the Genesee River. A bit south, near the railroad tracks, were Ormond and Leopold Streets where the few black families lived. Just beyond Hudson Avenue, a few blocks east, Poles and Ukrainians lived in one quarter and Italians in another. Our northern boundary was somewhat more indistinct. Some of the "better-off" Jews lived up there. At least they seemed better off because their houses looked a bit bigger and the adults spoke with less of a Yiddish accent then did our parents. Altogether, the general area was a kind of Eastern and Southern European jigsaw puzzle with one ethnic segment bordering the precincts of yet another.

There was little that went on in the neighborhood that did not have meaning, that was not part of some symbolic ritual or purpose or cultural practice. This was an unquestioned way of life: as long as we remained in the closed quarters of our community there was no reason for not accepting it. Most of these conventions and rules were sacred in nature but at the same time seemed to hold greater importance in terms of culture and identity. *Kashruth*, the strict dietary laws, controlled not only the nature and order of what one ate but also certain customs and styles among relatives and friends. That these eternal traditions existed at all encouraged among the more adventurous a truly delectable rebellion—a slice of crisp *bacon*, an iced *shrimp* cocktail, or just a plain *ham* sandwich.

In this regard, the neighborhood movie house, the old, seedy Lyric Theater, was a secular symbol and another metaphor of that era: the Saturday afternoon neighborhood movie and, as well for our parents, the midweek Bank Night, Keno night, or free dishes night. The Home's children were deprived of the Saturday afternoon with Ken Maynard, Hoot Gibson, Tom Mix, or other Old West heroes since, in the Orthodoxy of the institution, it would constitute a violation of the Sabbath. Actually, it was the wrath of the superintendent that they feared more than the wrath of God, since getting caught coming home from the movie would lead not so much to the moral anguish of transgression as it would to some painfully administered punishment. Yet at other times, the "Lyrics," as we called it, could usually be exploited as a possible source for our entertainment. If, of a midweek evening, there was nothing else to do, one of us might call the old lady who owned the theater and sold the tickets and politely inquire if "six or seven orphans could come to see the movie." For free, of course.

Penny Milk Time, No. 9 School, Rochester, New York, 1923 (Courtesy Stone Negative Collection, Rochester Museum & Science Center, Rochester, New York)

In retrospect, life, both in the Home and in the community was, in a way, tribal. You were born into it. It was part of you. You were part of it. Not only were you endowed with the customs and rules of Yiddishkeit from birth (and, if a boy, from the moment of circumcision), but from the outside, your caste as a Jew—as others defined you—was never in doubt. If perchance you somehow forgot for a moment to what tribe you belonged, even casual brushes with other nationalities or more rarely, real Americans, would tell you where you didn't belong. For the kids in the Home, this discrimination was sometimes even more stinging. Though he had achieved so many honors throughout his schooling and succeeded so well in life, Will still laments the anguish that went with being an "orphan" in the public elementary school. As he puts it: "The mental climate of the Home followed us wherever we went. It was a price. At school, everyone knew who we were . . . the kids from the Home got free cocoa or milk—other kids had to pay two cents. We weren't given two cents to pay so we could be like everybody else. And there were schmucky teachers then just like now: 'Now who is from the Home who can't pay for milk?' I don't think that I have ever gotten over that."

Being part of the tribe didn't necessarily mean that we always conformed to its customs. There is something wonderfully paradoxical about being a Jew. On the one hand, the customs and laws of Orthodox Judaism appear to be entirely unequivocal, absolute; on the other, there are inherent inducements for breach of custom.

David Hartman, a contemporary Judaic scholar, proposes that these paradoxical qualities are rooted in the ancient history of the individual Jew's curious relationship with his God—one that is akin to the relationship between the spirited child and the benevolent parent: in both instances, the mentor curbs his authority to encourage and enjoy the originality, the independence, and the initiative of the minor.[7] Putting this another way, Jews are always mindful and aware of the presence and power of their one God; simultaneously, they are conscious of the freedom to probe and test the limits of the bond that exists between God and themselves. We will see later how life in the Children's Home was in so many ways a living—and not infrequently, a flagrant and farcical—metaphor for this peculiar relationship. Within the austere and rigid climate of the Home there were many opportunities and incentives to creatively defy, bypass, twist, or otherwise see how far one could dare to go in challenging the rules that governed everyday life. For many, there was a certain sense of joyful deliverance and self-confidence that followed the success in pulling off one caper or another, especially when it could be done right under the nose of the piously Orthodox superintendent.

One purpose of this quick tour of a time and place sixty and seventy years past is to recreate a semblance of the social, cultural, and spiritual contexts for the lives of the elderly former wards of the Home portrayed in the coming pages. Doing history is, to be sure, an enterprise that is inevitably biased by selective recall, by the point from which one looks back, by intent and many other subjective variables: disclaimers are expected from those who recall other versions and details. Nonetheless, its intent is to prompt a readjustment of our modern, sophisticated lenses that, in looking back, tend to impose judgment on bygone conditions rather than understanding and insight.

Now, society is far more homogenized and marked by assimilation, at least as far as the second and third generations are concerned; then, the social world was carved into distinct ethnic sectors, the various immigrant groups carefully treading their way on the edges of the mainstream of society. Now, the responsibility for dispossessed children falls within the purview of the state or formal agencies created to offer a broad range of services; then, it was the community's choice or responsibility to do whatever it could for its dependents. Now, authority for the care of these children is often in the hands of trained professionals; then, this was rarely the case. In polarizing these differences, however, I am not implying that progress is necessarily equated with improvement.

In this grand tour we also have touched lightly on several themes that will evolve as we go forward: the importance of Yiddishkeit and its spirit of community for the lives of the children; patterns of life in the Home and the neighborhood; the importance of the contributions of both the leaders and the ordinary folk of the city; the origins of the families of the children and the conditions that prompted the placement of the children in the Home; and the changes that unwound over the thirty-odd years of the Home's existence until it closed its doors in 1947.

We will see these themes develop within the stories told by those men and women whose memories and reminiscences tend to link the past—their lives in the Home—with, for many, their present "golden years." The stories, the autobiographies, that the graduates of the Home shared with me so willingly destroy the psychological myth that we are destined to go on ever harvesting the results of the seeds planted in our earlier lives, that our personalities and outlooks are inescapably molded by the events of childhood. Without overlooking the painful woes and hardships of institutional life, we will witness the varied and extraordinary ways these people interpret their histories and weave their distinctively personal stories. They do so in a manner that preserves dignity and integrity, that serves to overcome adversity, and, above all, that creates a sense of mastery and worth. Much as they had in common, their individual stories are elegant and uniquely different improvisations on their collective themes of living.

We return to the conversation between Phil and Will for testimonies to the fact that people can share similar beginnings and, perhaps, even arrive at comparable realizations. Yet the meaning of the entire complex necessarily is shaped by individual differences in perceptions, sentiments, import, and impressions.

Phil points out that he and Will, although they don't see each other that often, turned out to be social workers and have always been like "surrogate brothers . . . the feelings are there." But he makes the point what *his* version of what life was like in the Home and what it meant to him:

> What I hated was the loss of autonomy. It was like a shroud over you. That you had to get up in the morning at five, that you had to do your chores, that you had to pray, that you had to go to breakfast, then more chores, then school, then more chores, then Hebrew, then vesper services, then you had supper, and then more chores. There was never time to be a child. . . . But I made up my mind that I was not going to be a victim . . . and was always ready to fight, mostly for other people not me. . . . My incentive to go somewhere in life came later from my relationships with other camp counselors [with whom he worked]. . . . I realized there was a big difference between us. I tried to be like them—it was a tough struggle but I did it.

Will, in turn, agrees that the Home was devastating insofar as his experiences burdened him with feelings of inferiority. Yet, he adds:

> Yet most of us did pretty well. See, there were good things that happened. We had opportunities. I maybe would never have gotten to college if it wasn't for the scholarship fund. If I were brought up on North Street with my aunt, may she rest in peace, I could have been a hood by now. And I will always treasure that opportunity. How much did the Home drive us to want . . . like, I wanted to achieve. I had to prove that I was somebody even though I could daven. Maybe that drove me into social work aside from other things. But I had to make it. I had to be somebody.

T W O

Orphanages
Origins

Oh! teach the orphan-boy to read, or teach the orphan girl to sew.
—Alfred Lord Tennyson

History is an alluring trap. When one risks reopening the dependable archives of memory, former certainties that give life its logic and order become unsettled and no longer hold. Thus, one is compelled to look again to rediscover how things "really" were, to rearrange and restore the logic and sequence of memory. I learned this lesson quickly and well while I listened to Will and Phil tell their stories about life in the Home and, subsequently, when other "graduates" generously shared their autobiographies with me. I would need to rethink and revise my personal recollections of the Home.

At the outset, I had no illusions that this study would be a project without complications. First, I discovered that I could not revisit those times and lives in the role of an impersonal spectator. Any pretense of the kind of detachment of objectivity that we like to believe purifies serious research dissolved immediately: as I already mentioned, many of the former kids, now my contemporaries, greeted me not as an aging professor-researcher but as the former "Howie" whom they remembered as another character in their unwritten autobiographies. Anna, for example, startled me after we had exchanged our greetings, when she reminded me that she still had the pin I had given her *fifty years ago*. "What pin?," I struggled to recall, until with a sudden blush, a page of memory turned. I was twelve and I did have a crush on Anna and, in my state of youthful ardor, I impulsively gave her my father's Odd Fellows lodge pin.

And so I had to adapt to being both an insider and an outsider in my endeavor to recapture these lives and times. I was an insider to the extent that together, we were part of a common culture at one point in time. But I was also a distinct outsider: I could not know, as they did, what growing up in an institution was really like, what it was like to endure childhood apart from one's parents.

This awareness made for yet another lesson to be learned, one that will thread its way through the recollected meanings of the stories that will be documented in these pages. Not only were my own memories and their inferences about those early years in question, but I also had to reconsider what I thought I knew—and even what I had taught as a professor—about the vagaries of child development. The stories that were shared with me cast doubt on both the theories and conventional wisdom that intuitively assume that an institutional childhood will lead to a later life beset with special problems: such generalizations fail to account for the countless accidents, twists, contingencies, luck in its various forms, and other uncertainties that would undermine such a straight and narrow path to adulthood.

These observations came to shape the purpose of this chapter and the next. Plainly, this study could not be merely a chronological account of the Children's Home and a biographical survey of the Home's children; such a two-dimensional view would be a static portrait of a place and its people that began and ended over particular time, a memento of another day. As I noted in the first chapter, even at the start as I entered the lives of Will, Phil, and a few others, I knew that I had to at least give credit to the cultural texture, its seams and folds and overlaps in which lives were imbedded. The intent, however, to capture the significance of *history* required the decision about where to start. It seemed that the earlier background of conditions in and out of the field of child care that led to the creation of the Jewish Children's Home in the first place was the proper place.

The authority of history becomes apparent once we begin to give serious thought to "what *really* happened and what did it mean?" Ordinarily, on glancing back in time, we tend to accept the past as a finished piece of business, as frozen in time as a scene in an old snapshot. But my conversations with the former residents reminded me of the obvious: the Home had its own history which, in turn, was inseparable from the history of the Rochester Jewish community. And this historical consciousness stirred an even more basic question: in historical terms, how did it turn out that institutional care would become an acceptable solution to the problems and needs of children; not just the children of Jewish immigrants in Rochester, but all dependent or surplus children?

Useful explanations can be found in broad theories that attempt to account for why, in the nineteenth century particularly, institutional care expanded and became an official practice.[1] One theory suggests that the institution was seen as an improvement over previous practices; a second theory views institutions as the expression of the desire of wealthy classes to exercise control over the poor; a third theory sees institutions as a means of strengthening the community during times of industrial change, or of providing discipline, training, and moral reform. In general sociological terms these theories capture possible trends or persuasions; they cannot, however, account for the distinctly personal motives and needs powerful enough to urge citizens to come forward and take on the responsibility of establishing the children's institution.

This last question was kindled by my growing appreciation of the significance and force of Yiddishkeit in the period in which the Jewish Children's Home was founded. I wondered first, perhaps naively, why *Jewish* organizations and communities turned to the institution as a refuge for their dependent children and, second, in so doing, why they continued to rely on the previous century's model of the congregate asylum, particularly at a point in time when progressive movements in child welfare were beginning to advocate more humane approaches such as the cottage plan?

The obvious answer to the first question is *historical:* as I will make plain in the pages that follow, the children's institution over time became the public solution to the problem of dependency. The acceptance of the congregate institution—a single shelter housing numbers of children—is, I will show, based on more complex reasons, including the place of tradition and the restraints of Orthodox Judaism as opposed to more liberal forms of Judaism.

As a starting point for this historical inquiry, it is important to note that although the Rochester Jewish Children's Home was more frequently called "the orphans home on Gorham Street," very few of more than 250 children who spent all or some part of their youth in the Home had lost both parents. The majority did have one parent; they were what were then called the "half-orphans." Parents' illness, poverty, and, in some cases, desertion, as well as a lack of relatives able to care for these children, accounted for the practical causes of their placement in the Home. These children were acutely dependent; the Home took care of their needs. A graduate of the Home expressed this equation in a matter-of-fact way: "My mother died, my father was barely making a living, my relatives had their own problems, and I was seven. What else was there to do but put me in the Home?"

True. "What else was there to do?" Despite this plaintive question, I could not help but wonder what it meant for families, within the Jewish culture, character, and custom, to relinquish their children to the institution. An old Yiddish saying has it that "to its parents, no child is superfluous." Silberman[2] reminds us that there is a distinctive nature to parent-child relationships in Jewish families wherein parents see their children as extensions of themselves. This may be called *naches*—difficult to translate but implying the kind of honor, fulfillment, and joy that only one's child can provide. The child's success becomes the parents' success; the child's failure, the parents' failure.

The question becomes even more poignant considering that the parents of these children did not leave their homes in Lodz, Vilna, or Brusilov to surrender their own children to an institution. Whether in search of the *goldene medina* or merely a job in a clothing factory, their hopes did not include the sundering of their own family. But, for the most part, the feelings and thoughts of parents or relatives whose dire circumstances led to the entry of their children into the Home are lost to time. The early records of the Home are less than sparse. They contain the parents' national origins and a scrawled word or two about the reasons for admission: "mother has heart trouble," or "father is dead, mother unable to support children." Later records are not much more informative.

As I grappled with these questions, the obligation to place the institution and its people in their proper historical perspective became increasingly apparent. Referring again to the objectivity-subjectivity issues in doing social history, I was aware of the natural tendency to look back to this era with a personal view similar to what William Manchester calls "generational chauvinism," or the tendency to judge the practices of past eras by standards of the present.[3]

From our modern child-centered perspective, children's institutions of previous generations are apt to be seen as some kind of archaeological curiosity. Whether one thinks about Dickens' Oliver Twist or other examples of the primitive asylum or orphanage, many harsh adjectives are likely to come to mind: punitive, unfeeling, regimented, moralistic, authoritarian, and so on. As we will see, all too often these terms are well justified. At the same time, to leave it at that, simply to relegate the earlier children's institution to a rude and primitive place in history, would be to overlook its importance to society and the purposes it served. Thus, it is essential to keep some issues in mind on going back in time to look at the conditions and patterns of institutional care foreshadowing the founding of the Rochester Jewish Children's Home.

First, granting that institutional life was harsh and often lacked even the rudiments of family life, we cannot reflexively conclude how the experience affected the later life of its wards. As Phil observes, "Our porridge came from the same pot, even from the same ladle, but we digested the stuff in many ways." For many residents, institutional life was more than a poor substitute for the family: for them, the Home signified rescue, security, survival, and opportunities otherwise out of reach. Out of adversity, others experienced growth and independence, or what Phil describes as "the need to keep our hands near the handle of our swords."

Second, we need to lend a critical eye to the times—the particular social era and its patterns and standards for child rearing. Any institution, including the Children's Home, is a social artifact, its form molded by what citizens and leaders knew and believed about how any child, including the dependent, ought to be raised. Likewise, it is important to take note of just how obligated society itself felt to care for its needy children. These attitudes would inevitably bear on the treatment, training, and disposition toward the institution's charges. I recall an alumnus of the Home summing up "how it was then" in that time and culture: "That's what being a kid was like in those days, except for the big difference that we were in the Home and the others weren't."

THE CHILD IN HISTORY

How the basic terms "child" or "childhood" are defined at any point in time is related to the treatment and expectations of minors—the dependents in particular.

Nowadays, we are pretty clear about what childhood is and the period of life that it covers. Moreover, the definition becomes even more fine-grained as clinicians, theorists, and researchers delineate with greater precision the stages of development ranging from the prenatal on into young adulthood. And, in turn, these stages are broken down into levels of cognitive, mental, psychosexual, physical, and moral development: any parent has available information that will pinpoint where the child ought to be according to any number of developmental schemes.

When we look back over our shoulder to previous eras we discover how little was the consistency or continuity about how "child" or "childhood" was regarded. The chronological boundaries of childhood—when childhood ended and majority was attained—varied greatly depending on places and times in history.[4] In some eras males became adults at age fourteen, females at age twelve. In other times, boys were apprenticed at the age of seven and girls were betrothed at the age of nine. As we will see, it was not unusual in the nineteenth century for boys to be shipped out as apprentices in their early teens. At the Jewish Children's Home, from its founding in 1914 to its closing over thirty years later, age sixteen, with few exceptions, was the mandatory age at which the wards were expected to leave and find employment: this was deemed the nominal age for maturity and independence. What it meant to be a child also varied greatly across time in accord with changes and shifts in the structure of society and the family. At one point in time, the child was depicted as an innocent; at another, as an obligated dependent; and in others as mentally incompetent, or even as a precious symbol of youthfulness. As the perceptions and definitions of the child changed over time so did the expectations and regard for the child.

Societies also tend to attach certain cultural symbols and metaphors to the concept of childhood that affected prevailing attitudes. References can be found to the child as "the poor man's riches"; as a token of the grace of God; as the living symbol of life's aspirations; or often as just a little devil. The doleful vision of the orphaned or dependent child in particular generally stirred more uneasy and disquieting omens.[5] The abandonment of these forlorn creatures, even now among the homeless, can stir our sense of vulnerability. At the other extreme are certain heroic myths, shaped by many allegoric visions of the orphan—personified by Oliver Twist, David Copperfield, and Jane Eyre—who rises out of the debris of desolation and abuse. And not the least, the orphan in our midst exposes some of the worst flaws of society. At one time or another, the orphaned child was held up as evidence of the community's failure to care for its own, as a sign of economic injustice, as a consequence of the moral breakdown of the family, or was portrayed as a potential degenerate who had inherited the depravities of his pauper parents. These perceptions persist as we now are horrified by even the newsclips of children on the streets or living in violent or sickly dwellings.

The symbols for the Jewish orphan held more sympathetic meanings. In the Yiddish tongue, *yosim,* a literal term for "orphan" borrowed from Hebrew, or more frequently, the diminutive, *yoseml,* is used to express the affection felt for the child; the idiom *nebach a yoseml* voices the pity or compassion for *anyone* suffering a terrible loss.[6] Often, the vulnerable state of the *yosim* symbolized for the Jewish people the tribal fear that the orphaned child might forever be lost to the faith or, more ominously, become converted to Christianity.

Economic and social conditions and prevailing attitudes about the family in past generations also had much to do with questions of obligation to and responsibility for the welfare of dependent children. What might now be judged as pitiless insensitivity or maliciousness on the part of particular human groupings actually mirrored their poor standards of family life, the demeaning effects of economic hardships, and the power of a paternalistic authority.

PATERNALISM AND PATRIARCHAL CONTROL

Both "paternalism" and "patriarchal" signify male power and governance, optimally protective but always absolute. These terms reflect a social doctrine that remained relatively unchanged well into (and some will argue that it is still present) the twentieth century. Its meaning for institutional care of dependents is apparent: it is the weight of paternalism that leads to the common stereotype of the orphanage or asylum as a stern, autocratic, and rigidly regulated institution. We think of the orphanage and Oliver Twist comes to mind, basin and spoon in hand, pleading, "Please, sir, I want some more," for which he receives a blow to the head rather than more gruel. This was cruel behavior by any standards; certainly there was no scarcity among many institutions of ill-trained wardens and hardhearted administrators of the likes of Oliver's master, Mr. Bumble. Yet, not all of Mr. Bumble's counterparts in other institutions were necessarily cruel for the sake of cruelty alone. It must be understood that strict order and regulations were standard practices that echoed the rules and practices that, within a patriarchal society, were laid onto most children even in ordinary families. This was society's decree, a legal as well as a cultural fact that defined children's required submission to adult authority. It was the ethos of the times that normalized methods of child care and supervision that we would now judge as severe and unfeeling.

This ethos we will see was a powerful influence guiding the nature of Jewish institutional life in both positive and negative ways. The nature of paternalism that was ordained by the laws and culture of the times was fortified (if not multiplied) by the enduring and commanding dictates of Orthodox Judaic traditions. For it is in the Halakah—the centuries' old Judaic law—where the obligation of the Jewish child to respect and obey his father and mother (or any surrogate) is explicitly spelled out.[7] Indeed, this will be a familiar theme and the expressions of a way of life in the reminiscences of our alumni.

THE DEPENDENT CHILD IN PAST TIMES

Like the poor, the dependent child, the orphan, the waif has ever been with us. The asylum or orphanage as a solution to this social malady was, within the span of civilization, a very recent phenomenon. From the time of the classical eras of ancient Greece and Rome until the eighteenth century, the surplus or unwanted child was simply abandoned not only by poor and depleted families but by the affluent as well.[8]

With all of its tragic overtones, the abandoned child is a well-known theme in mythology: the fable of Moses set afloat on a river in a basket, for example, or Oedipus cast out on a mountain by his father. The practice of abandonment itself was seen neither as an uncaring act by parents nor as something to be condemned by the community; in its time, it was used in what might then have been considered in the best interests of the child. Families suffering privation left their children in a public place expecting that the child might have a more promising life if taken in by others and raised as an economic asset—as a slave or a servant. The children of more affluent families were also vulnerable to abandonment for other reasons, including the plan to reduce the number of heirs to the family's property and therefore assure that a select few would enjoy their larger inheritance.

In the absence of humane solutions to the plight of the homeless children who filled the streets of eighteenth century Europe, Jonathan Swift wrote his social commentary, a bitter satire, in 1729. Called "A Modest Proposal, For Preventing the Children of poor People in Ireland, from being a Burden to their Parents or Country; and for making them beneficial to the Publick," this sardonic essay suggested that since children under twelve years of age are not saleable commodities, they be used as "most delicious, nourishing and wholesome Food, whether Stewed, Roasted, Baked or Boiled."[9] This practice, Swift craftily advised, would benefit everyone: the poor would get financial reward; the public would be relieved of the cost of otherwise maintaining these children; and the wealthy would delight in gustatory enjoyment.

Paradoxically, many children who were abandoned survived far better than those who became inmates of the first institutions, the religious asylums founded to provide care and shelter: those children who were gathered and closed into the asylum walls were immediately placed at risk. Given the primitive state of hygiene and medicine in that age, it was inevitable that any disease would quickly spread and become a deathly plague.

The first orphanages were created (as were many to follow) not by plan but by need. After infanticide was outlawed by the early Christian Church, overburdened, destitute parents would leave their young on the doorsteps of the Church as offerings and servants to God.[10] With the Church assuming the obligation to house these children, it then became customary for Western societies to place the burden of responsibility on religious denominations, both Christian and Jewish, to protect and care for increasingly greater numbers of excess or orphaned children. Altogether, the institution became society's determining solution to the problems of the dependent child with particular lasting implications.

A consequence of these religious origins of the orphanage was that wards would be subject to strong doses of religious training: the incentive to save souls and eliminate dependency was unyielding. Poverty was considered a sign of moral weakness or vice, making it mandatory that children could be converted and imbued with religious spirit as a remedy for moral depravity.[11] In time, daily religious instruction and ritual became an institutional fact in its own right.

The practice of institutionalizing children led to another outcome—a measure of immunity to accountability. When young dependents are placed in an orphanage they are not merely removed from their natural environment but, in this process, are also removed from the sight of society. Many children's institutions became an island, literally or figuratively walled off from the community they served. Thus, even in modern times, when group care settings are accountable to funding sources, boards of directors, or other citizen groups, the institution continues to retain a certain internal autonomy as to its mission and methods.

SHELTER AND CARE IN THE NINETEENTH CENTURY

Against the backgrounds described, our historical tour starts at the outset of the nineteenth century. At that time there were some indications of a new spirit that pressed for more humane approaches to the shelter and care of dispossessed children. It was a spirit shaped by a strict moral code that judged human qualities in absolute terms: success, achievement, wealth were symbols of strong moral character; pauperism, idleness, and debauchery of any kind were evidence of evil or moral failure. Consistent with such morality, the mission of charitable benefactors was to "rescue," "save," or "redeem" children, either from the possibility of their becoming moral degenerates or from the immoral grasp of their unfit or corrupt parents.

Since state and federal authorities were indifferent to the ordeals of the dependent child until the early twentieth century, it fell to the local community and its charitable and religious groups to devise ways to "rescue" these unfortunates. The orphanage emerged as one major solution. But to put the orphanage into its rightful perspective, other "rescue" schemes require brief mention: almshouses, indenture, and later in the nineteenth century, "orphan trains."[12]

The "poorhouse," more formally known as the almshouse, was created as a miserable warehouse for impoverished families, along with derelicts and the insane. Thousands of children languished in almshouses well into the 1920s despite many private and public efforts to extricate them from these quarters. Numberless children were conceived in this asylum, and for some it became their permanent home. Each city had its own statutes governing the kinds of children subject to rescue and commitment to the almshouse. In New York, the laws covered neglected or abandoned children, those soliciting charity from door to door, or those whose mothers were notoriously immoral. Massachusetts law "protected" children under sixteen who were suffering from the vices of their parents that might lead them to idle and dissolute lives.

Indenture, placing children in other families, was common practice first in Europe and then in America. It was both a social solution and a business contract. For some it was also a romantic and pleasing solution particularly when it offered a vision of these street urchins living in the rural countryside where, it was hoped, they would prosper amid the beauty of a pastoral environment. Overlooked, of course, was the absence of safeguards to protect the children from deprivation, overwork, and drudgery amid this rustic setting.

Once asylums and orphanages took hold as major forms of child care, a significant alternative arose in the mid-1800s. This was the "orphan train" project created by the young Charles Loring Brace, a theologian turned child rescue worker, who also founded the Children's Aid Society. Having little faith in the effectiveness of orphans institutions, Brace believed that "the family is God's Reformatory and every child of bad habits who can secure a place in a Christian home is in the best possible place for his improvement."[13] Brace also entertained an idyllic notion about the bounties of the great open spaces and the basic good-hearted nature of its rural folk.

Boys and girls of the city streets were rounded up and legal guardianship was established. If parents were alive they had to relinquish custody to the Society. Agents of the Society searched for likely homes in the towns and villages of Michigan, Illinois, Iowa, and Nebraska by posting advertisements ("Wanted: Homes for Children") in local newspapers. When the train steamed into the town, its children were transported to the local church where the citizenry awaited them to select a boy or girl from among the well-scrubbed group. The unlucky ones who were overlooked were returned to the train and were forwarded to the next town with the hope that the same procedure might result in better luck.

The "orphan trains" continued to roll until as late as 1929. Over 150,000 children found homes in the rural Midwest in the seventy-five years of the project's existence. While this project filtered off numbers of dependent children, the orphanage continued its steady growth.

ORPHAN ASYLUMS IN THE NINETEENTH CENTURY

The first major institution, the New York Orphan Asylum (NYOA), opened its doors in the early 1800s. This institution deserves closer attention because its methods and philosophy served as a model for the increasing number of other institutions that emerged across the entire country. By the end of the century, 613 orphanages were in operation. In 1909, at the time of the White House Conference on the Care of Dependent Children, 115,000 children were in institutional care and this number increased to 144,000 well into the twentieth century.[14]

The founding of NYOA requires attention for another salient reason: it reflects the significant (but often overlooked) efforts of women in improving the lot of dependent children in a time when conventional beliefs about the woman's role were put in these terms: "That *home* is her appropriate and appointed sphere of action there can be no shadow of doubt, for the dictates of nature are plain and imperative on this subject, and the injunctions given in Scripture no less explicit."[15]

The NYOA eventually came into existence as an unforeseen and unfortunate result of the misadventures of one ambitious welfare enterprise that led to the need for another. Compassion compelled a group of middle-class volunteer women to form "The Society for the Relief of Widows with Small Children." When several of these widows ultimately fell ill or died, out of their gratitude they bequeathed their children to their benefactresses. What were they to do with these orphans? The Society women were reluctant to violate their promise to these mothers or to lose touch with the dispossessed waifs. Their sympathies did not permit them to resort to conventional practices of indenturing the children or depositing them in almshouses. Many children were taken into the homes of the members, but this could only be a temporary solution. As Thurston records it: "After careful, and not hasty deliberation, their pious friends were called into council, especially Mrs. Sarah Hoffman, whose excellent judgment strengthened by much experience in charity, and commanding social position, rendered it peculiarly desirable that the movement should be made under her auspices, and it was determined that an appeal should be made to the benevolent public of New York for the means and agencies necessary for the founding of an Orphan Asylum."[16]

The NYOA was organized in 1808 with Mrs. Hoffman chosen as first directress; twelve other women became officers and trustees. Twelve orphans were admitted in the first six months and, by 1821, 152 children were housed in a permanent building designed for their purposes.

The constitution of NYOA expressed a moralistic philosophy that defined the officers of the institution as missionaries who rescue children and who carry out the moral obligation to convert these children into pious and useful adults.

> Amongst the afflicted of our suffering race none makes a stronger or more impressive appeal to humanity than the destitute orphan. . . . God Himself has marked the fatherless as the peculiar subjects of his divine compassion. "A father of the fatherless is God in His holy habitation." "When my father and mother forsake me, then the Lord will take me up." To be the blessed instrument of Divine

Providence in making good the promise of God is a privilege equally desirable and honorable to the benevolent heart.[17]

The missionary calling of these benevolent citizens was proclaimed in the rules and procedures that clearly defined how the rescued child was to be converted into a useful and virtuous adult, regulations that forecast the practices of institutions, including the Rochester Jewish Children's Home, founded over the next one hundred years. Control and management were the watchwords from the moment a child was being considered for placement. Only healthy children were received after being pronounced free from infection or incurable disease by a "respectable" physician. Friends or family were required to renounce all claims to the orphan forever; the Asylum would assume full responsibility for food, clothing, education, and "religious instruction, moral example, and habits of industry inculcated on their minds." The right to control the child had full legal support.[18]

Since "industry" was a major goal of institutionalization, the length of stay in the Asylum depended on the readiness of the child to earn his or her living. When this was decided, the child was indentured to a reputable person or family. Boys were put out as servants until the age of fifteen and then bound out as apprentices to "virtuous mechanics in hope of their becoming useful and happy members of the community and perhaps the future benefactors of the institution which nurtured their helpless infancy." Girls were bound out as servants from the time they could read and write until they were eighteen, at which point it was assumed that they would marry.

These rules cannot be considered unreasonable or discriminatory: it was not until the next century that society considered the need for Child Labor Laws, and so one could find very young children, even from intact families, toiling in mills, factories, and fields across the country. Ironically, asylum wards had the advantage not common in ordinary families—that is, the thought and care given to judgments about their individual readiness for indenture and the character of the people to whom they were bound out.

Consider that expectations of orphanage children in this time before the advent of psychology and child-centeredness were predicated on firm standards, virtues, and morals. Children behaved in accord with an explicit set of rules that governed cleanliness, attire, mealtimes, prayer, education, and play. Staff was also subject to these controls. Corporal punishment could be inflicted only by the superintendent, depending on his judgment about the need for discipline but within certain restrictions: only boys could be punished physically and always in the presence of another caretaker. One view of how these rules worked in just a portion of any day is expressed by a resident of NYOA; it may be used as a comparison with the accounts by the Home's children. The following is a direct transcript:

We had to rise at 6 o'clock in the morning the Big Bell for all to arise. We had to wash and get in Line by Six Thirty and we had to show our hands and faces to see if they were clean. We were arranged according to sizes. Then we had to march in the Dining room and the Girls on one side and the boys on the opposite side. After Breakfast we had to go in the assembly room and hold services. We had to sing Hymn without Hymn book and repeat Chapter of the Bible 23 Epistle, 14 chapter of John, Psalms I, Ten Commandments, Beatitudes and we had to study the Hymn in the Class when we had the Day School in order. After services in the morning we had to make the Beds and Clean up. Then it was 8 o'clock and time for Day School to begin. We had very bright teachers they must of bin College graduates. 12 o'clock was the limit for the morning Session and we all had to assemble and get Clean and go to Dinner.[19]

Another former inmate of an orphan home, who later became a minister, recalls his experience in a somewhat more melancholy tone:

In an institution the individual counts for nothing! Nor is the welfare, temperament, or disposition of any one child taken into consideration. . . . Life must be uniform, logical, and conventional. . . . The duties, tasks, and experiences of one day become the duties, tasks, and experiences of all the others. . . . The activities of every hour are planned. Promptly at seven o'clock we were marched to our morning bowl of oatmeal, coffee and dry bread which was served between German prayers and devotions. For religion held an important place in the daily routine . . . the girls were given the work of the dining room and kitchen; while the boys with pails and brooms proceeded to wash the floors. "Useful training" was the argument.[20]

THE HEBREW ORPHAN ASYLUM

The first Jewish asylum, the Hebrew Orphan Asylum (HOA) in New York, was founded in the mid-1800s. The accidental reasons and conditions for its origins are not dissimilar from those that led to creation of NYOA.[21]

At the turn of the nineteenth century, New York was a small bustling port city of over 100,000 inhabitants of which only 500 were Jews, descendants of the first migration of Jews in the mid-1600s. A group of Portuguese Jews was allowed to enter New Amsterdam on the condition that they would always care for their own poor. In the years that followed, the Jewish community was enlarged by Jews coming from Holland and England. Together, they maintained one congregation that provided fuel, medical care, and financial aid for the poor. Widows and the aged were cared for in their own homes. Orphans were boarded out or apprenticed to tradesmen.

Thirty years prior to the opening of HOA, men of the congregation formed the Hebrew Benevolent Society after debating their concerns about conditions within their Jewish community and how its more unfortunate members were being cared for. The members were shocked on learning that a Jewish woman had actually died in the poorhouse when it had been the duty of the trustees of the congregation to see to it that no Jew ever entered that dismal colony. A deeper concern was expressed about the risk that Jews of this growing community would lose their identity. There were no ghetto walls or discriminatory laws that would otherwise draw these Jews into protective unity; thus, it was feared that they might be tempted to forget their heritage and rituals or, much worse, succumb to the pleas of Christian groups to convert. Guided by the deeply ingrained commitment to the idea of social justice embodied in the principles of *tzedakah*, it was decided to use some excess funds to create the Benevolent Society itself.

Despite the scourges of yellow fever and cholera and the swell of Jewish immigrants from Germany and Poland, an asylum was not yet required for the orphaned and destitute Jewish children. They continued to be cared for by families of the first congregation and the synagogues that later multiplied in the community. By mid-century, however, the need for a home for orphans became pressing. The streets of New York were filled with homeless urchins and beggars, considered by the police to be "street rats." Was it possible, Jewish citizens wondered, that Jewish children were among this horde? Yet, action was not taken until an alarming editorial was published in the *Jewish Messenger:* a Jewish child had been placed in a non-Jewish orphanage and converted to Christianity![22]

Such fears prompted the opening of a small, temporary asylum pending the construction of a larger building. On behalf of the Jewish community, the trustees took legal and exclusive custody of orphans, half-orphans, and indigent children whom they agreed to maintain, provide for, educate, and instruct; at age 13 they would be bound out to be taught some useful employment.

Life in the HOA differed, it seems, from NYOA only in regard to the kind of prayers that were said and the God to whom they were directed. One of the first residents recalled the increasingly familiar daily routine: "get up, say your prayers, get your breakfast, go to school, come back, study your lessons, study Hebrew, get your supper, and go to bed . . . mush and milk, and hominy and milk, and mush and molasses, and rice and milk—and in the evening we had milk and bread."[23]

OTHER ASYLUMS

Although the men of the Jewish community were responsible for the founding of the first Jewish institution, many subsequent orphanages were products of and benefited from the compassion and the extraordinary efforts and leadership of women. Again, these were women of Jewish communities whose charitable activities were the only expression of initiative and capability that society would allow them.

Rebecca Gratz stands out as a remarkable example, a woman whose persistent efforts eventually were responsible for the founding of the Jewish Foster Home and Orphan Asylum in Philadelphia in the 1850s.[24] A sampling of her many contributions to the welfare of women and children drawn from the biographical dictionary, *Notable American Women 1607–1950*, Vol. II (Radcliffe

College, pp. 75–76), notes that, at age twenty, she helped organize in Philadelphia the pioneering Female Association for the Relief of Women and Children in Reduced Circumstances (1801). She was one of the founders of the nonsectarian Philadelphia Orphan Asylum (1815). She created the Female Hebrew Benevolent Society (1855). And during this time she raised the nine children of her sister who died in 1823.

Having served as the secretary of the Philadelphia Orphan Asylum she bore witness to the fact that, in the absence of a Jewish institution, many Jewish children were admitted to the Asylum, were raised as Christians, then released and indentured to Christians, finally returning to their former Jewish community to which they could no longer adapt.

Miss Gratz actively campaigned for support for a Jewish institution by writing tracts, stirring up friends, and arranging meetings in synagogues. It took years of steady effort to enlist other women in a movement to provide a home in which "orphans and children of Indigent Israelites may be rescued from the evils of ignorance and vice . . . and instructed in moral and religious duties and thus prepared to become useful members of society."[25]

A Ladies Society was formed that succeeded in opening a home for five children and struggled for twenty years to keep the Jewish Asylum going. Unable to secure adequate financial backing, they finally surrendered their administrative powers to men who would be more successful in raising funds.

Priscilla Joachimsen, another extraordinary Jewish woman and the wife of a very prominent public servant, was the guiding force who effected the founding of what later became the prestigious and progressive institution, The Hebrew Sheltering Guardian Society of New York (HSGS). Her husband was a federal prosecutor who secured convictions of slave traders, a brigadier general in the Civil War, and a judge. But Mrs. Joachimsen's prominence was not due entirely to her husband's status. On her own, she contributed to the establishment of a Home for the Aged and Infirm Hebrews and New York's first day-care centers. In the late 1870s she became president of HSGS, which she administered with the help of an all-women board of managers and an all-male advisory committee. Her remarks on the day of the opening of the institution summed up the commitments of these women: "We have to take care and nurse the neglected and abandoned Jewish children because we are *Jewesses.*"[26]

These commitments were essential since the women constantly braced themselves against the tide of community opinion that women did not belong in controlling positions since they were not capable of managing money, particularly public funds. Despite this battle for autonomy, the institution prospered: in the first year alone, 164 children were accepted. Even more important, the women managers were successful in instituting some unconventionally liberal new programs which, over time, came to be adopted by other institutions.

It must be said that in effecting these changes, the women managers not only softened harsh, ingrained institutional routines but diverged from Jewish (notably Orthodox) custom. One notorious example was the attempt to "Americanize" the wards of the orphanage by encouraging their involvement in the larger community, a plan that was also followed by the Rochester Jewish Children's Home that greatly benefited its children. To be sure, the children ate, slept, and received their religious education within the orphanage walls, but they attended public school, enjoyed recreation in the neighborhood, and went to outings in public beaches and parks. In turn, neighborhood children were encouraged to visit the orphanage.

Despite these changes, patriarchal controls were not significantly diminished. Michael Sharlitt, who becomes an informative visitor to these pages, refers in his autobiography to the "calculated paternalism" that was particularly reflected in the skimpy budgets that allowed for twenty-five cents per day for the care of a child.[27] Still, even with the persistence of "calculated" or uncalculated paternalism, the devoted efforts of Mrs. Joachimsen and her cohorts must have succeeded in encouraging a progressive climate that, over time, increased concern with the needs of children not only at HSGS but in other institutions as well.

In Sharlitt's memoirs we find evidence of such shifts in policies and programs occurring in the later years of the nineteenth century and on into the twentieth. As a pacesetter in the field of child welfare, his authority must be heeded: he was an orphan in the Hebrew Sheltering and Guardian Society in the latter 1800s and later served as its assistant superintendent. We will learn from him about the process of liberalization occurring at that institution that bridged the two centuries. His remarkable career in child welfare was accomplished when he later became superintendent of the Cleveland Jewish Orphans Home. Keeping pace with progress in child welfare, he was instrumental in overseeing that orphanage's transformation into the now prominent residential treatment center, Bellefaire.

As he recounts, he entered HSGS in 1887 when he was four years old. There, children were cared for, but at a very modest and austere level of maintenance by personnel who had little or no preparation for their work. Contagion—ringworm, dysentery, and trachoma—played havoc. Food, as was frequently the case, was meager: bread and coffee for breakfast, watery soup at noon, and to break the monotony of the evening meal of bread and tea, a piece of herring on Sabbath eve and an annual serving of two frankfurters when the Board of Directors met. All children dressed alike and recreation depended on their own creativity and imagination. Visits by relatives on the infrequent visiting days were carefully policed to prevent their bringing in food and sweets. But in Sharlitt's reminiscences we also get a hint of the temperaments and resolve that are bred within the restrictive confines of the children's institution and that will be found in the stories of the children of the Rochester Home. Many wards resisted becoming institutionalized by devising creative (and sometimes devious) ways of asserting selfhood. The ability to "beat the system" even in small ways, or to find a measure of success in school, develop talents, or create certain escapes (literally and symbolically) helped preserve a sense of inner unity and worth and not the least, a trace of humor that lasted into and fostered a worthwhile adulthood.

In this regard, consider the significance of Sharlitt's remarkable achievements: he was not only undefeated by his institutional years that were bereft of normal family life, but also drew from these early experiences in his endeavors to enrich the lives of later dependent and orphaned children. To be sure, this is one heroic story; but there are many others, perhaps less dramatic or influential, but no less indicative of spirit, strength, and will. Sharlitt's words echo the meaningful theme that winds through this study—the compelling influence of the Jewish community on the existence of these children.

> I am grateful that there was a Jewish community that made it a "must" . . . to accept responsibility for the incapacitated and underprivileged. True, when this story began, succor and service were rudimentary. . . . But there was a degree of sufficiency in Jewish organized life in this country in those early days to care for the extreme helpless, and as an orphan in the late eighties of the last century, I was a beneficiary of this traditional development of the Jew's desire to take care of their own.[28]

Sharlitt builds on a theme that will become more familiar—the undimmed spirit, the vitality, camaraderie, and strength of children otherwise controlled and regimented by their caretakers: "I have always been something of a dreamer, and in those drifting days I very likely played with the open skies by day and the stars by night, and the silver streak of the beautiful Hudson in the long summers. We boys would huddle together in the yard in intimate groups, tell our extravagant tales—and whisper the daring feats of bolder spirits. . . . So often such moments brought sweetness to the day."[29]

ORPHANAGES: THE TWENTIETH CENTURY

> The turn of the century brought some changes in the opaque clouds of blight, changes that must have had their origin in the slowly developing conscience of society. Education, particularly, opened up its opportunities. . . . Child labor legislation began its onward march. . . . And so it was within the walls of institutions for dependent children. There were no deep structural and policy changes at first, but the introduction of some new personalities, organizationally and marginally, made for a slow transfusion of a new spirit.[30]

In these words, Michael Sharlitt recalls the "new spirit" that marked the beginning of the new century, the era in which the Rochester Jewish Children's Home welcomed its first wards. Within this "slow transfusion," a few children's institutions quickly adopted this new spirit; most others were, in large part, untouched by these innovations in child care.

The few anecdotes of Will, Phil, and Sue in the first chapter dispel any notion that the Jewish Children's Home was entirely seized by the "new spirit" of the new century.

THE NEW ORDER IN CHILD CARE

We observed that the altruistic efforts of nineteenth-century child rescuers were largely driven by ingrained paternalistic doctrines aimed at regimentation, control, and the goal of strengthening the child's moral character. Regulation, religious training, the instilling of moral virtues were considered necessary for self-reliance and preparation for a productive and responsible adulthood.

With the rise of social reform movements in the late nineteenth and early twentieth century, a more humane attitude began to filter into the treatment of dependent children. At least in the eyes of the reformers, dependent waifs and orphans were no longer regarded as a homely class of urchins who had to be saved and given a proper moral and religious upbringing to shield them from vice and debauchery. The reformers' rhetoric now pictured these children as "indispensable in the battle for the nation's destiny . . . embryonic citizens who represented the cutting edge of the future."[31] As long as children were neglected by society, the American dream would not be realized. In less sentimental terms, others saw these ragged and unloved children posing the threat of crime and violence to society. Reformers of this era were not reluctant to exploit this fear to arouse the awareness of the public about the many other social problems.

There arose a new "gospel of child saving." Until this time, the "waifs" of society were treated as an undifferentiated mass: the delinquent, retarded, deprived, orphaned, and neglected were lumped together and managed as a common batch. As Ashby recounts, the shift to individualization was phenomenal:

> Between the 1880s and America's entry into World War I, fascination with the needs of children ignited an explosion of activity that produced juvenile courts, child labor laws, child guidance clinics, babies' health contests, free lunch programs, kindergartens, the playground movement, experiments in progressive education, numerous child study groups, a profusion of organizations (such as the Big Brothers and Big Sisters, the Boy Scouts, Girl Scouts, and Lone Scouts), the formation in 1912 of the United States Children's Bureau, and . . . new institutions and associations concerned with the special needs of dependent children.[32]

To be sure, this movement was not marked by consensus. Although the child rescue workers shared similar lofty goals, there was far less agreement about the means by which they might be reached. Many were convinced that traditional asylums were now out of date; nonetheless, across the country, the number of institutions increased at a dramatic rate over this period. There also were conflicting attitudes about the role that the state should play in the care of dependent children: although many supported the state's involvement, other reformers feared that shifting responsibility would only diminish the volunteer spirit of the reform movement. And while some argued for the placement of children in private homes, others were concerned that such a plan would become loose and careless and therefore more harmful than the controls imposed by institutional life.

The new rhetoric defining children as special beings, vulnerable and deserving of careful preparation for adulthood, had, with a few exceptions, little immediate effect on current institutional life. Doherty's report of a study of institutional care, published in 1915 (a year after the founding of the Rochester Home) by the Department of Public Charities of New York City, expressed serious concern about current institutional care for children.[33] Observing that some "high type" institutions do return to their communities children who are well trained and physically, mentally, and morally equipped to take their place in society, the study cautioned that there were too many institutions that were of such low standards as to preclude advancement and growth of their wards. In another group, managers held fast to methods of child care that long ago were discarded by progressive institutions.[34]

Doherty's report revealed the deplorable nature of these institutions. Medical care varied greatly; some asylums employed the daily services of a physician while others would call a physician only in the case of a crisis. Facilities for caring for sick children were "crude and inadequate" and physical examinations were rarely given. Dental service was entirely deficient. As the report states, "Some institutions have yet failed to grasp the idea that proper and frequent bathing of children is one means of helping ward off disease." Children were required to wash their hands but once a day and in some places several children used a common washcloth. It was not surprising "that the greatest number of these poor children were in a frightfully filthy condition."

The report went on to say that the same combination of food was served at meals over and over again—bread and molasses, tea and coffee—on dishes of agate and tinware and in dreary silence. Playrooms were painfully clean and barren and outdoor playgrounds were "fenced in like a chicken coop."

Low educational standards also were reported: "the situation resolves itself into a shut-in school taught by a shut-in staff" out of touch with the world around them. Gifted students were not inspired to seek higher education "and a very large percentage of retardation existed among institution pupils." What was termed vocational training "amounted to exploiting and overworking children who had no redress . . . a girl being compelled to work at a wash tub at five o'clock in the morning."

Predicting the "sacrifice of the children's futures," the advisory committee agreed on three contributing causes: the institutions' failure to realize the serious consequences of their neglect; the community's indifference to setting proper standards; and the failure of the State Board of Charities to use its power to compel these institutions to effect adequate standards for care and training of dependent children. Clearly, the previously mentioned theme of insularity, the freedom of administrators and staff to manage their wards as they wished without accountability to the community, was part of these causes. It can be said that in the field of care for dependent children, administrators and citizens' boards were probably far more "institutionalized" than were their wards, judging by how resistant they were to the prospect of developing more progressive and humane conditions for their wards. Then, again, these dismal institutions blended all too easily into the corrosive climate of industrial urban America where sympathetic caring was not common. The fresh, new Jewish Children's Home, not bearing the weight of such dismal traditions, might have appeared progressive by comparison.

Comparison does not work as well when the Home is set side by side with the few institutions that seized the promises of the reform movement and reshaped their fundamental philosophies and practices of child care. It would be more accurate to say that these changes were wrought, not by some kind of institutional consensus but, instead, by visionary and charismatic leaders. Dr. Rudolph Reeder and Dr. Ludwig Bernstein, to name the most prominent, singlehandedly, as the saying goes, dragged their reluctant associates into the twentieth century. Their reformations were publicly heralded; their programs served as models for years to come for other forward-looking institutions. Even now, their progressive ideas remain instructive for contemporary group-care projects.

DR. RUDOLPH REEDER

Dr. Reeder served as superintendent of the New York Orphan Asylum, already noted as among the country's first asylums in the early 1900s that set patterns of regimented, congregate child care. Reeder was an Ohioan who, after graduation from a normal school for teachers, taught in rural and urban areas. In 1900, he received his Ph.D. from Columbia University and soon after that was appointed to his post at NYOA. Although we can't say what influence his doctoral studies had on his style of progressive leadership, we do know that during that time many of the country's greatest minds were on the faculties of psychology, sociology, and education at Columbia.

Biographical data about Dr. Reeder are rather sparse. His obituary in 1934 noted that in World War I, he became a major in the American Red Cross and served in France. Subsequently he resigned (1921) from his position at NYOA and gave his time in Serbia to the needs of orphaned children through the auspices of the American Child Welfare Association.[35] He did leave his testament—his principles of child care—in his book, *How Two Hundred Children Live and Learn*, published in 1909. His theme or guiding motif of child care—caring within a disciplined, systematic approach—is expressed in the introduction to the book. There he refers to children as "seedlings" who need to be nourished in accord with scientific procedures. Reeder adds that his principles and methods are scientifically grounded in the record of his experience with school children, with his own five children, and with two hundred children at NYOA. The closer reading that we will give to his principles and methods will show, however, that despite Dr. Reeder's affection for science and progress, he could not escape the rigid moral ideologies and what we might now consider the prejudices of his times.

His book is nothing else but inclusive, covering what he believed were the needs of the growing child: diet, play and exercise, vocational training, education, punishment, moral training, motivation and the personal touch, and religious instruction. Reeder's emphasis on individual self-reliance and responsibility left little room for interpersonal relationships with family or friends. The flavor of his ideas is an interesting brew of nineteenth-century Victorian doctrines infused with doses of twentieth-century progressivism.

Reeder strongly opposed barracks or congregate forms of housing. He was convinced that the recently developed cottage plan provided the healthiest context for growth. One of several drawbacks of the congregate institution, he believed, was that food cooked for large numbers of children would become dreary and monotonous. Cottages, in contrast, each with its own kitchen, allowed not only for a varied and nutritious diet but also for the opportunity for the residents to participate in the planning and cooking. Eventually NYOA adopted his cottage plan and moved up-river to Hastings-on-Hudson.

Reeder held a fatalistic outlook on the kind of life facing the orphan once institutional life was over. Believing that more was required of this child than one fortunate enough to have had a family, he observed: "The orphan must fight his battles alone. He is not an endeared member of a family group, and usually receives little sympathy for his troubles. He is liable to hear censure only if he fails, and has few to rejoice with him if he succeeds."[36]

Independence and self-reliance would prepare the child to overcome the expected hardships. And this spirit, Reeder believed, could be attained only by way of rigorous experience and the Protestant work ethic in the work, training, and responsibility required of the child as a resident of the orphanage. But Reeder makes a telling distinction between the barren monotony of child labor common to that period and "wholesome work" that will give the child "a good deal of fun and no end of physical tone and appetite" as well as the opportunity to decide on a vocation for later life.

Reeder had something authoritative to say about the many conditions that would nurture and encourage the child's progress toward adulthood. The cottage plan and its eating arrangements figured strongly in this process. His statistics proved that, in a seven-year period, the number of children who were above the standards for weight and height doubled. This he attributed to the addition of such nutrients as graham flour, cracked wheat, dried beans and peas, salt mackerel, as well as the fresh vegetables from gardens tended by the children and "attractive desserts" such as rice and tapioca puddings.

"Let the child run and skip in Nature's own laboratory" was Reeder's alternative to the "dull, stale, and unresponsive" surroundings of the traditional institution. With a heady allure for the pastoral environment, he exclaimed that "a child so surrounded, and stimulated by the elixir of pure air and Nature's sweetness and beauty, becomes more active, more dynamic than the child that is in contact with the fixed and monotonous." In more prosaic terms, Reeder recommended a formula for play, work, and school that will leave no room for "waste time." Priority was given to play, as an "influence upon the mental and physical vigor of adult life." Reeder's ideas were more than precious rhetoric, however; after the rural cottage plan was inaugurated, the orphanage hospital fell into disuse when, after five winters, the threat of contagious sickness vanished.

Preparation for independent, self-reliant adult life was guided by Reeder's precise vocational and economic objectives: "how to earn money, how to save money, how to spend money, and how to give money." Children were paid certain wages that increased with responsibility; with their earnings, they learned to make purchases for their personal clothing and other needs. Each child was expected to keep an itemized expense account to be submitted for inspection each month. As well, the boys and girls contributed to the support of children in a mission school in Calcutta maintained by the Woman's Union Missionary Society.

Reeder acknowledged that attendance in public schools might expose his children to the competitive nature of the larger world, but he remained convinced that the dependent child required a different form of training. Because of their deprived backgrounds, the institution's children needed remedial assistance. And, since these children would have to depart the institution at an early age, "they will be obliged to make their way in the world by the work of their hands rather than by their wits . . . they must learn to do things."

His plan was fundamentally pragmatic: the child's schooling was firmly tied to life outside school and was seasoned with the importance of experience and responsibility. Learning about dozens of eggs or bushels of apples or gallons of molasses was not an abstract mathematical endeavor; rather, it involved everyday experience with these items. "Every important event or development in the life of the home, plowing, planting . . . starting and running incubators . . . incidents and accidents—are all fraught with educative stuff."

In this era of transition the psychological, mental hygiene perspective on the developmental needs of children was beginning to gain favor. Still, the importance of such personal virtues as honesty, responsibility, and self-reliance had not entirely diminished. Reeder favored corporal punishment, fines, and loss of privileges when other authorities were beginning to think of this method as barbarous. This discipline, he stressed, was used not to maintain order or to inflict pain. As he put it, "every child has a right to know that there is such a moral force in this world as authority; that it is necessary to his well being, and that it is as unyielding as a law of nature"—a principle, it seems, whose time is coming again.

Reeder did not overlook the influence of environment on moral training. The moral standards and atmosphere of the institution itself were critical: "Its molds and dies give shape to all who pass through." He deplored the breakdown of moral values that was occurring in society, attributing the cause to the deterioration of the home, the schools, and the church and the nature of urban life. "Juvenile depravity," he believed, also was a result of the "immigration of a million or more foreigners annually, parents too ignorant to learn our language, with children quick to grasp the privileges of American Liberty but without the sense of self-control or civic responsibility which safeguard it."

That religious training is mentioned last does not suggest that it was any less important in Reeder's institution than it was in the traditional orphanage. He did not hesitate to include religious instruction as part of general education, believing that schooling suffered when religious content was eliminated. However, Dr. Reeder departed from the convention of subjecting the child to daily rituals of prayer and services; he advised that "religious instruction should be as clear and intelligent to the child as instruction in geography . . . the monotonous mumbling of prayers which carry no meaning to the child should have no place." For Reeder and his wards, religion was a further means of developing morality, or a sense of accountability and responsibility, not to an abstract principle, but "to a Divine Personality."

DR. LUDWIG BERNSTEIN

Some similarities can be drawn between Dr. Reeder and Dr. Ludwig Bernstein, the superintendent of Hebrew Sheltering and Guardian Society (HSGS). Both were well-schooled administrators who espoused progressive ideas far ahead of their times. Both were strong advocates of the cottage plan. Both used personal power and the authority and convictions of their knowledge virtually to overhaul and refashion every element of their institutions. Yet their philosophies and their respective understandings of child development differed in important ways.

Reeder did not entirely let loose the tenets of the nineteenth century, whereas Bernstein was reaching into the emerging new knowledge of the twentieth. HSGS retained many traditional aims of the institution—the goals of producing virtuous, moral, and self-sufficient adults—but tempered them with a remarkably modern awareness of the individual needs of the child. For the first time he made active use of the benefits of group interaction. Most important, the changes that were wrought showed how informed leadership can revolutionize fixed and encrusted policies and programs.

As his program took form, Dr. Bernstein documented his efforts in an article, "Some Modern Tendencies in Jewish Orphan Asylum Work," published in the *American Hebrew* magazine.[37] Here he outlined not only the unprecedented changes that he had implemented, but also the educational, psychological, and philosophical rationales for his endeavors. But to gain some appreciation of just how progressive these changes were, it needs to be said that the year was *1908* and that the orphanage in which these innovations were wrought then housed almost 1,000 children!

Michael Sharlitt offers his personal and intimate portrayal of Dr. Bernstein:

As a genuine pioneer, with something of the fervor of the old prophets the new director was down to the depths of his heart an educator. . . . He was conversant with half dozen languages, having obtained his doctorate at Columbia University. . . . He was a learned man if there ever was one . . . with the core of his learning suggesting the culture-proud German, though he was not born in Germany. Added to his superb intellectual qualities was a fine singing voice, which we children were later to enjoy not only in religious services, but in the social functions which became so pleasantly a part of the new pattern of life.

"The Doctor," as we called him, was almost squat in stature. He was always impeccably dressed, glasses on chain, and favored a substantial-looking walking stick. Strangely . . . he did not suggest warmth, though this may have been the composite result of deep scholarship and a philosophic separation from the intimate things of life . . . [the] tone of the entire place was lifted at once. Not only was the monotonous routine partially overcome, but new horizons for the children were fixed, the philosophy and realistic challenges of broad community living stealthily interjected.[38]

Dr. Bernstein argued that monotonous rules and rituals only benefited the supervisory personnel and created an unnecessary breach between the adults and the children. It was not sentiment alone, but the endeavor to build character, that prompted him to launch a program that, by some years, foreshadowed even the remarkably reformative ideas and efforts of such innovators as John Dewey, Jane Addams, and the founders of democratic social group work.

Like Dr. Reeder, Dr. Bernstein strove to create a humane and healthy environment in which his wards could be trained to acquire specific standards of behavior and attitude. But Bernstein was singularly concerned with the quality of relationships occurring within that environment: he had faith in the idea that it was through healthy processes of communication and interaction that children would develop and mature into successful adults. The club—an interest group—was the medium by which this process could be realized. By instituting a variety of clubs, he could draw together the supervisors who controlled and disciplined the children and the children themselves. The club, he believed, creates an opportunity, a common ground upon which both the supervisors and the children could talk to each other about matters other than restraint and control. As the value of this radical plan became evident, the initial resistance of the staff subsided. The club leaders were impressed enough to organize themselves into groups to preserve a common purpose and to keep in touch with the relatives and parents of the children.

The clubs were carefully graded in accord with educational standards. The variety of clubs that were organized after a period of careful experimentation were remarkable by any standard. Depending on children's interests, they might be focused on biography, literature, debating, art, the problems of everyday life, moral issues, and entertainment to name just a few. For the first time, the club encouraged boys and girls to intermingle and experience and learn about natural relationships. At the heart of this endeavor were two aims of Dr. Bernstein's version of "modern education"—*individualization* and *socialization*. In his own words, "It is only where the growing character comes in contact with other numerous growing characters that there is the greatest likelihood for development of strength and firmness. . . . [There is] an endless variety of characters to study and how innumerable are the ways of polishing off all the sharp corners by rubbing against one another!"[39]

A proper education for the children of the institution was of course a major aim of Dr. Bernstein's administration. But in contrast with Reeder's intent to control the training of his children, the wards of HSGS were expected to attend public schools and "as a matter of principle" were given the opportunity to take at least a one year's course in public high schools, technical institutes, or Normal Colleges. With good progress, they were allowed to continue their studies in various institutions of higher learning and were encouraged to complete their advanced education. In addition, public education was supplemented in the institution by classes in religious instruction, musical development, and manual skills.

Within HSGS, these programs led to the lessening of the autocratic form of administration and supervision that typically controlled institutional living. A limited self-government plan was introduced "in harmony with sound educational theory and practice," but with considerable misgivings on the part of the institution's staff. The boys, first, were asked to elect their own delegates and representatives and a Boys' City Republic was formed. Bernstein reported the fear of anarchy that some staff believed would follow; after a brief period of transition, however, the boys showed that they were capable of managing the challenge. Officers were installed (mayor and councilmen) and duties were carried out according to a constitution. Now the children were no longer called "inmates" or "orphans" but, instead, "citizens" who would take charge of many activities of the asylum. Bernstein speaks of the "cultivation of a spontaneous respect for higher authority, obedience to established law," "a spirit of manhood and self-reliance," and "changes in the mental and moral attitude toward the community and society" as desirable alternatives to their submission and blind obedience. Optimally, the young person can learn "to evolve, to clarify, to rationalize into moral precepts . . . what would otherwise appear to him to be oppressive laws." Such goals were also shared by proper families not too long ago when it was considered that personal virtues would shape what was then called "character," a philosophy of idealism that supported the optimistic aim of developing in children habits of moral responsibility and citizenship.

It is worth observing that these seemingly outmoded notions once again are gaining attention. Now that the more recent individualistic psychologies—concerned with goals of "inner harmony" and "self-development"—have, to some extent, run their course, at least a few thinkers are reconsidering the costs of a preoccupation with self-centered perspective. Bellah and his colleagues[40] make the point that, in the pursuit of individuality, we have lost the moral language needed to make sense of our public and private lives and the web of moral understandings and commitments that tie us together in a community.

The importance of community living was expressed in the adoption of the cottage plan by other institutions early in this century. The New York Juvenile Asylum, previously located in Manhattan, established The Children's Village near Dobbs Ferry on the Hudson River. In the 1907 annual report, Superintendent Charles Hilles lauded the benefits of the "cottage home type of school," echoing Bernstein's ideas of *individualization* and *socialization*. Hilles was convinced that the cottage home offered greater regard for differences among individuals. "The central idea running through the whole is the value of personality . . . it helps to refine moral ideas, provides a pastoral home influence . . . a clearing and shaping of the mind of its ward about what the foundation of his life should rest upon."[41]

Informal group living—small clusters of children along with their house parent—while not a substitute for conventional family life (which few of the wards might have had the good fortune to experience anyway), provided its own social structure that nourished individuality and growth. Dr. Leonard Mayo, eminent in the field of child welfare for seventy years, recalled his experience of growing up as the son of the superintendent in an institution for wayward boys, Berkshire Farms in upstate New York, at the turn of the century.

Noting that the Berkshire child could always find someone to whom he could relate ("if not the cottage mother, then the coach or the teacher"), he described his overhearing the cleaning lady, Mrs. Gray, giving a straight-from-the-shoulder lecture to one of the difficult kids, Herman, a "hard nut" who had resisted the best efforts of all the professional staff. Herman did turn himself around, and Mayo later asked him how it happened. Herman's answer was certain: "It was Mrs. Gray. She's interested in me and wants me to go places."[42]

Although the majority of the asylums held fast to the century-old traditions of child care, advanced programs such as those promoted by Reeder, Bernstein, and Hilles began to shape a larger movement aimed at professionalizing institutional care. In accord with the glowing aura that the new sciences were casting, institutional care was taking on the ambitious countenance of a "scientific method."

By 1910 the definitive text was written: *Cottage and Congregate Institutions for Children.*[43] This book announced that the age of simple philanthropy was passing and that the founding of the children's institution should be based not just on the good-willed efforts of child savers but on proper funding, the advice of experts, and the considerations of committees created to deal with questions of policy, methods, and equipment. Studies were required to determine the actual need for an institution, the proper auspices (public or private), and financial support (endowments, religious subsidy, annual funds, or public treasury). Which classes of children (and their sex and age) should be received—delinquent, dependent, or deficient? In addition, the book laid out in precise detail advice about the structure of the institution, its cost, layout, and other architectural factors.

This overview of the various reformations occurring in the first decades of the twentieth century—structural by Reeder, democratic by Bernstein, organizational by Hilles—is but a fragment of the history of child welfare. Transcending these changes, Bernstein's ideas of individualization and socialization, as he put them in practice, offered an entirely new way of defining the needs of the child, recognizing that these were more than just training, food, and shelter.

Dr. Bernstein and the HSGS readily adopted and enlarged on this radical new thinking; the Rochester Jewish Children's Home did not. Both institutions were sponsored and supported by their respective Jewish communities and served dependent children of Jewish immigrant families. But I would argue that it was sectarian differences *within* the Jewish faith that encouraged, if not determined, the distinct philosophy of child care that each institution pursued. HSGS was committed to Reform Judaism, the Jewish Children's Home to Orthodox Judaism. The former implies change and momentum, a studied readiness to adapt religious practices to the requirements of changing social conditions; the latter is equated with the preservation of traditional practices irrespective of changing conditions or the social environment.

While I was writing this history, I asked Will why he thought that the Home resolutely held to tradition. His answer was quick, simple, and to the point: "To teach us how to *daven*." Literally, his statement referred to learning how to pray. But he meant it in its more powerful metaphorical sense: to teach us how to be devout and steadfast Jews, entirely dedicated to the Orthodox faith.

Both Reform and Orthodox children's institutions regarded religious instruction as central to the care and training of their wards. There was a difference, however, in the extent to which religious doctrines governed the operating principles of the institution's programs. Institutions following the liberal themes of Reform Judaism were therefore open to and accepting of new ideas on child care as they came along; religious training took its appropriate place as one element in a larger purpose. This was not the case with the Orthodox institution: Orthodoxy drove the program and all other routines orbited these ancient and ingrained doctrines. As we will see in the next chapter, this split in religious ideology was strikingly apparent in Rochester. The orphanage founded by German Jews who were committed to Reform Judaism preceded and co-existed with the Jewish Children's Home, but there was little contact or connection between the two. The one attempt at unification (since both homes were serving children of immigrant parents) foundered as a result of slight differences about the critical matter of kashruth, the Orthodox dietary laws.

I have offered my historical perspective on the events and the figures shaping the evolvement of institutional care of dependent children in the United States. Beyond whatever historical interest this account may have, my intent is to show, first of all, that children's institutions were not entirely malicious instruments of an uncaring society. To be sure, in all too many cases they served as a waste bin for surplus children or the waifs who were feared as threats to the well-being of the particular community. But until the rise at the turn of the century of a more enlightened concern about the welfare of the child, the institution was seen as the principal alternative to the family when the family, for reasons of poverty, neglect, sickness, or death, could no longer provide even minimal proper care. And even with the enlightenment occurring in child care, the institution continued to be seen as a practical alternative for many years.

In this regard, I also hope to soften both the harsh and instinctive reaction many have on hearing the words, "institution" or "orphanage" or "asylum" and the stigma or pity they automatically impose on one who happened to have been a ward of such a place. To speak of institutions as "good" or "bad" is beside the point: they just were a creation of a society as it was. Many of the former residents of the Home express this reality in various ways that add up to "that's how it was then. That's how kids grew up."

There is a touch of irony in whatever negative feelings we may hold about children in institutions since, within the crises facing modern society, the institution arises in some minds as a reasonable solution. This proposal will receive more precise attention in the last chapter. For now, I note a recent article by Joyce Ladner, a professor of social work: "Our current child-welfare system is in a state of crisis. Its policies are woefully out-of-touch with the sorry realities that now confront many children. So harsh are these realities that I believe it is time to reintroduce, in a new and more humane form, an institution many hoped would never be needed again: the orphanage . . . for a growing number of children, they offer a safer, better refuge than the current alternatives—foster care or a return to the biological family."[44]

A similar conviction is expressed by Dr. Charles Aring, now an emeritus professor of neurology, in his article "In Defense of Orphanages,"[45] based on his firsthand experience of growing up in the standard orphanage. Although he also recalls simple, coarse, and insufficient meals, cheap clothing, strict discipline, poor schooling, and an excess of rote religious training, he cautions that "from these various deficits it should not be inferred that I was unappreciative of the home I was given," and goes on to note the "credits." They include security, cleanliness ("owing mainly to our own efforts"), the advantage of many playmates, and good health ("everyone was *expected* to be healthy"). The major benefit, however, was the sense of living in an "extended family"— a theme that will appear frequently in the stories of the Home's children. Interestingly, he adds his recommendation that institutions be established to maintain the benefits of the extended family for the dependent children. "I can imagine a facility for housing not only orphan children but also a limited number of healthy elders who might be interested in their own development after retiring. It should be a facility modeled on the extended family of bygone years."

Dr. Aring's successes are yet another reminder of the fallacy in hastily judging the graduates of these orphanages as "victims," "traumatized survivors," or in other ways damaged goods. Such a judgment also falls into an instinctive assumption about what is "good" (the nuclear family) and what is "bad" (the institution). The accounts of life in the Home will portray more paradoxical and complex versions of growing up. Looking back some sixty years on her early life in the Jewish Children's Home, Bertha says it well:

> I would have never been a victim. I think I was born with a chip on my shoulder. [Speaks about loss of mother and why she was placed]. So in a way it was a mitzvah [good fortune] that there was a place to go because I had aunts who had their own kids and you know goddamn well that they cater to their kids before they cater to you. So in a way it was a godsend and it was what you made of it. You could either be a sniveling little nothing or you could be mischievous and upset people around you.

In this story of the Home and its children I have sketched the background—the social, cultural and ideological field—against which the ground of the Home can be positioned. It is now timely to return to Rochester to consider the circumstances and the people involved in the founding of the Jewish Children's Home itself.

THREE

The Home
Origins and Meanings

Development among children of respect for their elders, regard for duty, obedience to authority and the law, and above all, a belief in God is the program to which the Jewish Children's Home on Gorham Street is committed. Every function of the home is designated to prepare the youngster for good American citizenship, under Orthodox Jewish training. Self-reliance is the keynote of the training.

— *The Story of Our Home*, 1921

It is doubtful that this official proclamation by the Jewish Children's Home received much notice by widowed parents or other relatives who surrendered their children to the care of the Home. Though most of these folk probably lacked the words to say it, they no doubt would agree that "good American citizenship, under Orthodox Jewish training" was what they wanted for their children. For in this new land, to get ahead it was not enough just to be a good Jew. In fact, one had to be much more than a good citizen to make one's way as a Jew in the face of quota systems, restrictive covenants, and other prejudices.

These ambitions, the civic and the religious in combination, had considerable importance for the sequence of events that led to the founding of the Jewish Children's Home, the event and its implications that will be the centerpiece of this chapter. There was indeed a need for the care and shelter of the dependent offspring of immigrant families struck by harsh adversity. If only decent care and shelter were required, such needs could easily have been met by the Jewish orphanage already long established in the community. Still, it failed, according to the judgment of the community's elders, to meet the test of Orthodoxy despite its other unquestionable qualities. In their eyes, the creation of the Jewish Children's Home was an imperative.

Life in the Old Country offered little preparation for the requirement to assume the combined role of secular citizen and pious Jew. In the countries of Eastern Europe, being a Jew meant bearing the burdens of this identity: isolation, loss of basic rights, subjection to suspicion and fear. Those years of suffering and grief are captured in a rich and vast literature, in novels, plays, and stories.[1]

Many immigrant parents said little about their early lives in the Old Country. My parents were typical: my father revealed very little; my mother even less. At sixteen or seventeen, he set out from his shtetl, Brusilov in the Ukraine, leaving his sister and parents, crossing Europe on foot to join his older brother in a small town in northern Ontario. Why he left, I don't know, although there were plenty of compelling reasons. To escape service in the Czar's army? Or perhaps to avoid the dire penalties he expected to suffer for his youthful socialist exploits in prerevolutionary Russia. Years later, he got word that his parents had perished, probably in another pogrom, and that his sister was the victim of a Stalinist purge.

Some of those who set foot in the New World were immediately transformed by its wonders. Garson Rockoff, who was the temporary superintendent of the Jewish Children's Home during the summer of 1927, recounts his memories of coming to America as a child. Writing in 1938, he recalled: "Twenty-seven years ago I came out of a land of medieval darkness, oppression, and fear. Twenty-seven years ago I was brought into a land of sunlight and freedom. I witnessed a parade of noble Americans passing in review before me saying, 'Here we are. We are happy and free. We are ready to serve our fellow citizens.' My adopted country gave me shelter and education. It gave me citizenship and a chance to grow."[2]

It was far less romantic for many adults who had to find ways of adapting to the new customs of this secular, industrialized, and urbanized country. Difficult as it was to hold to the practices of Orthodox Judaism, becoming an American was an even greater trial. Irving Howe described it this way: "One culture they carried deep *within* themselves, within their spiritual and psychic being. The other they bore *upon* themselves, like an outer garment."[3]

Although scarcely the *goldene medina* that had been hoped for, life in America did allow for a few hard-won benefits. Nonetheless, to get a bit of what was "good" about life in the New World meant also to pay a certain price. If one did find work as a presser or a peddler in the squalid sections of the city, the immigrant Jewish family also discovered the hazards of juvenile delinquency, tuberculosis, desertion, influenza, and alcoholism. The growing number of orphans, half-orphans, or other young candidates for asylum care was the consequence of failing to make the grade.

The history of the Rochester Jewish community during the time in which the Children's Home was founded is well documented by the studies of Rabbi Stuart Rosenberg.[4] Recalling the spirit and the native features of that immigrant Jewish community described in the first chapter, I want to draw from Rabbi Rosenberg's account and other historical documents to sketch the events that led to the emergence of the community and with it, the founding of the Jewish Children's Home.

The years following the 1880s (until immigration laws shut off the flow in 1924) were the times of the great migration. The new arrivals were in all respects "foreigners," aliens, "greenhorns." Their appearance, mannerisms, and religiosity were perhaps more threatening to the Jews who had already found their place and position in the Rochester community than to other Rochesterians. As far as the latter were concerned, the Russian Jew or the Polish Jew or the Galician Jew was just another species of the mass of outlanders settling into and changing the countenance of their city. In the resident Jews these poor foreigners stirred a certain unease.

As noted, the German Jews were well settled and even somewhat integrated among their gentile neighbors. But now in their midst and in growing numbers was another caste of people who, nominally at least, were their Jewish brethren, adults and children who lived and carried on in literally outlandish ways. They were visibly poor, many uneducated and unskilled. Moreover, they were Jews who insisted on isolating themselves within the narrow margins of their traditional Orthodox beliefs, customs and practices. The laws of *tzedakah*, "charity that means justice," impelled the German-Jewish community to extend help and welfare to the new arrivals. But, as also observed, the Orthodox community chose to create and take responsibility for its own charities; the founding of the Rochester Jewish Children's Home was, of course, a major instance of the community's pledge to serve its own people in accord with its own traditions.

THE JEWISH ORPHAN ASYLUM

That "other Jewish orphanage," the Jewish Orphan Asylum Association of Western New York State (JOA), was first organized in 1877 and represented the concerns of German-Jewish residents of Syracuse, Buffalo, and Rochester.[5] Dependent children were evident in these towns but not in sufficient number to justify local orphanages. The Association was financed privately through membership contributions and bequests. In the fall of 1879, six children were accepted for care and were boarded in a private Rochester home.

In 1882, the Association decided to establish an orphanage in Rochester, at midpoint between Buffalo and Syracuse. Two years later, a large house with ample grounds was purchased along the Genesee River Gorge, just a mile or so north of where the future Children's Home would be built thirty years later.

The arrangement of the new orphanage was, in its original form, similar to that of the subsequent Children's Home: at that early time congregate structures were still in fashion. Eight or ten children were admitted and although the number grew, it never exceeded forty or so residents, about half the average population of the Children's Home.

A woman who had been among the first group admitted said that life in the

JOA was much as it would have been in a private home.[6] The superintendent's children mingled with the residents and all received equal treatment. The children attended religious services and Sunday school at the Temple and were enrolled at No. 20 school, the same elementary school that the residents of the Children's Home would later attend. The children played in the neighborhood until the large cow bell was sounded at 5 P.M. to call them in for supper. Although they were confined to the grounds after their meal, other neighborhood children could visit.

The steady advancement of the child-care practices of JOA deserve further comment since it sharpens the contrast between the two institutions. Clearly, religious doctrine was intertwined with motives for progress. Both asylums shared certain common characteristics: dedication to the welfare of dependent Jewish children; locations roughly within the same geographical boundaries of the immigrant community; and commitments to raising children within the traditions and beliefs of Judaism. What eventually distinguished the two institutions, however, were their respective versions of the essence of Judaism. The Jewish Orphan Asylum, sustained by the tenets of Reform leadership and principles, was open to the progressive ideals of the era and the professionalization of child welfare; the Jewish Children's Home, on the other hand, remained faithful to the practices dictated by the Orthodox tradition.

The 1909 White House Conference on the Care of Dependent Children recommended that, in lieu of family life, institutions should adopt the cottage plan. There is no proof that the Board of Directors of JOA (prominent German-Jewish businessmen and professionals) ever acknowledged these recommendations. However, when the Board resolved to build a new orphanage, believing that the old building was no longer suitable, a new institution embracing the concept of the cottage plan was built in 1915. It was built on four acres of attractive land in the more gracious southern section of the city, and therefore some distance from the center of the immigrant Jewish community. Ironically, about this time, the Jewish Children's Home was settling for a solemn-looking, traditional, nineteenth-century type of congregate institution. To be sure, boys and girls were housed in separate buildings but meals were prepared in one kitchen and all the children ate in one large dining room.

The cottage plan, described by Richardson,[7] comprised three colonial buildings, each a self-contained unit. Designed in good taste, the cottages contained a kitchen, two pantries, a dining room, recreation room, and, on the upper floor, three large dormitories and an isolation room. The cottages were attractively furnished and a cottage mother and her assistant were assigned to each building. In addition to offices and the superintendent's apartment, the administration building held a well-equipped gymnasium. A playground and vegetable garden, tended by the children, filled the space behind the buildings.

Children at JOA received medical attention and monthly physical examinations by staff physicians, regular dietary guidance, and psychological testing every two years by local clinics. The children continued to attend local public schools nearby—elementary, secondary, and vocational. Reform religious services were held at B'rith Kodesh Reform Temple and Hebrew lessons were given daily. Kashruth, the Jewish dietary law, was enforced, but apparently not up to Orthodox standards, which eventually derailed a plan to merge the two Homes.

Emerson long ago commented that "an institution is the lengthened shadow of one man."[8] Having described the shadows cast by superintendents and directors such as Reeder and Bernstein, I must also comment briefly on Armand Wyle, the superintendent of JOA because of the effects of his ideologies on the evolvement of JOA. As well, even a brief review will say something about the nature of "scientific" approaches to child care in that time.

Earlier in his career, Wyle had worked under Dr. Bernstein at the Hebrew Sheltering and Guardian Society. There he was in charge of social work and was credited with being the originator of the Children's Republic.[9] Prior to assuming the superintendency of JOA, Wyle had been the head of the Hebrew Orphan Asylum of Newark, New Jersey, beginning in 1909. He took over control of an orphanage in virtual chaos, imposing moral training on "unrestrained and insubordinate children . . . owing to stupidity and inaneness which characterizes many of the orphans."[10]

In his first annual report to the Board,[11] Wyle was by no means modest in advising the Board about his professional competence and authority. In forthright terms, he informed this group of citizen-benefactors that the age had passed when "well-meaning and generous hearted men and women" provided shelter, food, and clothing for orphaned children. "In this age of specialization," he went on to say, "child caring has become part of intensive study and training." Apparently terminating any further discussion, he concluded that "to go into the minutiae of modern methods would require volumes."

Character building, the attempt to induce self-reliance and resourcefulness, was Wyle's objective. This was achieved through a limited form of self-government, something called a Family Group led by a Big Brother. Family Councils were held after religious services Friday nights when children, according to Wyle, were encouraged "to express freely, but respectfully, the point of view of the children they represent." Wyle subscribed to "Nature's Laws," and children were "corrected" when there was any infraction of these laws.

Wyle's plan to simulate "the normal dwelling," that is, to duplicate family life in the institution, didn't exactly correspond to the elaborate system of governance he set in motion; the latter more accurately resembled a massive bureaucracy than an intimate family. All sorts of Commissioners were appointed: for Agriculture, to supervise the productivity of the Home's farm; for Social Affairs, to arrange birthday celebrations; for Education, to distribute books and to assist children whose report cards showed B's; for Safety, to arrange calisthenics, fire drills, and athletic events; for Efficiency, to assist cottage mothers by pointing out discrepancies in their thinking and practice; and, for Law and Order, to assure that children accept correction in good spirits.

In his subsequent reports, Mr. Wyle described his "well-balanced curriculum" that, as he had it statistically worked out, divided the residents' week into precise percentages: sleep, 39½%; physical exercise, 18¼%; mental activity, 25 ¼%; moral understanding, 10%; and spiritual teaching, 7%. He affirmed that "there are no waste moments" in his institution.

By 1920, Mr. Wyle appealed to the Board to refuse admission of "abnormal children"—meaning the delinquent and "feeble-minded"—to the Home. It would be unfortunate, as he put it, to force children who were deprived of their natural guardians to associate with "any type of child from whose occasional contact you would take the utmost pains to keep your own children." In fact, Wyle argued that only the morally and social defective, the delinquent, and other "difficult" children should be placed in institutions, believing that "proper Jewish homes" could be found for every normal child. It is worth noting that there is nothing to show that the Jewish Children's Home ever gave much attention to "scientific" ideas such as those of superintendent Wyle. At the same time there also is no intimation that the Children's Home discriminated among its wards or screened out "abnormal" children.

In the next ten years, into the 1920s, the population of JOA continued to decrease because the newly founded Jewish Children's Home was absorbing most of the Rochester applicants and Syracuse and Buffalo were providing their own services to children. Also, some families were reluctant to place their children in JOA because of its distance from the central Jewish community: visits to their children on weekends required parents or relatives to drive or ride the street car, acts that would violate sacred Sabbath rules.

A severe decline in admissions resulted in the closing of JOA in 1928. Mr. Wyle apparently did not accept this practical explanation for the closing, for he transformed this event into an opportunity to claim more lofty reasons. The closing, he claimed, was in accord with his conviction that institutional care is not as good for children as placement in good homes.[12] There is nothing to show that the leadership of the Children's Home ever publicly acknowledged the closing of JOA or that the example set by Mr. Wyle in any way raised question about whether the Children's Home should continue to exist. Nor, apparently, was it moved by the report issued five years later by the Jewish Children's Bureau, the successor to the JOA, lauding the closing of JOA and the benefits of foster care including "normal family life" and the development of individuality.[13]

Mr. Wyle left his own testament to what he believed were his substantial contributions to child welfare. But now, after almost seventy years, Phil offers his view of Mr. Wyle as an inveterate patriarch. Phil recalls a time when Armand Wyle was visiting the Jewish Children's Home and the superintendent, Jacob Hollander, introduced him to Mr. Wyle: "It was in the dining room of the Home and I believe I was eight or nine years old. The cruelty stays with me. He responded to the introduction by grabbing both my cheeks in his fingers, twisting and turning until I cringed in pain. I remember Jacob Hollander stating to me in his [Mr. Wyle's] presence that 'you don't have to be afraid of him since he is not your superintendent.' "

THE JEWISH CHILDREN'S HOME

On Monday, September 14, 1914, there was dedicated what was first called the Jewish Sheltering Home. The name was soon changed to the Jewish Children's Home and the institution continued its mission for another thirty-three years.

Two years prior to the opening of the Home, in October 1912, a group of men—all good citizens and businessmen—convened to set in motion the plans for the new Home. Outstanding and perhaps the most influential in organizing the Home was Abraham D. Joffe, known as the "grand old man of Rochester Jewry," who, after the inauguration of the Home, became its first vice president.

A Hebrew scholar, businessman, and philanthropist, A. D. Joffe, as he was known, studied theology in his native Lithuania in preparation for entry into the rabbinate but subsequently chose business as his career. After migrating with his family to Baltimore in 1880 he moved to Rochester and involved himself energetically in Jewish communal activities, particularly those concerned with children's education. It was his $1,000 contribution, a sizable amount in those times, that enabled the organizers to purchase the building at 27 Gorham Street. This was but one of his many commitments. He helped found and taught classes at the Hebrew School, established the Hebrew Library and the Hebrew Free Loan Society, and was equally responsible for the organization of the Home for the Aged. For many years he lived nearby on Gorham Street to give his time and help in the operations of the Home.

Although the front pages of the newspapers of that historic day in 1914 carried the accounts of the battles that were raging in still distant Europe, *The Rochester Herald* of September 14th did not overlook the opening of the Home. Accompanied by a photograph of the first structure, a major story headlined "Will Care for Jewish Orphans" carried the subhead, "A. D. Joffe Purchases It and Presents $4800 Mortgage. $2000 more subscribed to the Home."

Rabbi Solomon Sadowsky, whose residence faced the Home on Gorham Street, gave the opening remarks. He was followed by Rabbi Chertoff, who contrasted this important day with the atrocities occurring in Europe: "While the great nations of Europe are engaged in destroying life . . . we are building homes for orphans while they are making orphans." But he cautioned the listeners—one thousand attended the ceremony—that they must support this Orthodox orphanage, one of the few in the country, since it would require $5,000 a year to maintain it. The monetary gifts, most ranging from fifty cents to ten dollars, added substantially to A. D. Joffe's contribution.

The newspaper article filled in other details about the new Home. A single building, purchased from a Mr. Louis Adleman for $12,000 and converted into

Founders of Rochester Jewish Children's Home (From *Story of Our Home*, 1921)

an orphanage for an additional $1,000, enclosed the kitchen, office, library, dining and reception rooms on the first floor and dormitories on the second.

A cottage in the rear housed the first superintendent, about whom there is some mystery or certainly absence of information. According to Rabbi Rosenberg's account of the opening of the Home, Mr. Morgenstern, a principal of a Hebrew school in Youngstown, Ohio, was presented as the first superintendent. His tenure, for unknown reasons, lasted only two years. There is also an occasional account of a Mrs. Horney that can be found in the recollections of the first residents. Either as matron or superintendent she would punish the children by hitting them across their backs with the flat of a knife. One of the children reported this to a board member and Mrs. Horney was subsequently fired. At any rate, neither Morgenstern nor Horney received any mention in the formal histories or commemorative publications of the Home. The superintendent for all time is Jacob Hollander.

Despite the newspaper article's depth of detail, the integral reason for founding the Children's Home was either overlooked or distorted. As the article put it, the purpose of the Home was to "take care of the overflow from the present Hebrew Asylum (JOA) on St. Paul Street." Since the census of JOA then included only twenty-seven wards, the term "overflow" was scarcely accurate. Nor did the new Home actually draw many children from the Reform Home.

Did the intention to establish a second Jewish orphanage call for any justification or public pronouncement? It is unlikely that any of the founders felt that the local press, a secular instrument at that, should be told about the theological or ideological discrepancies between the Reform and Orthodox persuasions; even if journalists were interested, would they understand? And if they understood, would it be wise to let the gentile world know too much about internal differences? Any divisions that existed between the German and Eastern Jews, or for that matter, between Polish, Russian, or Lithuanian Jews, were cultural, inside issues, something that "we" owned, that was part of "our" heritage. A few years passed before the eloquent Alfred Hart, the Home's president, principal benefactor, mentor, and guide, did offer his articulate defense for the need of two orphanages. Speaking of "our little ones from Orthodox parents," he asked, "Why not raise them as their parents would have done if they lived, with all the sacred customs so dear to them?"[14]

Within a month after the grand dedication, seven children entered the Home and three more followed in the last months of 1914. But of the ten, not one was an orphan and only one other child was transferred from the Reform Home, another coming from the nonsectarian Rochester Orphan Asylum. Who were these first wards of the Children's Home? And what were the dire events in their young lives that made it necessary for them to become the first of the almost 300 children whose formative years were governed by the institution?

Like the children who followed in the next fifteen years, all ten youngsters were the unsettled children (in its literal and figurative meanings) of parents who had emigrated from Russia. Like most of the children of this period, their families were shattered by acute and crushing hardships. Half the children suffered the death of a parent, most often mother; these survivors were the "half orphans." In these instances, the remaining parent lacked either the resources or the personal well-being to care for their bereft children. In other cases, the family was nominally intact but one parent had become chronically ill and was hospitalized in a medical or state mental hospital. And in a few cases, desertion caused the anguished need to institutionalize the children.

It is important to note that a gradual shift occurred during the last fifteen years of the Home's existence when first and second generation Jews were becoming parents. Beginning in the 1930s, the records show a gradual rise in the number of children who were casualties of families shattered, not as before, by calamities visited upon them, but by conflict and divorce within the family itself. Labels such as "unmanageable" or "delinquent" began to appear.

There is some irony in the fact that the Home's children typically were called "orphans"—by folks in the neighborhood, in news articles, by school teachers and others—since, over the entire course of the existence of the Children's Home, only very few of the children were true *orphans*. In the first half of the Home's lifetime, only 12 of the 165 children admitted had lost both parents; in the second era, only four of the ninety children admitted (and the four were siblings from a single family) could accurately be called orphans.

Looking back from the present when the ordinary act of, say, buying or selling a car requires more documentation and notarization than one can bear, a child at that time could be relinquished and admitted into an institution in simple, unceremonious ways. An abbreviated form called "General Record of Inmates" most often was the sole token of the child's affiliation with the Children's Home. This form was sketchily filled in with facts about birthdates and places, sex of the child, physical and mental health (usually summarized as "good"), and the child's status as a public or private charge. It is fair to assume that plans and decisions about placement of the child were carried out in informal discussions between officials of the Home and the parent, relatives, or representatives of the public charity or courts.

The first two children to cross the Home's portals at least did not have to travel far since their mother's home was on Gorham Street. They were brothers—Manuel, eight, and Abe, eleven—and were the sole offspring of parents, who like those of the other children, had come from Russia. Unlike the others, the boys were born in England; there is, however, no indication of the length of the parents' stay in England or why this was an interim stop between their old home in Russia and their travel to America. "Father," prior to his recent death, had been a jeweler and, as the admission form succinctly stated, "Mother," who was now thirty-eight, "can't care." The children were admitted as public charges. Both boys remained in the Home for five years—that is, until Manuel reached sixteen, the mandatory age of discharge. Presumably, he and his thirteen-year-old brother returned to their mother's home. As will be noted further, the space between entrance and discharge, as far as most of the children's records are concerned, typically was empty of detail or comment.

The records of the next group of four sisters proved to be the exception. Probably because of the seriousness of the family's entanglements with various social agencies, at least a simple chronicle of events was documented in one of the few case histories compiled in those early days. This family was decimated by the desertion of father and the subsequent death of mother, conditions made all the more disquieting because of the absence of any further explanation in the case history. The record's author merely noted that three of the youngest children of the family of seven daughters had already been adopted by separate families. The remaining four were placed in the Home by the Commissioner of Charities of Rochester shortly after the mother died. The father, whose occupation was listed as a shoemaker, had served time in prison, and was currently being sought by authorities for bigamy. Another exception posed by this family: the children were among the very few who were adopted from the Home.

The oldest, Anna, was thirteen when she entered the Home. She was discharged two years later to the care of her aunt but lasted there only a short time and was then placed in a private home ("very fine people"), could not adjust there, moved to a third family "where she was also a failure," and then moved away to an unknown address.

Bessie was eight when she was admitted. She also remained in the Home for two years and was adopted by a Jewish couple in another city. When she was fifteen, she quarreled with her adoptive parents and returned to Rochester to live first with her aunt, then her sister, and finally in a private boarding arrangement.

Dora was admitted at age six and, after two years, was sent to the Child Adoption Committee of New York City and was soon adopted by a family in that area. Rachel, ten months younger than Dora, lived in the Home for four years and was then discharged to the care of her aunt. Unable to get along with her aunt, she went on to live successively with three other families and finally left to take a job in New York City where she resided alone.

After the four sisters, Fannie was the next child to be admitted. She was ten years old and the only child of parents who, for unknown reasons, were still living in Russia. The admission form mentions only that "Grandmother too old and too poor to care for her. Has no other guardians." Fannie lived in the Home until 1921 when, at the prescribed age of sixteen, she was discharged.

William, also age ten and an only child, was transferred into the Home as a public charge from the Rochester Orphan Asylum by the Monroe County Court. There are no data about how long William had been in the previous Asylum; the record only states that his father had died and his mother was unable to support him. William also stayed in the Home for the maximum period and was discharged at age sixteen to his mother.

Rounding out this first band of children were three siblings: Abel, age six, Rose, age eleven, and Sam, fourteen. All three were born in Russia and were the survivors of another devastated family. An uncle placed them in the Home since their mother was a patient in a state mental hospital (described as "unfit to care for children's physical needs") and their father, an iceman, had deserted his family. There is no indication of how or in what sequence these events played out. Abel remained in the Home for eleven years and then went to live and take employment with a local resident. After six years, when Rose turned sixteen, she left to live in a private home. But Sam tolerated the Home for only one week and, as the record put it, he "deserted." His record contains no further explanations.

Like archaeological relics of an earlier age, these bare fragments of data, revealing nothing about what must have been colossal events in the lives of these children and their guardians, tantalize and stir our curiosity. Coincidentally, the records from which these facts were drawn were also relics, stored and forgotten along with other musty documents in a back corner of a Jewish social agency. Only the keen memory of a senior secretary brought these records, literally, to the light of day.[15]

But I was able to learn something about the early years from Henry and Irving, who are brothers in their mid-seventies. Their recollections, still vivid after almost three-quarters of a century, poignantly depict the moment when their family life, precarious as it was, ended and they became wards of an institution. They tell us what it was like to suddenly find themselves alone in an entirely alien world, charged with new rules, rituals, and procedures.

The two men welcomed me into Henry's gracious but modest home in a suburb of Rochester on a summer's afternoon. Comfortably furnished, his home was a kind of archive of a family's existence; photographs and personal mementos of earlier times filled the rooms with a vague nostalgia, for Henry was now its sole occupant, a widower whose children were grown and had moved away. A bookkeeper before he retired (Irving had been in the tire business), Henry was as precise in recounting the events surrounding their entry into the Home as he no doubt was in keeping his accounts.

"Let's start from the beginning," he said and spoke about their tubercular mother who had been sent to a sanitarium in the Adirondacks—the usual "cure" for TB patients—and returned to Rochester after she underwent a "remission." In 1921, when the boys were eleven and eight, "things got rapidly worse, she had to take to her bed for most of the time." He goes on to say:

> In 1921 we saw her off on a train to Denver, the National Jewish Hospital. A day or two later my father decided to put us in the Home so the two of us were taken (they can't remember by whom) to Jacob Robfogel's home on Gorham Street, of one of the Directors. He called up Hollander (the superintendent) to say he has two children here. Send them right over. They called one of the boys and told him to get a couple of mattresses, pillows and blankets and they set us up in the corner house. Two other brothers and the caretaker lived there. The procedure was in

those days to isolate incoming children for two weeks, to make sure there was no communicable disease. Two weeks were up and we were sent to the regular dorm. A woman was there, a taskmaster, wanted everything done *just right.* Insisted everyone toe the mark. She was rough. Taught us how to make the bed a certain way—hospital corners (Henry laughs). Showed us how once. If it was not OK, she'd rip off the sheet. *Do it over again!* She was rough. Our mother died two months later.

I asked the expected question, What was it like for a kid of eleven to be so suddenly uprooted? Henry and Irving glanced at each other and shrugged. This wasn't a particularly difficult question. As he put it: "That's the only way we had. We didn't know any different at home because of our mother's situation. This is the place to be so we were there! Maybe if we had a little more brains I would have thought about it. But where would the brains come from?"

"Maybe if we had a little more brains!" Was Henry telling me that he had already shrugged off that anguished chain of catastrophic occurrences— mother's devastating illness, father's instant (as far as Henry sees it) decision to surrender his children, and the brothers' isolation and quarantine just as he shrugged off my question? Or had these boys merely followed the rules that applied to the children of that time? Indirectly, Henry seemed to underscore the second explanation by referring to another youngster who was placed in quarantine around the same time. "Louie, the oldest of three brothers, hated the place and walked home several times. Just went home, nobody stopped him. Brought him back the second time and somebody must have told him something to keep him there. No more trouble." Was that the way life worked for children then? An adult tells you to do something and you do it and that's it. Or is there more to the story?

IMPLICATIONS AND MEANINGS: A LOOK AHEAD

There is more to Henry and Irving's story that will find its place in later sections of this book. But in the telling of their story, a new cadence and tone is struck in this account of the Home and its children. To this point, we have taken a direct path across the chronicle of events that influenced and inspired the founding of the Children's Home.

Whether we call it "The Home" or "The Orphanage" or "The Asylum" or "The Institution," any of these terms conveys a sense of concreteness, an impression of a monolithic structure fixed in time. It is also, in a manner of speaking, a "cold" term that implies bare form and structure and that arouses stark images of gray walls and somber surroundings.

Perhaps obliquely, Henry and Irving's reminiscences tell us something more about the vital or "warm" characteristics of the Home that reflect the lives that the institution and its physical structure enclosed. "Warm" can allude to the quality of friendships and caring relationships that were shaped within the Home; it also can refer to the friction aroused when numbers of children are collected under one roof and subjected to harsh discipline and control. In either case, it speaks to the vitality of the setting that is too often eclipsed by stony appearances or narrow minds.

If we listen carefully to Henry's stories and those of other former wards of the Home, we may hear what seem to be the voices of two distinct individuals. The first is the actual voice, the words of the elderly man or woman telling us about those early times and the adult years that followed. Often touched with pride, these words describe how, despite the lack of preparation for adulthood, a full and productive life was achieved. With rare exceptions, the children of the Home succeeded in attaining the status of "good American citizenship, under Orthodox Jewish training." A second voice, if we pay attention, filters through the utterances of the adult, the sad voice of the forlorn child who was torn from familiar (though too often less than wholesome) surroundings and literally set down in isolation. How can the two voices be reconciled? For some, it never was. For Henry and others the Home appeared to serve its special purpose. It was, as Henry put it, "the place to be" for children whose fractured families left them with no other "place to be."

This was the practical purpose of the Home, the dividend of the efforts of a few of the religious and business leaders of the Jewish community. The intent was quite simple and unadorned: to create a refuge, a place to be, for the bereft and dependent children of the small community. But although it was unexpressed and unplanned in formal policies or official documents, it turned out that the creation of the Home served, over the course of its existence, several other important human purposes.

In chapter 1, I described how the Jewish Children's Home was a conspicuous element of this immigrant community, a symbiotic bond that enriched and benefited both.

To be sure, the Home fulfilled its practical mission by providing a modest if not somewhat bleak shelter for the dispossessed children of the community. Yet, in the absence of knowledge about what might have occurred otherwise, we do know that this endeavor created the opportunity for these youngsters eventually to return to their community as useful members in their own right. For the most part, they took their place as responsible citizens who worked, married, raised families, and otherwise contributed to the well-being of their locality and city. Some became prominent professionals; Will and Phil are but two good examples of alumni who entered the professions. We will see that graduates formed an alumni association that, through personal contact, planned activities, and material means did much to enrich the lives of succeeding generations of the Home's children.

There are many fragments from the past that tell us how much meaning the Home had for many other members of the surrounding community, my family among them. If it was not a community center as a formal organization, it was the center of my community and that of many other youngsters who lived nearby. There were no gates to enter or obvious restrictions to overcome; a child only had to walk up the gravel driveway to play some ball or to just sit on the long bench along the auditorium and fool around. The Home served variously as a playground, a social club, a place for religious observances, a source of entertainment, and, in modern day parlance, somewhere where one could just "hang out" with good friends. It even offered opportunities for outsiders to achieve certain rights of passage: I endured my bar mitzvah ceremonies at the Home's small synagogue and earned a few merit badges as a Tenderfoot in the Home's Boy Scout troop in which, as well, my older brother discovered his leadership abilities as scoutmaster of the troop. Clearly, the founders of the Home did not have me, my brother, or other neighbors in mind when the institution was conceived; that it just happened to be there, however, directly shaped and nurtured our childhood in profound and touching ways.

There were other unintended but meaningful transformations that came about as a consequence of the Home's existence. Successful businessmen turned out to be philanthropists (although there is nothing to indicate that any one of them ever appropriated that majestic title) by virtue of their unstinting devotion to the Home and its children. These citizens did not mark out sharp divisions between their business and personal lives and their commitments to the Home or other charities. There is more to be said about these men and women but, for illustration, let me cite a brief passage that reflects this full commitment, an extract from Alfred Hart's slender but telling book, *Higher Ideals:* "Charity is not a duty. It is a privilege and an opportunity open to those anointed with the blessings of life. Let us keep charity and love in our hearts not alone for those who are needy but for every man, in every station of life, of every religious belief, and of every nationality."[16]

The Children's Home provided the ordinary Jewish women of Rochester with the opportunities to enjoy an alternative to, and, at the same time, an extension of, the nurturing and caring domestic roles that were assigned to and accepted by many women of that era. The medium for such opportunities was the Mothers Club, first organized in 1919 as a spontaneous and grassroots response to the needs of the Home's children. Adeline Rubenstein, recalling the leadership and activities of her mother, Mrs. Brudno, observed: "These were all just common ordinary wives of working men like my father who was a house painter. In those days women didn't work like today. There were the Perlmans, and the Bittkers, and Mrs. Kleinberg. . . . They acted as mothers to the children . . . as close as the women were, they never called each other Becky or Elsie. It was always Mrs. Kolko and Mrs. Perlman and Mrs. Kleinman and Mrs. Placksen."

Young adults also had their place in the stock of community folk who became aware of and responded to the plight of these institutionalized children. No doubt, the Jewish Big Brothers and Sisters Club provided a meeting ground for young men and women, an opportunity for social life, and, as it turned out in some instances, courtship and marriage. But its major virtue was the kind of personal and organized services the Club afforded the children.

No one forgot the Club's "third Sunday" entertainment for the children, the best show in town. The hard wooden folding chairs were noisily opened and set in rows in anticipation of a glorious afternoon's entertainment. Musicians, dancers, magicians, ventriloquists, Punch and Judy shows, game booths, bingo, the WPA orchestra, minstrel shows, or even "Rabbit" Maranville of the Boston Braves, and Indian Chief White Beaver were among those who at one time or another enlivened the drab and unpretentious auditorium of the Home.

There also were other clubs and organizations—the Aleph Eien among them—that took something from but gave much more back to the Home. Beyond these formal organizations and auxiliaries, however, were the other ordinary citizens of the Jewish community mentioned in the first chapter, whose only connections with the Home in the form of gifts, parties, and treats were prompted by joyful events in their lives. For the children, these were enjoyable diversions. For the providers they served in many ways as an unsanctified ritual, an expression of benevolence and blessing that strengthened their sense of well-being and good fortune.

Within the context of history and culture, a remarkable bond was quickly cast between the Home and the Jewish community it served and, responsively, was served by. The children of the Home were at the heart, both literally and figuratively, of this community enterprise. And so it is timely to conclude this chapter with a brief follow-up on the lives of the first ten children who, not by choice it must be said, became pioneers of a sort.

As already noted, we are left with the few documents that tell us about the facts of admission and discharge but little about life in the Home as it was. Thus we have to depend on the miscellany of mementos that were randomly retained, largely in the columns of the monthly *Home Review* newsletter and in the bits and pieces found in their folders. It is unthinkable that full-blooded lives can be reconstructed from such fragments; yet we can gain a glint of insight into the bits of these lives that these fragments represent.

We start with the first two children admitted. Abe falls heir to several symbolic themes. That he was given the number 001 on the register of children entering the Home signified that he was the pathfinder for the almost 300 children who became charges of the Home. It is also symbolic that he was one of the first to benefit from the opportunities for higher education offered by the Home. After college, Abe went on to law school, from which he graduated in 1931 when he was twenty-eight years old. This was a rare achievement in those times, particularly for a poor Jewish boy. Education beyond high school for most of us—including those who had intact families—was not part of our vision nor did many parents cherish such expectations for their offspring. In the days of the Great Depression, getting a job was what counted. Advanced education was the privilege of the elite of our society. Apart from teachers colleges and normal schools, free or low cost secondary education then was not available in our state.

Abe's letter to the Home following his graduation from law school, expressing gratitude for the gift sent to him, put it this way: "Now that I am freed of the burden of study, I hope to spend more time in the interest of the Home. Let me assure you that I will never forget the Home nor the debt I owe it." Abe kept to his promise. After he opened his law practice in Rochester, he was active as a member of the Alumni Association, was elected its president in 1938, and treasurer in 1947. Emblematic of his ooi status, Abe was granted recognition when, a year after the closing of the Home, he was given the responsibility of offering an honorary presentation to the former superintendent, Jacob Hollander. Abe married in 1941 and, two years later, fathered a son.

Abe's brother Manuel chose a different career. In 1928, at the age of twenty-two, he started his own business as an electrician specializing in house wiring and motor and radio repair and manufacture. In the advertisement that he placed in the *Home Review* he guaranteed that his prices were reasonable and that "no job is too small or too big." Manuel also was active in the Alumni Association and was elected its president in 1941. He became engaged to Rose in 1931, married two years later, and in 1939 fathered a daughter.

The common metaphor, "cast to the winds," aptly applied to the seven sisters, four of whom were surrendered to the Children's Home in 1914. Reunion, however, is the theme that informs us about their lives twenty-three years later. Under the heading, "Family Reunited," a brief article (that kindly overlooks the earlier adjustment problems of the sisters) in the April 1937 issue of the *Home Review* tells the happy story of what occurred after the children were separated and placed out for adoption with families in West Virginia, Rochester, Buffalo, New York, and Syracuse:

> As Anna and Rachel grew older and left the Children's Home, they became interested in learning the whereabouts of their sisters and, in time, the six older girls were reunited. No trace of Libbie, but they never lost hope and always made inquiries. Recently, Libbie was informed by her parents that she was adopted and that she had a family of several sisters in Rochester. Libbie's name was changed to Naomi and she was married. She contacted Buffalo Jewish Social Services and asked assistance. A worker corresponded with the Jewish Welfare Council of Rochester and arranged to have Betty (Bessie) go to Buffalo. Anna Wolfe (of the Jewish Welfare Council) and Jacob Hollander were present at the happy reunion.

Bessie (now Betty) and Rachel (now Rae), both married and parents, remained affiliated with the Home through their commitments to the Alumni Association. Betty served as treasurer and vice president during the late 1930s and was elected president in 1943. Rae, who resided in New York City, was an original member of the New York City branch of the Alumni Association and visited the Home several times with her daughter.

Fannie's life after she was discharged at age sixteen remains as vague as were the conditions prompting her entry in the first place. Left in her records are some photographs and studio portraits of a lovely, dark, photogenic woman, poised and confident as she faced the camera. Apparently she moved to New

York City, since a letter from that area appeared in the *Home Review* in 1928. Praising the newsletter that commenced publication a year prior, she added: "How I would love to be at the Alumni banquet not for the eats alone but to see all the dear faces that were linked to my childhood at the Home. Will send my dues and contribution."

The chronicle of William's life is truly sparse, yet intriguing. This youngster who had been transferred to the Home from the Rochester Orphan Asylum apparently left the city sometime after his seven years in the Home and his discharge to his mother. He also Americanized his surname. Still in his early twenties, he continued to write to Mr. Hollander, offering him advice about how the *Home Review* newsletter could be improved and how Mr. Hollander might better administer the Home. He suggested that the children should be given lectures by businessmen about the value of money, savings, and investments. "Also lectures about life, how to make the most of it and avoid its pitfalls and snares." William also proposed that girls be taught how to sew, take care of the home, and avoid spending money foolishly. And last, "Teach the boys sewing, at least the rudiments of darning which saves quite a bit of money."

The lives of the last three of the original ten children, Abel, Rose, and Sam, casualties of desertion, reveal some interesting contrasts. After eleven years in the Home, Abel, as noted, found employment. No other tokens of his adult life are recorded other than his affiliation with the Alumni Association and his marriage in his later twenties, a formal affair officiated by Mr. Hollander. Rose married and moved to Chicago, but did not loosen her bond with the Home. After receiving her first copy of the *Home Review* in 1928 she wrote, "It made me homesick. I felt like packing my suitcase and coming home." She did "come home" many times over during her thirties, at one point to a party held in her honor and later to arrange an ice cream party for the children. To the time of the Home's closing, Rose continued to send her alumni dues plus small monetary gifts in the memory of her mother.

Sam's story takes its own turn. Although he "deserted" the Home after only one week (one should remember that he was already fourteen, close to the age of what was considered adulthood), the Home apparently persisted as an important anchor for him. He became, in fact, one of the first members of the New York City branch of the alumni. But as the following excerpt from a 1940 issue of the *Home Review* tells us, his independence that urged him to "desert" in the first place also made for some fascinating adventures:

Sam visited the Home on his arrival from Palestine. During the World War [well ahead of the entry of the United States] he joined the Jewish Legion and fought with them in Palestine under Col. Paterson and the late Vladimer Jabotinsky. After the war he settled in Palestine in the Legionnaire Colony. In recent riots between arabs and Jews he was a member of the Haganah Police Force, a corporal. He had arrived from San Francisco and was on his way to his wife and child in New York City. He had travelled through the desert to Baghdad and from there went by way of the Dutch Indies and Pacific Ocean. The only route he could travel took seventy days.

A year later, Sam was guest of honor at an alumni picnic and later traveled to Rochester to attend other alumni fetes.

As a prologue to a more elaborate version, we have skimmed across what, in the loftier scope of events, might be considered a minor or provincial drama. Though this drama is composed of some residual fragments of human experience, it is nonetheless compelling. It is about an event that also was routinely occurring in many other cities: a Jewish orphanage was founded and the first cadre of ten children, hapless victims of the calamities of their families, was admitted. The birthright of these children, the actors in this drama, was deprivation and the failure, illness, death, or desertion of their parents. The Home as a home for these children was, as we learn, scarcely utopian. Its emphasis on discipline, control, and regimentation bore little similarity to the modern institution with its therapeutic and developmental milieu. The denouement of this account was the lives of its wards, many of whom were deceased when this study was initiated, others still thriving and willing to tell their stories. It will become even more evident—even without having to say "all things considered"—that like the first group of ten, most lived "average" lives while others' took more extraordinary paths. At the very least, they met the standards of "self-reliance" and became the "good American citizens" that the Home hoped to produce.

There are some things to keep in mind as we go forward, however. There is a natural predisposition to question whether or why these graduates succeeded, given that their beginnings were not what we, in our times, would want for the vulnerable child. In the attempt to figure out the "ifs," "whys" or "how comes" of the fact that the majority of these graduates managed their lives with a measure of success, we must take stock of our own conditioning and unquestioned presumptions. Popular literature, popular psychological theories, and our fascination with the exceptional occurrence, lead us, almost automatically, to assign people who have suffered certain hardships to special categories. In the case of the Home's children, we might spontaneously assume that, because of their "traumatic" early years, their lives just could not be "normal" and judge them according to a simplistic equation that tries to have it both ways: if one who had suffered hardship eventually fails, it is *because of* the adversity; if this person succeeds, somehow this occurs *in spite of* the adversity. The unquestioned assumption is that a direct cause-effect relation must exist between what had been and what came to be. Probably because it muddles our thinking when neatness is what we want, what tends to be overlooked is the complex mix of survival instincts, resiliency, and the effects of pure chance. An example of the last is the alumnus, Stan, who, on a whim, took a civil service exam, was granted extra credits for his military service, passed the test, and entered a career that wholly altered his self-image and meager aspirations.

The enigma that arises when one attempts to make sense of others' lives was very present in my conversation with an alumna who had been placed in the Children's Home when she was seven or eight years old. After her mother had died, her father, not in the best of health and earning very little, apparently had no other recourse.

Clearly she was primed to respond to the "what was it like?" question I posed all the graduates—a response that was startling in its intensity, unrelieved even by the mordant humor or the pride of survival that I heard in the stories of other former residents. She decried her years in the Children's Home with naked bitterness and resentment. She sincerely and tearfully wanted me to include in my study just how demeaning and damaging the Home had been to its wards, citing one example after another. She was exhausted, wearied by the resurgence of grievous memories and feelings. I wondered what to say next.

Here was the enigma. I was trying to take in, grasp, this sorrowful lament while we sat across from one another in the gracious living room of her home in a lovely suburb. Also, she had mentioned soon after I arrived that she was looking forward to her retirement in the coming years, after a caring and productive adult life. She was proud of her accomplishments as a professional in the human services field where she served troubled children and adults suffering, perhaps, hardships not too dissimilar from her own early years. And she and her husband spoke about the "naches" (parental joy) they felt about the successes of their grown children.

And so, I knew what I had to ask. In careful and calm terms I wondered how or if she saw some relationship between the childhood she had just condemned and her adult life?

She stammered in trying to respond, searching for the right words: to be clear and articulate seemed to be just one of her high standards. But her response at first seemed to be incidental to my question, a digression about how not long ago she had, for her own reasons, talked to a counselor—as if this event explained things. As counselors do, he asked about her childhood, something she usually didn't give much thought to. Dutifully, she told him the facts that apparently left him bewildered. As well as she could remember, his abrupt reaction was something like, "yours is the most pathological childhood I have ever heard about."

The room became still. And then, after a moment and a bit wistful, she asked of no one, "Was it, really?"

I proposed a few pages back that while the Home had the many attributes of the "cold" institution, it also embraced the turmoil of being human in which lives unfold in complex and indeterminate ways that often defy satisfying explanations and confident conclusions. What did it really mean to be a child and to grow up in this institution? The individual stories hold the answers.

FOUR

Facts and Figures

> The persons directing the Jewish Children's Home endeavor to bring into
> the lives of the youngsters the characteristic love of family as evidenced by
> the Jews, having in mind the dictates of Talmudic teachings. The Talmud
> gives very specific instructions about how orphans should be treated and the
> Home makes a conscientious effort to conform. . . . Among these instruc-
> tions are these: "Talk to them nicely. Handle them with honor. Take care of
> their finances. Give them a good education. By doing so the child is consid-
> ered as your own."
>
> —*The Story of Our Home*, 1921

To the extent that memory serves and documentation is available, I have
sketched the nature and ethos of the community in which the Children's Home
was nested and the conditions—historical, ideological, and religious—that led
to the founding of the Home. The statement opening this chapter that ex-
presses the Talmudic foundations for care of dependent children directs our
attention to the conditions, operations, and nature of life within the walls of
the Jewish Children's Home.

Ahead are the narratives and recollections of the "kids" whose early years
were sustained and regulated by the Home. To provide a demographic frame
for their accounts, it is important to give brief attention to some facts and
figures: the facts are numbers and frequencies and patterns over the Home's
thirty-year span; the figures, key individuals who created, administered, and
sustained the institutional world occupied by the children. How this world
worked will be the focus of the next chapter.

THE FACTS

Compared with many Eastern United States children's institutions mentioned in earlier chapters, the Rochester Jewish Children's Home was a small and
modest operation. Almost 300 children spent some important part of their

youth (the entire part for many) in the Home during the thirty years of its existence. Consider that this number was much less than the census on any *one* day of the New York City's Hebrew Orphan Asylum or the Hebrew Sheltering and Guardian Society.

Altogether, 285 children were admitted to the Home between 1914 and 1946. It would be more accurate to say that the Home accepted 146 applications for admission during this period, that number representing the actual number of families requesting or required to seek the services of the Home. In the early years surviving parents or relatives most often prevailed on the Home to accept their helpless children; in the later years of the Home's existence, the children's court and social agencies increasingly became the referring sources.

A word about the sources of this information and what follows. There is no evidence that a formal or systematic attempt was made to preserve any of the records of the Jewish Children's Home. The reason is uncertain. Perhaps this neglect was due to the fact that record keeping in the early years of child welfare was handled in a rather casual fashion that contrasts with present professional standards and high levels of accountability. At any rate, the search for these documentary vestiges of the Children's Home was a minor archaeological project. A scattering of handwritten ledgers and record books—contributions to the scholarship fund, children's bank accounts, and the like—was found in the archives of the University of Rochester. As noted, the children's individual records, carefully organized, each neatly sheathed in its own manila envelope, were found in the back corners of the closet at Rochester Jewish Family Service. The fascinating booklet printed in 1921, *The Story of Our Home,* and the richly illustrated 1939 Silver Anniversary commemorative publication also were found in the University's archives.

The children's records frequently contained only two official short forms (frequently incomplete) to verify the existence of the child. Imprinted with the official seal of the State of New York Department of Social Welfare, one form was labeled the Report of Admission to Institution or Agency for Children, the other, the Report of Discharge of Child from Foster Care.

The Home itself maintained its own official record, a large, cloth-bound, battered ledger, a veteran of three decades of service. Each page bore the heading of the original name of the institution, the Jewish Sheltering Home; apparently, having paid to have the ledger printed, there was no good reason to go to the expense of having it redone. The pages, numbered sequentially, determined the number given children on admission. Except for the age and sex of the child, the homeland and current residence of the parents, most of the other spaces on the forms were left vacant. Always completed was the section on responsibility for the payment for the child's care. Who was supposed to pay the $4.00 per week, the parent or a public institution? In the 1930s, a brief but more formal admission form was added. It duplicated much of the data contained in the other documents but added a declaration to be signed by the parent and witnessed. It is not known how or why this ambiguous contract between

OTHER INDIVIDUALS OR ORGANIZATIONS INTERESTED IN CHILD

....

....

....

TRAITS OF CHILD

Honest	Careless	Obedient
Studious	Slow	Stubborn x

HEALTH RECORD

Previous diseases of child

	Date			Date		Date	
Measles	....	Pneumonia	....	Influenza	....		Malnutrition
Mumps	*1.9.3.*	Diphtheria	....	Scarlet Fever	....		Tuberculosis
Smallpox	....	Infantile Paralysis	....	Typhoid Fever	....		Convulsions
Whooping Cough	....	Chickenpox	....	Diseased Joints	....		Rheumatism

Smallpox vaccination ....   Dick Jan. 1932 pos. T-AT 3 doses 1932 neg
Wasserman ....   Shick 1932 neg

Remarks: *German Measles — Mar 7, 1935* ....

.... Rheumatic Fever - 1938 ....

....

....

I, ...███████████...................... parent, relative or guardian of........███████████
hereby grant to the Jewish Children's Home complete and exclusive care and control of said child, granting them full power
and authority to exercise all rights of parents and guardians. It is agreed and understood that the Jewish Children's Home
in no manner assumes responsibility in case of sickness while under the institution's care or in case of accident or mishaps
of any nature that may befall the child while under the institution's care. I also give the institution full authority to decide
about operating on the child if this is found necessary.

The Institution reserves the right to return or discharge the child upon recommendation of the Executive Committee.

Signed..███████████████████

Witnessed..*Hannah Hartman*

I investigated this application and recommend that same be accepted:

rejected:

Signed ....

Admitted: **December 8, 1931**

Discharged to:	Address:	Date:

Health Record and Application Form and Contract between Children's Home and Parent or Relative, 1930 (Courtesy Archives of the University of Rochester Library, Rochester, New York)

the Home and the parent was introduced. Clearly, the parent's rights are compromised: they lost control on one hand, but on the other hand, were forced to resume responsibility for the child should the Executive Committee so decide. I found no evidence that this agreement was ever tested; yet its legalistic innuendos do not abide with the open, receptive spirit, the qualities of *tzedakah* that infused the earlier mission of the institution.

A glance at the catalog of diseases in the Health Record checklist reminds one of the risks children faced not long ago and the impending threat of epidemic they posed for institutional life. The other checklist, Traits of Child, is indeed a curious and inconsistent collection of peculiarities that revealed little about the child in question. For example, the youngster whose record this was, who was checked as "stubborn," was referred by the County Court. The court record that accompanied his admission calls him "ungovernable" since "he neglects and refuses to obey the reasonable and lawful demands of his grandmother in violation of Sub. 3, Sec. 486 of the Penal Law of the State of N.Y." In December of that year, 1931, this "ungovernable" boy, five years old, was abandoned by his divorced mother to be cared for by his ailing, overburdened grandmother.

Perhaps as a nod to the professionalization occurring in the field of child welfare in the 1930s, occasional formal case histories appeared in a few of the children's files. For the most part, they were extensions of "case studies" initiated earlier by referring agencies such as The Society for the Prevention of Cruelty to Children or the Jewish Welfare Council. Such a case history record was largely a catch-all that included family history, physical history, and intermittent entries about school progress and behavior. Most of the entries were anonymously written, unsigned or uninitialed until the last years, when part-time caseworkers left their marks.

Considering what these records include, emphasize, and omit, they offer some interesting insights about expectations that resulted in moral judgments about specific behaviors, performance, achievement, or their lack. "He is not making good progress, indolent and inefficient at school, but helpful and interested in Home's activities." "Very attractive, alert looking girl. Sweet smile, pleasant personality." "Takes great interest in personal appearance. Neat, enjoys changing hair styles." "Unattractive in appearance, scraggly hair, complexion poor. She is accepted by children in Home but they do not seek her company."

Character and behavior are what counted. Since no frame of reference, no particular psychology of development existed, there was no reason to probe the child's feelings, thoughts, or other personal expressions. Conforming to the rules and staying out of trouble was the mark of the ideal child. Here, for example, are someone's recorded impressions of an adolescent girl who, years before, had witnessed her mother's death: "She has not mentioned it for a long time . . . it was decided that in view of the good social adjustment she has been able to make, the matter of her mother's death should not be opened unless she should express a need for help."

"Good behavior" was equated with "doing well" and with certain virtues— among them, neatness, punctuality, and obedience. Age did not seem to count in judging the child's behavior: whether four or fourteen, behavior was judged according to a uniform standard.

The children's files bore other historical fruits in the form of random keepsakes and tokens. Whoever finally gathered and organized these files was thoughtful enough to retain these simple scraps; they are the only vital signs of the existence of a child whose only other testament was a name left on two official forms. Yellowing newspaper clippings showing the Home's children

A Bar Mitzvah Boy with *Talis* (prayer shawl) (Courtesy Jewish Family Service of Rochester, New York, Inc.)

Passover Celebration (*Rochester Journal American*, March 30, 1934)

Purim Celebration (*Rochester Journal American*, April 19, 1935

Rosh Hashonah Services, Jacob Hollander and Resident (*Rochester Journal American*, September 1933)

Chanukah Celebration (*Rochester Journal American*, December 1934)

celebrating significant Jewish holidays—Passover, Purim, Rosh Hashonah, and Chanukah—represent just a few of the ways the Home symbolized Judaism for both its Jewish community and the city as a whole. Old postcard photos capture the bar mitzvah *bochers* (boys) in their new suits (complete with knickers) and prayer shawls or religious robes. Other photos, stiffly posed studio portraits, commemorate events whose meanings are lost in time.

One of the richest finds was the complete collection of the monthly newsletter, the *Home Review,* mentioned in the first chapter. Carefully bound in hard covers, the collection was safeguarded over the years by Sylvia, a widow of an alumnus who, many years ago, had been given the honor of being the custodian of the collection by superintendent Hollander.

A product of the zeal of the Alumni Association, the *Home Review* first appeared in 1927. Henry, who previously spoke of surviving the quarantine of his first days in the Home, was its first editor-in-chief. He inaugurated a monthly column called "The New Era: A Column of Discussion," that covered such topics as the need for a new clubhouse, the importance of the alumni, and a tribute to Alfred Hart. In the July 28 edition, Henry's editorial celebrated the first anniversary of the newsletter and restated its purpose. Noting that a year ago alumni members proposed a paper that "would accurately contain all the Home's and its auxiliaries' accomplishments," this eighteen-year-old editor went on to exclaim the purpose of the newsletter in a rhetorical style now lost:

> And what is that purpose? To spread to the out-of-town members their own and the Home's news; to spread the news to all persons connected with the Home. What an amazing desire for such mere boys! What brilliant thought! Thinking of the psychology of forming a great brotherhood. Thinking of the possibility of boosting the great worthiness of the Home by spreading its accomplishments and news. With these thoughts, what organization wouldn't succeed? . . . Thus, we say, in a fitting end to a glorious tale [that] has a great idea, a great purpose, and a great paper combined not only for the Alumni's but also for the Home's future welfare.

Editors changed over the years but, without pause, the four-page mimeographed newsletter continued to "spread the news to all persons connected with the Home" until Volume 22, Number 6 of October 1948 announced: "On July 1, 1948, the Jewish Children's Home officially closed its doors after giving child care service to the Jewish community of Rochester for upwards of 35 years."

Returning to the "facts" of the Home's existence, it was largely during its first fifteen years that the Home fulfilled its original mission of care of the dependent children of the immigrant Jewish community: almost two-thirds of all of the children served by the Home were admitted during that time. By 1925, the average number of children in residence reached the peak of seventy-three. This number gradually decreased in the ensuing years. After 1929, more children were being discharged than admitted each year and by 1940, fewer than forty youngsters were in residence.

Chant of Kol Nidre Sounds Opening of Yom Kippur

Yom Kippur Services (*Rochester Journal American*, October 12, 1940)

The reasons listed in the section, Cause for Commitment, were tersely noted on the admission form, leaving it to the reader to imagine the anguish, the tragedies the few words masked. "Mother is dead. Father sickly and cannot take care of child." "Father died of wrong operation." "Mother died. Father serving time for non-support." "She has no guardians. Grandmother too old and too poor to take care of her." "Parents dead. Relatives poor." "Mother dead. Father has no home." And one of the few lengthier explanations: "Mother admitted to state hospital 1921. Drs. say there is no hope of ever recovering sanity. Father is tailor. Quiet man not given to saying much and not very bright mentally."

Generally, all children of these devastated families were placed in the Home since relatives or extended family were equally destitute and barely able to care for their own children. Groups of three or four siblings were not uncommon; broods of five or more children were relinquished by a half-dozen families. This meant that a few very young children—two or three years old and in total, twenty-five under four—were also swept into the Home along with their older kin. Thus the need for the Baby Cottage in the early years. Altogether, half of the total population was between five and nine years old, another third, between ten and fourteen.

As noted, during the 1930s and 1940s the reasons for admission began to change. With more children leaving than entering, "orphans" and "half-orphans" were gradually increasingly replaced by the "child of the broken home." Eventually, almost half the children came from homes shattered by separation or divorce, a symbol of social change in its own right. Now the section of the official form, Cause for Commitment, introduces a new set of curt explanations: "Parents separated; children neglected." "Parents separated; bad home influence on child." "Child has no proper home. Mother left children with father, she is interested in another married man. Father unable to provide." "Divorced mother works during day. No place to leave child." Then, continuing to foreshadow coming social change, in the mid-1930s, a few new and more serious reasons are added: "Boys transferred from foster home after probation for stealing." "Delinquent, could not adjust to foster care. Childrens Court saw JCH as alternative." "Committed by court, habitual truant."

As might be expected, there were shifts toward the increase in the proportion of boys to girls and in age at admission, a few over fifteen years old. Where problems of behavior and adjustment began to supplant dependency as a reason for admission, it was more likely that only the "problem child" of a family would be referred for placement while the other siblings remained at home with their parents.

It is worth noting that in remaining records there was no indication that the administration of the Children's Home directed any notice to these changes in population and function or indeed to their implications. In the final chapter I will speculate on how these circumstances were linked to the seemingly unexpected closing of the Home in 1947.

"Skimpy" is the best that can be said about remaining information that could say anything instructive about the almost invisible parents who surrendered their children to the Home and, as the formal agreement states, granted the Home "full power and authority to exercise all rights of parents and guardians." This is not entirely surprising and it cannot be inferred that parents were unimportant or uninterested. We are looking back to a time when the kinds of psychologies of family life and parent-child interaction that are now so dominant were not yet invented. The issues then were considered in far more practical, if not survival, terms: dependent children required shelter, protection, and care; on opening the gates of the Home to these children, parents remained outside, their roles, for good or bad, subordinate to the planning for their children's care.

As mentioned in the first chapter, these were people who overcame untold hardships on making their way to the New World. All the parents who relinquished their children during the first period of the Home's existence were born in Europe, in most cases in Russia or Poland. In the later years, particularly after 1935, there was an increase in the number of American-born parents. Our understanding of the Children's Home would be enriched were it possible to have access to first-person accounts of the immigrant parents' loss and sorrow. Sydney Weinberg, in her book on the lives of Jewish immigrant women,[1] offers one poignant example of these tragic lives. A daughter recalls the aftermath of her father's tubercular death: "What was my mother to do? There were no jobs for women. She cooked at weddings, she plucked chickens, took in boarders. . . . She became a janitress in the Talmud Torah . . . scrubbing the classrooms and halls, making up the stoves to heat the offices. . . . Now you know why my mother had a bitter tongue."

Although there is not much that can be said definitively about parents' relations with the Home and their children, we do know that most lived within easy walking distance and were free to visit their children. As Lillian, an alumna, told me: "Mothers and fathers did visit. That's where the touch was. Hollander didn't keep the visiting hours for only Saturday or Sunday. Never. It was always open, any parent could come any time and see their child. The parents used to bring fruit and candy. I know that because I had nobody to bring me food."

Parents received scant notice in the *Home Review* and found their way into the pages of their children's case records only when they were considered less than pleasant—at least by the harsh, moralistic, and judgmental standards of the nameless persons who made such entries as: "A talkative person given to bragging a great deal, dapper, irresponsible." "Very neat in personal appearance but is an extremely shrewish person." "Constitutionally inadequate. Uncouth in dress, dirty in personal habits. Little strength of character." "Tall lanky man, comes from family of low moral standards. Negligent and inefficient."

The majority of the surviving parents (in the early years, three-quarters of the total families) were in their thirties, although there were several younger mothers and a few fathers scattered in the forty-year age range. The husbands were neither a skilled nor educated lot. Where employment was indicated in the records, the tailoring trades accounted for the largest group; the rest held such menial occupations as iceman, peddler, huckster, painter, and bill poster. Only in the last years do we find a few working in such skilled trades as plumber, dry cleaner, baker, and furrier. Of the few mothers who were employed, factory work was all they could find.

Altogether, the lingering impressions of these parents are something less than flattering. Yet these sketchy images conceal the backdrop of living against which they need to be placed—the formidable demands of everyday life that confronted the immigrant family. As Irving Howe writes in his book on immigrant life, even when the family was not burdened by death or illness, their existence was exacting:

If the Jewish family was a major force making for stability in the immigrant world, it was also peculiarly open to the seepage of alien values. So many demands were made on it that sooner or later it had to show signs of strain and coming apart. . . . Anyone reading through the "Bintel Brief" ("Bundle of Letters") column in the *Forward*, where readers declared their troubles with unnerving candor, might suppose that thwarted loves, broken homes, soured marriages and heartless children were the norms of immigrant life.[2]

My curiosity about the role of these unnoticed parents was partially and unexpectedly satisfied when, as part of the routine of collecting data, I gave closer readings of the sparse data in the "Reason for Discharge" and "Age at Discharge" sections of the children's records. These figures cast a more kindly light on the responsibility and caring of these parents; they had not disappeared after all nor had they abandoned their children. As it turned out in a majority of cases, they were nearby, trying to provide a home for their children.

To be sure, the years filling the space between admission and discharge confirmed that the institution was, for most of the children, the only constant home that they would know. This was especially true for those wards who were only two or three years old when they were received and young adults when they graduated. Most other children lived at 27 Gorham Street for five to ten years, a fair-sized chunk of their young lives.

Over half the children remained in the Home until age sixteen when, in accord with the Home's policy and definition of maturity, they were supposed to leave. A few did stay on for a few more years, some as supervisors, others for reasons or problems of transition. Parents re-entered the picture (if, in fact, they were ever fully out of it) when, in most of the cases, children returned to their parents' homes. This was usually the case and often the reason why a child would leave the Children's Home before reaching the age of sixteen. In these instances, widowed or deserted parents, as the record briefly noted, at last "made a home" for their children either as a result of their remarriage or attaining a more stable life.

It is significant that about a dozen of the graduates went on to college, benefiting, as we will see, from the Home's scholarship fund. This was a number unmatched by intact families of the local Jewish community. As noted, New York state did not offer free or low tuition college programs. And the University of Rochester's annual tuition of $300 was considerably beyond the means of Depression era immigrant families. An equal number of graduates found employment, often with the assistance of the Board members; both the Kolko Paper Company and Hart's chain of grocery stores were important to the careers of these youngsters. One last statistic: of all the applications for admission over three decades, only four or five children were rejected.

Clearly, there are few significant trends in this more or less quantitative chronicle of the Children's Home. Even the contrast between the Home's

Facts and Figures

Executive Board, Rochester Jewish Children's Home, 1939. *Seated, left to right:* E. Frankel, H. Z. Harris, S. Sturman, Ida Hart, President, H. Kolko, 1st Vice-President, Mrs. M. Amdursky, 2d Vice-President, B. Robfogel, Secretary. *Standing, left to right:* N. Natapow, J. H. Rubens, M. Levinson, Endowments Treasurer, J. Hollander, Superintendent, F. Bieger, Operating Fund Treasurer, H. Wronker, Chairman Physicians Staff, M. Cohen, Building Fund Treasurer. *Portrait:* Alfred Hart. (Silver Anniversary publication)

population in the first and second half of the Home's life is largely an expected drift reflecting changes in family characteristics. Certainly the absence of statistical records makes a difference. Nonetheless, other than the use of these data for record-keeping, there wasn't much to measure. Most applications were accepted. Children were not classified according to comparative categories; even age was a doubtful variable. Administration, policy, and program remained constant, by some degree unaffected by the transformations occurring in the community, child care, and society in general. In one respect, this might be defined as rigidity; but in another, it could be seen as stability.

THE FIGURES

Recalling Emerson's aphorism, the Rochester Jewish Children's Home, an institution, was, amid many significant individuals, the lengthened shadow not of one but of three dominant figures. Three powerful men, distinguished and visible members of the Jewish and the larger Rochester community, made common cause in their commitment to the Jewish Children's Home. At the same time, they were singular men, self-made in a tradition of that era, each from a different immigrant origin. They were, as one early resident of the Home called them, the "Three Musketeers," independent, powerful, and effective men who concerted their diverse talents to shape the form and function of the Children's Home. Jacob Hollander, born in Jerusalem, was the superintendent of the Home from 1919 until its closing in 1947. Alfred Hart, native born of German-Jewish parents, was president of the Children's Home from 1918 until his sudden death in 1936. Hyman Kolko was born in Poland and as an infant immigrated with his parents to the United States. Over most of the Home's existence, Mr. Kolko served as a board member in a variety of leadership roles—as secretary, vice president, and finally, president.

The three were fascinating men, each of a different temper and disposition. All three shared in the deepest spirit of Judaism; although Hollander and Kolko were Orthodox Jews and Hart Conservative, each man was also driven by a personal religious mission or vision that guided both spiritual and worldly enterprises.

They were extraordinary men to be sure, but largely so in how we define them from the modern vantage point: then, philanthropy was its own reward; now, philanthropy is inseparable from personal gain—tax relief, deferred giving, named endowments and trusts that earn a kind of immortality, and so on. They were not unusually outstanding or national public figures of their time; their individual biographies would in many ways conform with those of a generation of leaders, perhaps a generation of distinctly Jewish leaders and philanthropists. The virtues they displayed—hard work, integrity, honesty, and independence—all bound by a devout faith, epitomized the paragon or ideal types that orphanages hoped their wards would emulate. It is not surprising that these men were so deeply attracted to the Jewish Children's Home, given their convictions about what they believed to be the proper training. Their promise was to assure these vulnerable children a righteous life based on a solid religious upbringing.

These men themselves were sustained and supported by a broad range of community leaders who comprised the relatively stable Board of Directors of the Home. I am scarcely able to cover the roster of these benefactors who provided time, leadership, gifts to camp and scholarship funds, and entertainment for the children. I will note first, for example, Ben Forman, who began as an immigrant tailor and went on to build Rochester's prestigious high fashion department store. There was Mrs. Meyer Amdursky, wife of the owner of the Joseph Avenue kosher meat market, who was vice president of the Board and responsible for the Hebrew Ladies Free Loan Society. Abraham Neisner, whose first five-and-ten-cent store in Rochester multiplied into a national organization, contributed regularly to each child's bank account. And at the nucleus were the physicians, Drs. James Markin, David Wolin, Harry Wronker, I. Messinger, and I. Hurwitz, who were ever available to the medical needs of the

Home's children. They gave equally of themselves and through their involvement left their special imprint on the lives of the children whose early existence depended on this institution.

Jacob Hollander (1890–1972).

How to describe "Jake," as he was known by the Jewish community or "The Boss," a title more cautiously used by some of the kids? There was no question in my mind or the minds of everyone I talked with that Jake Hollander was the commanding figure, the central player in this chronicle. Because he was so visibly and actively known, because he affected the lives of so many, because he was a different man to different people, the question about how I would (or should) portray superintendent Hollander in recognizable and consistent ways was inescapably open to doubt.

Numerous profiles of Hollander survive in testimonials and newspapers that attest to his life's work. In recollections and discussions with alumni and others, there was no dearth of opinions, anecdotes, and feelings about Mr. Hollander; just mention the Home and his name appears in one guise or another. His deeds, jokes, his role in and out of the Home, his dogma and values—all were colorfully and obviously available. Jake Hollander indeed was an evocative character; the problem is that the images he evokes are many and diverse. What is clear is that there is not *one* Jacob Hollander, nor one consistent portrait of him.

As we will see later in the graduates' personal recollections, these incongruities are reflected in the diverse ways he was judged or how they felt he affected their lives. For now, the sketch of Jake Hollander will depend on a few examples that represent the contrasting sentiments held about him—as a saint of sorts by some outside the walls of the Home, as someone less than benevolent by others who were in more intimate contact with him.

A lengthy posthumous tribute to him as a founder of the Rochester Hillel School in its 1973 yearbook praised him as "remarkable because he dedicated his life to high ideals and the community, and he influenced others to do so as well . . . he left an indelible mark on all who have known and loved him." An article in the *Rochester Jewish Ledger*, "Who's Who in Rochester," December 12, 1947, written after the closing of the Home observed:

> Some think of him as the man who is perennially raising an astounding uproar in Community Chest report dinners by always coming up with over a 100 percent mark on his quota—a super salesman for charitable causes. Others regard him as a puckish little man with bright youthful eyes, as full of buoyant vitality as any of his youthful wards on Gorham St. . . . "Jake" as he is known by his many friends, is all of these and more. . . . He loves to talk about the children in the Home . . . he will boast of their achievements in the outside world as if they were really his own children.

One alumnus remembers his discipline well: "We considered him mean. But he was following the biblical precepts—spare the rod and spoil the child. He'd put a chair in the middle of the dorm and he'd call the kids and he'd whack them with rage. Some of us kids got together and decided next time there was a Board meeting we were going to tell them about Mr. Hollander whom they revere so much . . . but we didn't have the nerve and knew what we'd get after that."

The words of another alumna reflect the ambivalent but powerful feelings this man stirred: "Everybody loved Hollander. Some hated him but were afraid to say it. You know why I didn't hate him? In my stupid mind I felt that he kept the family together. He didn't keep the family together. We kept ourselves together."

But Mr. Hollander's son Morton holds a different image: "I always saw the nice things he did. I was always with the children in the Home, whether I attended morning services or evening I was with the kids. He was always there for giving advice to the children. On Sabbath he would always speak to them, give them a blessing. Remarkable. If a kid had to be punished they were punished."

Finally, one of the elders of the Jewish community tried to offer a somewhat apologetic but balanced portrait:

He was accused once of hitting a child with his belt and accidentally the buckle got out of control and did something, cut or something like that. . . . There was a little investigation but nothing happened to him. . . . So if he did it once in awhile I would have to say he had to be made of iron not to do it more often . . . some of the kids were very incorrigible. . . . The other side of the coin is that he was a good administrator in running the Home. He was good at public relations in getting people of the Jewish community to get themselves involved. He had a difficult, difficult job. And he did it practically all by himself.

Admittedly, my own memories of Mr. Hollander are shaped by the perceptions of a ten- or fifteen-year-old boy. I picture a stubby man, large bellied, balding and wearing what I saw as his trademark or crest—the square patch of black mustache under his prominent nose. His quick walk, arms stiffly at his side, seemed determined: no matter where he was heading it had to be momentous. Thus you couldn't know whether he was going to his quarters for a nap or whether he was on the trail of some miscreant since his eyes were always scanning the space around him. It was safer to be out of his sight. His patriarchal omnipotence was magnified each Sabbath as he dominated the altar, always attired in his dark religious robes, constantly peering above the prayer book, searching the rows of the Home's children for any hint of improper behavior.

Although he was usually stern in demeanor, the presence of visitors would produce a genial, almost-loving smile. It was at these times that he would display a brand of affection not strange in those days; the child whose sad fortune it was to be within reach got what was called a "knip" described previously by Phil on his introduction to Mr. Wyle—the child's cheek clipped between thumb and forefinger and sharply twisted.

He spoke with a distinctive and strong accent that, because of his origins, differed a bit from the more common Yiddish-inflected, Eastern European locution of my parents. When you heard, "Vot are you doink?," you knew who was asking a question that had ominous import. In my later teens, he called me "deh menajeh" (the manager), referring to my devious efforts to persuade his son, my friend, Haskell, to borrow his father's 1936 Hudson Terraplane for a spin after the Sabbath ended.

These are impressions that no doubt differ from those of others who also knew "Jake" in their own special circumstances. But from the records, tributes, newspaper clippings, and the *Home Review* we can get a fairly straightforward summary of some facts about his life. His birthplace in what was then called Palestine immediately marked him off from most of the other Rochester Jews of either Eastern or Western European parentage: every biographical account makes special mention of his Palestinian background.

His parents, born in Poland, emigrated to Palestine about 1890 and Jacob was born a year later. Like most others in his position (Drs. Reeder and Bernstein were exceptions) he had little training or preparation for his career in child care. He received his primary education at Rabbi Blumenthal's Zion Children's School in Jerusalem and then studied at the Yeshiva Torath Chaim, a rabbinical school from which he graduated in 1911. He was twenty years old.

Upon graduation he married Jennie Horowitz (ever known as "Shaindel"), the daughter of a respected scholar. Because of the threatening conditions in Palestine affecting the Jewish pioneers, he and his wife sailed to America. Offering no further details, his biography mentions that he taught in New York City for a short while and was then called by the Binghamton, New York, Jewish community to become director of the Hebrew School. In the absence of a rabbi, he also served as spiritual leader. In 1919 he was offered the position of superintendent at the Rochester Jewish Children's Home. The *Jewish Ledger* reported that he had so endeared himself to members of the Binghamton community that they promised to invest in a business for him if he would only stay.

His arrival in Rochester as a rather youthful twenty-nine-year-old superintendent of the small Home marked the consolidation of a lifelong career in child welfare. Yet it was a career tinged by at least two paradoxes. The first was already noted: the discrepancies that persisted between the adulation tendered him by the larger community, where he was acclaimed for his work with, among many others, Associated Hebrew Charities, Zionist district of Rochester, Rochester Hebrew School, Jewish Welfare Council, Mizrachi, Interreligious Court Commission, and Federation of Palestine Jews of U.S. and Canada, and how he was regarded by the members of the community that was the Home. The second paradox is the discrepancy between Mr. Hollander's involvement and leadership in the field of progressive child welfare and his role and responsibility as a child-care administrator.

The commentaries on Mr. Hollander that began this biography illustrate the first contradiction: although he garnered unquestioned admiration and affection from the community outside the Home, he was not as fortunate, as the previous personal quotes show, when it came to the more intimate environment of the Home. Still, Jacob Hollander's mettle was evident in his perpetual balancing act. I asked a former resident, also named Jake, if something didn't suffer in his endeavor "to be all things to all people"—husband and father, patriarch of the Home, fund-raiser, community worker, and so forth. For Jake, Mr. Hollander was an extraordinary, unforgettable individual who was able to be everywhere at once. "He was interested in everything about everybody. He was strict and yet he cared deeply about everybody and he busied himself with every aspect of the child like, uh, the schoolwork, the religious work, the religious schooling. . . . He was the Home. The whole thing was built up by him. He was the dominant figure, kind of one-minded in his ways. And if you weren't disposed that way then you had a tough time."

The paradox related to the schism between his external activities in the expanding field of child welfare and his internal control over the unyielding Orthodox philosophy and operations of the Children's Home is partially explained by the innate resistance of Orthodox Judaism to secular doctrines. The divide between the two exemplifies Irving Howe's view of the Orthodox Jews' ability to preserve their culture deep within while bearing surrounding culture as an outer garment. Thus, Hollander and other Orthodox leaders could genuinely participate in several secular roles without compromising their fundamental faith. Let us consider just a sampling of his secular-professional roles.

Frequent items in the *Home Review* referred to his annual attendance for twenty years at State Conferences on Social Work, National Conferences of Jewish Social Services, and the National Conferences on Social Work. A report in 1928 concerned his attendance at the National Conference of Jewish Social Service in Cincinnati. Facetiously, the article went on to say, "By recent changes in management of the Home, it seems that 'new' ideas were acquired by the Home's head," explaining that Max (alumnus) was engaged as supervisor of boys in place of Mrs. Greenwald (the cook). In 1931 Mr. Hollander was appointed a member of the Nominations Committee and member of Program Committee for Superintendents of Children at the New York State Conference of Social Work. In 1937 he was re-elected member of the Executive Committee of the State Conference of Social Work. In 1938 he was chairman of the Regional Committee of the Association of Children's Institutions and presided over discussion of child-planning and casework methods at four regional assemblies. And in 1941 he was a member of a panel of the New York State Department of Social Welfare to give consultation and guidance to child-caring institutions in the state.

Mr. Hollander, as more than just a casual observer, could not have been oblivious to the remarkable progress that was being made in the field of child welfare. The 1930s and 1940s were times of enthusiastic growth in the knowledge about child development and psychology, in progressive practices in institutional care, and the foster care movement. But "he was the Home," and his control counted. Certainly the Board of Directors and, as we will see, individuals such as Alfred Hart and Hyman Kolko had some say; but their commitments to the virtues of a religious upbringing strongly complemented Mr. Hollander's. Still, how the Home was run and regulated was always by his edict and control. There was no such thing as a table of organization now found in modern institutions that allocates specific responsibilities to an assistant director or to others in charge of youth services, education, recreation, or religious training. Jacob Hollander did it all. By doing it all he thereby became the undefinable man, the man of the many images and personas I mentioned at the outset, the man who is remembered variously as saint, villain, or benefactor.

Alfred Hart (1883–1936) and Ida Hart (1891–1978).

Together and totally, Alfred and Ida Hart are borne in mind as a humanitarian and philanthropic household for over a half century, and as benevolent and devoted patrons of the Jewish Children's Home and many other Rochester charitable institutions. The tributes tendered this couple are considerable; yet I discovered none as earnest as the elegant little essay written by Sophie Rolick Stekloff as recently as 1987, fifty-one years after the death of Alfred Hart. It was neither an anniversary nor any other special event that compelled Sophie, seventy-five years old and an alumna of the Home, to write her tribute. Timeless memories of this man and her love for him were the roots. After sketching Mr. Hart's many ways of caring for the Home's children, she concludes: "Mr. Alfred Hart lived a short life of over fifty years but will never be forgotten. His inspiration, generosity and kindness shown to us children embodied the qualities of a natural father. This is how we will always remember him—a real father."[3]

At first glance, the account of Alfred Hart's life reads like the stories of many other self-made entrepreneurs of the era covering the first third of the century. To be sure, he was an enormously successful businessman, the founder of the self-serve grocery that anticipated the modern supermarket. He started with one neighborhood store in 1917; additional stores were opened at an almost exponential rate—three in 1919, seven in 1920, twelve in 1922, and sixteen in 1923. In six years, fifty stores were in operation; less than ten years later in 1932, he owned 140 stores located in Rochester and nearby villages and towns. Mr. Hart was a brilliant and careful master planner. Still, there was more to him than his mercantile wizardry. His ingrained humanitarianism governed how he carried out his felt obligations to his customers, to his employees, and others.

Mr. Hart was born in Oswego, New York, in 1878.[4] His father, Moses, had immigrated from Germany and set up a grocery business; his mother was from England. Young Alfred supplemented his public school education with courses at the Rochester Business Institute and then obtained a clerical position at a major department store. After promotion to bookkeeper, he joined with his brother Leo to form a printing business but after five years left to establish his first grocery store, the first of the profusion of Hart's Stores bearing their familiar orange and green signs. He was then only in his early thirties and already married to Ida Rubens.

Certainly he must have been a determined and goal-directed man, given the marvel of his financial achievements. Yet, he is remembered in many other ways. "He was a very gentle person," recalls his daughter Hazel. She added, "Don't think of him as a tyrant, not at all. You always wanted to do to please him because he was such a sweet, gentle-natured person. In our family, mother was the disciplinarian." He was, as well, "a marvelous dresser, a great stylist. He had a flair for the good things in life that he really enjoyed."

Hazel believed that her father's powerful religious beliefs grew out of his desire to express his thanks to someone because of his success in business. Alfred was more concerned with the rituals of Judaism than with Orthodoxy. "He believed in all the rituals and he practiced them vehemently. Every day of his life. He would go to the Temple at 6:30 every morning." As he grew older he became more religious and eventually became one of the founders of the new Temple Beth El, believing that the other Temple was not religious enough.

Mr. Hart is remembered by another source as one whose philanthropy was certainly concerned with Jewish needs, "but was also more ecumenical than people gave him credit for."

> His charity was not confined to Jewish institutions. I believe he became religious because of such a strong sense that some divine being was responsible for his monetary success. He wanted to share his success with others—Jew and gentile. When I was associated with the company (Hart's Stores) business, I remember thousands of requests coming from every organization—religious, educational, cultural—throughout Monroe and surrounding counties—Boy Scouts, churches, museums, synagogues, etc. Each bona fide request was satisfied with a check.

To the children of the Home and to me, Alfred Hart was a kind of legend, a benefactor whose largesse and active involvement in the life of the Home touched everyone's life. But this man was to us especially charismatic because he afforded us symbols of wealth that we in our part of town would rarely see—a splendid mansion on elegant East Avenue and a sleek Pierce Arrow, always chauffeured by Louie. I rarely saw Mr. Hart in person but his limousine, parked in front of 27 Gorham Street, was always alluring because of its immaculate tan and chocolate brown sheen and, wonder of wonders, headlights that were stylishly molded into streamlined front fenders.

Many graduates cherish the enchantment of their brushes with Alfred Hart and his mystic world—some that sound a bit apocryphal. Arnie recalls: "Why he called me I don't know. I'd come in there through the back way on 1200 East Avenue. I'd help Mrs. Hart in the kitchen and she'd say will you take me to such and such a place. Yeah, I'd drive the Pierce Arrow. Class, what the heck. She used to hand me ten or twenty dollars but I never asked her for anything."

And Sue, one of the many children who dined at the Hart home, reminisces about the pre–Pierce Arrow days of the 1920s: "Hart was wonderful. I remember riding in his electric car. They used to send for me every Friday night. I would teach their kids Hebrew on 1200 East Avenue. The chauffeur would come and get me and I'd have dinner at the l-o-o-ong table."

We live in an era when executives' schedules are meticulously planned and protected. Seemingly, Alfred Hart, a superb executive and manager of another time, was able both to anticipate and to respond to what, from a modern perspective, appears to be infinite demands and needs. And apparently he was able to fulfill these demands with ease and graciousness. For this reason, it would be foolish to pretend that this sketch in any way represents, among his many other commitments, Alfred Hart's role as president and major benefactor of the Children's Home. And so, I leaf through the pages of the *Home Review,* not to declare the quantity of his contributions, but to give some examples of the variety and quality of his devotion and bestowals.

> 1927: Fulfilling his promise to come every Saturday afternoon to speak with them, Mr. Hart spoke for the last five Saturdays on various phases of Jewish morals and behavior. Talks thoroughly enjoyed.
>
> 1928: Took children acting in Purim play to Rochester Theater. Had ice cream afterwards. Presented Home with ten mandolins. Class started.
>
> 1929: Paid for fares for staff and children of Home for boat trip to Coburg, Ontario, gave prizes. Sent box of beautiful autumn flowers for New Year greetings (this was an annual gift along with flowers donated for the Passover seder).
>
> 1930: Three boys were his guests at Father and Son Banquet at Temple Beth El. Twenty boys and girls his guests at Beth El Minstrels, treats afterwards. Newly formed boys' baseball team called "JCH Harts." While on a trip to Atlantic City sent saltwater taffy to children.
>
> 1932: Donates $2000 to needy Rochester families. Sent Easter remembrances in the form of $5 checks to 400 families recommended by Catholic Charities, World War Vets, Social Welfare League. Each check accompanied by personal letter.
> Spoke at funeral services of Joseph Alderman, an alumnus. Was pallbearer at funeral of A. D. Joffe.
>
> 1933: Gave $100 to Camp Fund. Will award gifts to children whose names appear most often on Honor Roll.

Alfred Hart's philanthropy could not be measured in amounts or frequencies. His caring and devotion were expressed in the smallest gesture—a Chanukah toy or an ice cream treat—as well as the lavish endowment. Known but rarely documented were the many jobs in his company that were opened to graduates who, on reaching age sixteen, had nowhere else to turn for employment, particularly during the Depression days.

The culmination of his benevolence was, in 1934, the new synagogue he had built on the grounds of the Home, given in the memory of his parents, Moses and Jessie Hart. In appearance, it was a pleasant but unimposing structure with small stained-glass windows and white simulated pillars, just large enough to hold the Home's children and a few visitors. For us who regularly attended Friday night and Saturday *shabbes* services, it was truly a shul (synagogue) compared to the barren, all-purpose auditorium where services had been held to that time. My symbolic entry into manhood, my bar mitzvah, remains special since it was one of the first to be celebrated at the new synagogue.

In 1936 *The Rochester Democrat & Chronicle* reported that Alfred Hart died unexpectedly at the Waldorf-Astoria Hotel in New York City. He had been in ill health for the past few years but his condition had improved considerably in recent months. After a lengthy tribute and commentary on Mr. Hart's successes in business and his philanthropy involving so many dimensions of the community, the article closed with this commentary:

> In his work with the children of the Jewish Children's Home, Mr. Hart found his greatest joy, contributing to all activities of the Home and alumni. He sent checks to each boy confirmed, to every newly married couple or baby born to alumni members, and every year each child was remembered on his birthday with a gift. He was in touch at all times with Mr. Hollander regarding each child and all activities of the Home. Part of his daily routine was to call Mr. Hollander to talk over matters concerning the Home.

A series of resolutions, tributes, and other commemorative events followed his passing that attracted representatives of social agencies, government, and various religious groups. In 1937, a memorial plaque was unveiled at Temple Beth El at a service that filled the place of worship. Soon after, his tombstone was unveiled at Mt. Hope Cemetery. Kaddish, the prayer for the dead, was recited (as it had been for that entire year) by Isidore, a true orphan of the Home, a young man who, as we will see, was already all too familiar with the mortality of the human soul.

In the same year, Ida Hart was elected president of the Board of Directors of the Children's Home, a post she held until the Home's closing ten years later. But in Hazel's recollections, the transitions that her mother had to make were not without anguish. As a widow, she had been a recluse, in mourning for two years; with some sadness Hazel was reminded of her mother's darkened room that was closed to her and her sisters. She added that once Ida came forward from her grief, "her main objective was to perpetuate her husband's name and works. And she did. She was absolutely devoted to him. Everything she did had an Alfred Hart connotation to it until she died, including the Alfred and Ida Hart Theater at the Jewish Community Center. . . . The largest single benefactor was Ida Hart. She named the theater. Very capable."

Indeed, her innate qualities were noted by the community who considered Ida Hart one of the "Women of Attainment."[5] She was described as a woman "whose work in the community is so closely identified with all that is aimed to help mankind, has won the love and respect of all who know her . . . Mrs. Hart is a 'worker for humanity' considering the immensity of her social service work."

Re-elected annually as president of the Board of the Home, Ida Hart made sure that Alfred's beneficent traditions were carried on. Flowers continued to be sent for the High Holidays and the Passover seder table. Ice cream parties and all kinds of entertainment were provided. She regularly presented the Alfred Hart Award for Honor Roll Achievement to the deserving children. She continued to work closely with Mr. Hollander concerning the affairs of the Home. She served as hostess, along with daughter Hazel, for various Board functions and was a speaker at luncheons of the Mothers Club and other auxiliaries. And with the repercussions of World War II, just one affirmation of her activities was volunteered by an alumnus of the Home who was stationed in Iceland. Young Louis wrote: "Knowing you, Mrs. Hart, by the good work you have accomplished past and present and always indebted to you, I find this letter hard to write. Always doing something to help others, I know that you had to find time to stop and write to me. I shall never forget this . . . and I hope that you continue to be happy in your work."[6]

At the memorial services for Max Weinstein, the only alumnus to be killed in action, Ida Hart presented his mother with a Gold Star pin, while another alumnus read the chapter, "Faith," in Alfred's *Higher Ideals*. And she awarded a War Bond to Staff Sergeant Israel Jacobson, another of the many alumni who served in the armed services, in recognition of his earning a Silver Star in battle.

In the eulogy for Ida Hart at Temple Beth El on March 10, 1978, Rabbi Kanter spoke of her devotion to her religious faith, her husband, and the welfare of others. He underscored the breadth of her affiliations extending beyond Rochester's boundaries that included her friendships with Eleanor Roosevelt; Teddy Kollek, mayor of Jerusalem; and Golda Meir, Israel's prime minister. The rabbi noted as well her love for beauty and her aesthetic sense, a "great lady . . . whose graciousness went out to people wherever she was."

Hyman Kolko (1895–1976).

If we think of Jacob Hollander as the "Boss," the man at the wheel who guided the Home with a firm hand, and Alfred Hart as the benefactor who enriched the spirit and substance of the Home, then we might consider Hy Kolko, who completed the trio, as one the community's *balbatim*, the Yiddish version of the take-charge leader of authority and responsibility.

I recall Hy Kolko as a not too easily approachable adult, perhaps because I tended to compare him with his brother, Abe, a gentle and open man living nearby who would regularly trudge across our backyard on his way to services at the Home synagogue across the street. Hy was a square, bulky man whose serious countenance was not relieved by small, round wire-rimmed eyeglasses:

there was something totally consistent about him in manner, appearance, and attitude that perhaps accounted for why he was remembered as "Napoleonic" or a bit of a "Caesar." As Will recalls, "He was a really terrific guy as long as you did it the Hy Kolko way. But he did good." And good he did do as a driven, high-powered, unstinting force in the Jewish community over many decades.

The Jewish Children's Home was but one of his many charitable enterprises: virtually from the opening of the Home to its closing, for over thirty-five years, Hy Kolko served the Board as secretary or vice president in his no-nonsense, business-like manner.

My curiosity about the motivations of the *balbatim* of the Jewish community, those who gave and did without palpable reward, prompted me to ask his daughter, Ruth Vinney, what drove Mr. Kolko—was there some compelling force? She recalled:

> He was very active in all things in Rochester. He was the founder of the Day School, Hillel. He was president of everything, of Beth Joseph Center that he helped build—probably for twenty-five years. He was very active on the JYMA and the Jewish Home and Infirmary. He was on all Boards and had a lot of presidencies. The Home was just one of many. . . . I will tell you, we are very proud of him. But the family suffered. We never saw him. . . . The community and his business came first. And he gave away so much money that his business suffered. . . . He even took a second mortgage on his home in 1948 to give more to the new state of Israel.

"If you ask where my father got it from," Ruth went on to say, "he got it from his mother . . . it was how she thought." Ruth and I were talking across the kitchen table, coffee and pastries adding to our ease. From the open wall of windows of her lovely modern home in a Cleveland suburb we could look out on her splendid garden. But as she described and drew us back into the lives of her grandparents who lived behind the Kolko Tailor Trimmings store at 246 Joseph Avenue in Rochester, time became disjointed by old grainy memories of our Rochester street.

> My grandmother, she was a saintly lady. A true old time Jewish woman with a great heart and a concern for her fellow beings. And she made it a project during Depression years to make baskets in her home, *erev shabbes* (Sabbath eve). She would call Alfred Hart and ask him for all his seconds on Thursday. . . . She made these packages for all the people. She made it a personal project to find out where all the people were who had no food. . . . She would never tell us the name of the people. And we were to deliver them at night after it got dark. Just put it by the back door so they would not know who brought it . . . it was the ultimate in *tzedakah*.

Ruth explained how the Kolko Paper Company came into being. After high school, her father planned to enroll at the University of Rochester to study law—"a really big deal for a Jew to go to the U of R but he was the cream of

Jewish young people in his day." But since many of the classes were offered only on Saturday, Hy would not violate the Sabbath rules.

Grandfather Kolko apparently believed that his self-assertive son should do something on his own so he asked a relative "who did something in paper to teach Hyman the paper business." This was before the first World War and Hy, living at home, kept a stock of paper in the basement and delivered to neighborhood stores using his pushcart. Eventually he bought a building nearby as a warehouse and within a short time grew rapidly and moved his business to another part of the city.

As was the case with Alfred Hart's stores, Kolko Paper warehouse was a source of employment during the Depression for the Home's graduates. It also served as a kind of sheltered workshop for certain of the Home's kids whose personal limitations precluded their finding employment in the regular job market.

Altogether, Kolko Paper was more than a successful business. It was, according to Hyman's son, Mort, a "social phenomenon, a historic phenomenon." He described how various family members, brother, uncles, and others, worked there for thirty, forty, over fifty years. They "interacted as a family, drew pleasures as they might have been from that experience and still made a profit and to my knowledge never had a significant meaningful dispute that broke the family up."

Hy Kolko's ability to create a climate of conciliation and accord served him well in his relations with the community and its leadership. Ordinarily, strict Orthodox Jews such as Mr. Kolko would have limited status in a community dominated by Reformed and Conservative leaders. But as his children affirmed, he was the one person who could bring the various factions together. "He had as much acceptance as any Orthodox person could have and had as much of a participatory relationship with the community as anyone could."

Mort considered that his father "focused his immense energy on institutions rather than on people because of a deep conviction that institutions helped build people. . . . His approach was more benevolent and paternal than we see in people today."[7] In this regard, Will thought that Hy Kolko, in accord with his beliefs, wanted to do more *for* the kids than *with* the kids—that he wanted to train them to go out and get a job. "That's it." And so, in scanning the *Home Review*, his frequent contributions appear to have a more of the "doing for" rather than the "doing with" quality. They included regular monetary gifts to the various funds including Camp and Scholarship, flowers to brighten seder services, support for the Coburg boat outing, new sets of prayer books, addresses at alumni dinners.

Ironically, Hyman Kolko, after thirty years as a Board member, was elected president of the Jewish Children's Home in time to preside over the closing of the Home just a year or so later.

The virtues of self-reliance, hard work, and religious dedication that Hollander, Hart, and Kolko shared complemented those of other members of the

Board. Since minutes or any records of the Board's meetings could not be located, I cannot show that the members were always in accord or necessarily sanguine. Still, the fact that the membership remained remarkably intact over long stretches of time suggests that there had to be a special bond. No doubt confidence in Mr. Hollander's superintendency and the esteem for Alfred Hart's leadership combined to strengthen this bond. Among the typically curt announcements of the Board's annual meetings and banquets listed in the *Home Review,* there is one that in a droll way touches on this bond of amicability. It might be of interest that the date of this item, August 1928, just happens to fall within the Prohibition Era. "BOARD OUTING. Biggest outing ever given in form of a boat ride to Coburg, Ontario. Left at 8:30 A.M. There was entertainment and a speech by Alfred Hart. Arrived at 11:30, went to a park for races and games. Hy Kolko won fat man's race. While returning to boat it was noticed that some members of the Board were carrying heavy cases that looked suspicious. Later, hilarious singing and laughter heard from stateroom 12. Best picnic we ever attended."

One striking difference that I discovered through my conversations with descendants of the first Board members was that at least a few of these benefactors were exceptionally indifferent to the rewards of status or acclaim. Nate Robfogel, a Rochester attorney, spoke with pride and warmth about his father, Ben, one of the Robfogels in a paper business that competed with the Kolkos. The senior Robfogel's tenure on the Board dates back to the 1920s and he served in a variety of influential positions. Nate said that although his father's community work was remembered he really didn't get much attention:

> This was because he disdained and eschewed taking any title. He would not be president of anything. You might get him to serve as assistant treasurer or assistant secretary at best. He never liked *yiches* (Yiddish for earned status or prestige) or recognition of that kind. He liked to work and that was his shtick. . . . The only time we could ever get him honored was when my brother and I tricked him into getting some recognition through a Jewish national fund when they named a forest after him in Israel. He was not happy about that.

Bud Rubens recalls his father, Jack, in similar terms. Jack Rubens, long associated with Hart Stores, was elected to the Board in 1938 and served as Scholarship Fund Treasurer for many years: "My father was a funny man that way, the kind of man that if he made a contribution would not accept having his name put up someplace. He was very generous, but didn't like the social aspect of it all . . . the idea of having your name listed for giving a gift."

Again, writing this chronicle from the present, when philanthropic activity typically is titrated through trusts, foundations, and accountants familiar with the regulations of the Internal Revenue Service, it is difficult to capture the true spirit of *tzedakah,* the sense of personal responsibility for the misfortunes of others, which compelled the benevolence and generosity of these people.

The magnitude of this native philanthropy will become even more striking when, in the next chapter, I will consider the contributions of the women of the Mothers Club, the Big Brothers and Sisters, and Aleph Eien and other organizations, the casual offerings of ordinary Jewish citizens, and, not the least, the alumni of the Home who knew best what the kids needed.

Although the benevolence of the members of the Jewish community deserves to be celebrated and memorialized, it is important to say something more about its meaning for the wards of the Children's Home. The most obvious was their realization that they were part of a family, a community that cared about them. There were other benefits, of course, ranging from the financial support necessary to enable the Home and its programs to survive, to the incidental, but significant, treats, entertainments, trips, outfits, and other things that made the rigors of institutional life for the children somewhat more tolerable. As well, special gifts allowed some children to pursue advanced education and all to attend summer camp.

Beyond the giving, however, the very character and virtues of the givers, the personalities, standards, and religious convictions of these men and women, as previously suggested, shaped the mission, routines, and discipline of the Children's Home. Directly—that is, by the Home's procedures and policies—and indirectly, by example, these men sought to influence the religious and moral development of the Home's children.

This observation is in accord with the thesis that has threaded its way through these pages: at their best, institutions for children (orphanages and asylums), prior to and extending beyond the emergence of modern child-care practices were guided, nay, driven, by an unwavering commitment to the development of specific virtues rooted in fundamental religious necessity—Catholic and Protestant as well as Jewish.[8] I say "at their best," since, as noted in previous chapters, institutions that existed only to warehouse children (many also under religious auspices) were all too common.

The religious principles that infused every dimension of institutional life by definition could not be disturbed or altered by newly fashionable ideals in child welfare that placed psychological well-being ahead of spiritual education of the child. "The dictates of Talmudic teaching" mentioned in the credo that introduced this chapter are not, after all, whimsical notions that submit to changing times and ideas.

And so the boys and girls of the Home were given ample rations of consistency, regulation, exact expectations, and examples of what was right and wrong, good and bad, or self-reliant. More than just the pedantic indoctrination of ideas, these virtues were, over time, embodied in the actions of the men and women who, in effect, controlled at least the early years of the children of the Home. We can't say yet whether all agreed with Sophie Rolick Stekloff's judgment that men like Alfred Hart "embodied the qualities of a natural father"; still, whatever fellowship they shared with the Harts, the Kolkos, the other members of the Board and, not the least, the women of the Mothers Club and men and women of Big Brothers and Sisters, encouraged a sense of identity and what it meant to be a Jew and a citizen.

FIVE

"It Wasn't Family but It Was Home"

It wasn't all that bad. The Big Brothers and Sisters went a long way to make
it good for us. And the alumni and the Mothers Club. They were like a
family. And a lot of people growing up in their own homes didn't have some
of the things we had.

—Miriam, an alumna

Historical studies frequently generate their own special metaphors. This story
of the Jewish Children's Home is no exception: a metaphor that continues to
command attention is that of the dismal Dickensian orphanage in popular perceptions of child-care institutions. To be sure, their lineage (whether it is progressive or archaic) springs from a historical necessity and dilemma: What
should society do about the persistent presence and plight of the dependent
child, the waif, the orphan, the casualty of every blight, plague, war, or the
victim of indifference and coldness? The solution to this problem in every era
had to be a social improvisation of one kind or another based on how culture
defined childhood, personal responsibility for the care of the child, or, for that
matter, the value of life itself.

Acknowledging that this harsh metaphor does represent the nature of the
orphanage, the intent of this chapter is to show that this judgment is scarcely
the whole story. The many variations, ambiguities, and paradoxes of institu-

TWO VIEWS

Strain between the two ways of perceiving and understanding—the "objective" or "outside-in" and the "subjective" or "inside-out"—will remain a constant theme or issue in the ongoing discussion. By definition, neither side can be judged as "true" or "accurate" in regard to what the Children's Home was like: each perspective is swayed by whoever is reporting the "facts," the vantage point from which the report is being made, and the message or impression—whether tacit or deliberate—that the reporter wants to convey.

I can make these disparities clearer by two examples: one, an *official* or legitimized likeness, the author unknown; the other, the personal impressions of the author who lived through, who knew the experience firsthand.

The first is a paragraph taken from the handsome brochure published in 1939 to commemorate the Silver Anniversary of the Home. Although the writer of this charming, almost sentimental appraisal of the Children's Home is not introduced, it is safe to say, however, that it was composed from the outside looking in. "This is a story about children, about tiny tots, about shy little girls; dark-eyed and blue-eyed, cute winsome, lovely. And about boys, little boys, manly boys, wide-eyed and inquisitive, some mischievous, some quiet, serious minded, as though intuitively aware of life hazards that lie ahead. Little fellows in a Big, Big world. . . . This is a story of heroic work, molding character, shaping lives, building bodies, training minds."

Contrast this perspective with a second view, that of Sue's, or of Suzie's of the famous Kitchen Band, as she was known during her early years in the Home. The words are excerpted from her "manuscript" of *27 Gorham Street,* the seven pages that constitute her valiant struggle to write her book on life in the Home as she remembered it. Sue, so gracious and elegant in the seventh decade of her life, shared these pages with my wife and me after a sumptuous, gourmet Yiddish brunch at her Florida quarters. She hoped that I would include her story to tell people that her Home, the Jewish Children's Home, wasn't just one thing, nor was it just good or just bad. In her own words:

> Growing up with about 60 people daily is an experience in itself. The sadness, the glad times, the frustrations, the helplessness could either make you or ruin you. If you couldn't cope with it, it would ruin you. . . . There were the good times, too. Public school, religious school, piano lessons, dance classes, bar mitzvah, birthdays, picnics, movies. We all walked in double lines with Hollander at the front but Rhea and I pretended we didn't belong by walking up front and fast, ahead of the lines. . . . Everybody took care of one another. We would fight for our brothers and sisters. It's like the survival of the fittest. I was the survivor. I was the tough one. . . . I could go on and on about my life from 5 to 16. People ask me to this day, "How did you endure it?" Unless you've been there and you experienced each day yourself, no one can imagine what was good times and what were bad ones. We still refer to it as the Home. Never growing up with a birth mother after age

five, I considered all the matrons to be mothers—in other words, whoever took care of you was your mother!

The two frames of reference enclose sharply contrasting portraits of the same place. Together, they agree there was a physical structure and space— once a collection of buildings, the dwelling for forty, fifty or more children at any one time on the south side of Gorham Street. Separately, neither portrait, the brightly lit, idyllic garden of happy tots nor the grayed-down sketch of endurance, can tell it all. But even now we begin to touch two relatively variant realities that shared the same time and space but, with the irony noted, each embracing a form of its own. The first is the public reality. This was the firmly positive perception of the Home, softened by the glow of goodwill and devotion and created by the adults who founded, administered, and actively supported the Children's Home. The other reality is shaped by the reminiscences of the alumni. We will see that it is a more calloused, rough-edged, sardonic reality. It is sometimes skeptical, other times playful but always heedful of both the dismal and dear that made up the experience of Home life. That second reality, reconstructed by our elders' memories, tells about a child who once occupied several worlds turning and crossing on different orbits. There was, of course, the *synthetic world* created and regulated by the prevailing adults; among the children was the *shared world* of "having to get along together"; and within the child was a self-created, private, often *solitary world*. As noted, this chapter illuminates that first world as the universe within which the other two revolved.

ANATOMY OF THE HOME

That the Home was an autocratic society governed by one figure is evident. Our modern, child-centered, egalitarian attitude may stir a trace of disapproval on looking back, but could the Home have been other than patriarchal in its culture? To be sure, democratic or child-oriented programs such as Dr. Bernstein's or John Dewey's were being tested in special places. But in the Orthodox Jewish community of Rochester—or of Newark, Chicago, or other cities—patriarchal control was expected and respected.

By definition, the patriarchal culture guarantees its own perpetuity. Opposition and controversy are not easily tolerated; specifically, the son (never mind the daughter), whether symbolic or actual, does not rise up against the father. It is perhaps more precise to say that an uprising should not *look like* an uprising for, as we will see, "sons" and "daughters" did intentionally frustrate patriarchal rule in canny and often antic ways.

The code of noninterference or compliance also guides behaviors of equals— the stratum of the ruling patriarchs. Thus, Jacob Hollander was free to run the institution not only with the considerable help of Mr. Hart, Mr. Kolko, and the

Board, but with their acquiescence. Garson Rockoff who, as a young teacher, administered the Home briefly in 1927 when the Hollanders visited Palestine, recalls Mr. Hollander "as a disciplinarian and his word was law to everyone— the cooks, the matrons." Lil, a former resident who, after graduating, returned to work in the office, remembers that there were few strains between Mr. Hollander and the Board. "He was very manipulative. Whatever he wanted, he got, especially when Al Hart was president."

Lil's follow-up of this sober report anticipates the kinds of comic, at times tragic, and often victorious ironies that we will hear in graduates' stories of otherwise fact-of-the-matter events. No matter how powerless or pained they felt, many could always reach around and find the other side of the tale. Her commentary on the power of the Home's administration finished, Lil's grand grin lit up our conversation as she told about a stunt that proved, at least to the girls involved, that in the face of stern, adult control, you can be shrewd, you can befuddle them, and even get away with things—even a thing that verges on sacrilege if not sin in the eyes of the patriarch.

> The Board met once a month. I'll never forget one Board meeting on Christmas Eve. The girls [in their house across the yard in direct view of the Board meeting room] decided that we were really going to be sinful and hang our stockings like the goyim [gentiles] do. We had the candles lit and were eating Cohen's Specials [for thirty-five cents, you would get a corned beef on rye, a sour dill, potato salad]. The Board looks over and sees the candles. Somebody stood guard, so all of a sudden we're all in bed laughing like crazy when one of them showed up asking what was going on over here.

A "one man operation" meant that the structure of the Home was as lean and sinewy as it could be. Hollander was the superintendent, in control. The permanent staff included Hannah Hastman, for thirteen years (beginning in the late twenties) the devoted, dependable secretary/bookkeeper; Al Jentiss, the gentle, quiet nightwatchman; the cook; the boys' matron; and girls' matron.

"Matron," with its straitlaced, stern connotations, was the operative term, not the more maternal "houseparent" or "housemother" used in cottage-type centers. There were "boys' supervisors," recent graduates and favorites appointed by Hollander to oversee the younger kids, to get them up and going in time. Records show that in the last years social workers made part-time appearances at the Home. Will doubted that these workers were trained, recalling that they mainly kept the records up to date. But, "Yes," he remembered, "they did get Lillian Kaplan who was trained, but she didn't last very long." Hebrew teachers, dance teachers, and others gave their classes and left.

Utilitarian. Functional. Efficient. These words characterize the skeletal frame of the Home, the assigned roles that made up its organization and structure. Still, the absence of anyone bearing a title or role that might even hint at a familial attitude didn't mean that the children were unable to create surrogates of some sort.

Dorothy recalls that Hannah Hastman "always gave us gum that the Beech Nut company sent over." Although some kids wondered whether Hannah could be trusted, whether she told things to Hollander, she was always there; but as Hannah herself put it, "I had no life of my own," and after a prolonged illness and hospitalization, had to preserve her health and leave.[1] She was, if nothing else, entirely devoted. After emphasizing that every organization and the Board were "putty in his hands," she wrote that

> Hollander was a constant wonder to me in those days . . . he would have made a great cult leader because "When Jake spoke, everybody listened." Me too! I hated to say "no" to him, which is why I worked such endless hours and spent so much of my life at the Home. He always made his staff feel that they were the most capable, trusted employees . . . he left the running of the office to me, handling the finances, ordering the food. When he was gone, which was often, I had immediate contact with Alfred Hart, Hy Kolko, or the doctors. Everybody put the kids' needs before their own and many of the older children were always ready to lend a hand with the younger ones.

Hannah, elderly and legally blind when she wrote to me from her Florida apartment, recalls the Home after half a century much in Sue's terms: "Most of the children came to the Home from unhappy, sometimes tragic backgrounds. But I believe every one of them grew up to consider the residence at 27 Gorham Street their 'Home,' and in later years their 'Home Away from Home.' All stopped in on weekends and holidays just to say 'hello.' Jake Hollander was their 'father' and all the other children their family. It became their Home always."

Al Jentiss was the nightwatchman and janitor. The summer afternoons with Al, where he sat on the long bench that stretched the length of the Home's meeting hall, the kids bunched on either side, remain as quiet, serene memories. He rarely said much, and what he did say was simple and reassuring. He was an odd figure, especially since he was something other than Jewish (anyone who was not Jewish was "something other," it didn't make any difference what). Al's quiet ease was enough to calm the silly jerkiness of a bunch of ten-year-old boys. Another alumnus had other thoughts: Why, he asked, could the humble janitor offer the kids so much more than the esteemed superintendent who was charged with responsibility for their well-being? "The janitor was the most sensitive guy in the joint. Al was the sweetest guy who took the kids under his arm and he'd let them push the mop or stay with him when he was mopping. That's what I resented about Jake. Why couldn't he be as giving?"

The kitchen of the Home, as I remember, was dominated—totally and sometimes with frenzied zeal—by Mrs. Greenwald. The image I retain of her in the act (and an act it really was) of brandishing a large kitchen knife while shouting Yiddish curses is, in part, a caricature that helps embellish the story. Stan verified that she was a good cook but she really did throw knives. He vindicated her completely, however, observing that "I don't blame her, I used to bother her." Arnie recalled, "She was the queen of the kitchen, the kitchen queen we used to call her." But as another remembered, "She was a sweet lady."

Ahead, we will be spending some time in that kitchen since the subject of food—eating, cooking, preparing, and stealing—filled a fair part of the kids' lives. It was not deprivation in the way we think of the craving, gruel-fed orphan; the children got a fair share of their institutional food. What counted, as we will observe, was food not only as a pleasure but as a prize earned through ever-inventive forms of deviousness. Parenthetically, while I can't prove any connections, it is worth noting that beginning with my first dinner with Will, Phil, and their wives, most of the graduates I met with made sure there was always something to "nosh" on while we talked.

The matrons were the only women with whom the children—the girls, for the most part—shared something close and consistent, but not necessarily intimate. "Matron" is what they were; their role was to carry out the strict policies dictated by the superintendent.

Recollections of the boys' matrons were sparse, mostly associated with duties and discipline. Recall Henry's memories, recorded in chapter 3, of the imprint of his exposure to the iron will of Mrs. M. during his first days of quarantine in the Home. Phil's recollections are similar, though not as forgiving as Henry's. "We had a matron whose name was Mrs. M. She was a bitch of the first order. I remember, she looked like a witch, skinny." Will disagrees: "Mrs. S. was worse, she was a widow, supervisor of the Baby Cottage." Phil continues: "You would be on your hands and knees scrubbing, washing and dusting and Mrs. M. would come along—the original First Sergeant. She found one speck of dust and you did your chores all over. What an ugly lady. People ask, where did I get affection from? I didn't get it from Jake Hollander or from the matrons. . . . (to Will) It was your sister, Bertha, a wonderful, affectionate, caring person."

Since bed-wetting was not an infrequent mishap in either the boys' or girls' dorms, some matrons were the ever-vigilant monitors of this grievous act. The stories of how matrons would scornfully "whip off the wet sheet" and expose the damp and shamefaced child were told uncomfortably, like a badly timed joke.

The girls' matrons were recalled more vividly since the children in the Girls Cottage were forced into frequent and close contact with whomever happened to be the resident matron. There was very little change in personnel over the span of more than thirty years.

Miss Daugherty was the most constant of all, starting as a nurse in the Baby Cottage in 1921 and then taking charge of the Girls Cottage in 1929. After a few years, she left and then resumed her position for a time in the 1930s. Ruth, who lived in the Girls Cottage for nine years, recalls Miss Daugherty graphically: "She was skinny, grey hair. She was inclined to be very strict. I won't say she ever treated me as a pet—she didn't have any pets. Everybody was the same. But I never gave her a problem. We had to get up at six in the morning. . . . I used to think, the biggest thrill will be when I don't have to be wakened by an alarm."

On another evening, Anna (who returned my father's lodge pin) generously arranged a barbecue at her suburban home so that I could meet her husband, grown children, and other alumni who, over the years, remain her friends. In this circle, Lil added her view of the matron: "We were allowed to be in just so many rooms. Miss Daugherty closed up the whole front of the house. She never slept upstairs. She had her own room with a cot set up. You weren't allowed to go to bed upstairs. You might disturb the beds. The only time you go into bed was when you were running a temperature—a good temperature. Then they let you go upstairs to bed because she was afraid you'd give anything you had to the rest of the kids. Which I did. I gave measles to everybody."

Again, their stories of struggle or deprivation were tempered by the added tale of some personal risk, a theme, sometimes absurd, of how "I made it through." Anna, picking up the playful mood, recalled *her* adventure with Miss Daugherty, a story that stirred some hilarity. Anna's married daughter grinned but with a curious twist at what must have been a revelation.

> We worked in the big kitchen and decided we wanted to make some fudge. One of us would swipe something, I would swipe something and eventually we got all the ingredients. In the girls' basement there was a laundry room and a stove where we cooked the starch. So we were making fudge. Daugherty comes down and says she smells something cooking. I threw the pot in my locker and we said we weren't doing anything, just sitting there and reading. By the time she left and I got to that fudge—my locker, my shoes—for weeks I couldn't get out the fudge.

Others recalled Mrs. Dillenbeck and spoke more fondly of her. She took over as matron in 1933 and, as Sue mentioned earlier, was something close to what they thought was like a mother: I repeat, not a mother, because they weren't sure about what that was, but "something like." On another morning in Rochester when we had breakfast together at her favorite diner, Sue's sister, Sophie, also talked well of Mrs. D.: "She was wonderful, understanding, looked after us, made dresses, from old dresses she made new dresses. I remember one day my sister Sue got her period. She was only eleven years old. Mrs. D. cradled her. She guided us, talked to us, mothered us, told us what was right and what was wrong. Encouraged us to go to school, to be neat and clean, and dress properly in business life."

But it was Bertha who, indirectly to be sure, made it clear that in the patriarchy that was the Home, there was no one who could really be your mother. If one could be at once regal and Yiddish, it was Bertha; like an outsized Bette Davis brandishing her cigarette and with a bit of a Yiddish meter, her domain was her little Florida retirement apartment. Bertha first talked about Mrs. Wall, not mentioned by anyone else, the "*schvartze* laundress, the sweetest woman alive." She added: "Every time I got punished, every time I cried for something, I went down to her and she would take me in her arms and she'd say, 'now look child,' and explain things to me. And then one day she said something which I will never forget and passed on to my kids, 'The least said is the easiest mended. When you are angry, you watch because once it comes out, you can't take it back.' "

But Mrs. Wall was not a matron and no doubt came and went, did her laundrying with little notice. When it came to confiding in the real matrons, that was something else. "If you dared complain about something and it accidentally got back to Hollander, that was a no-no. So you learned to keep your mouth shut unless you're being cute, which I was a lot of times, just to get under his skin. But other than that, you kept your mouth shut."

Yes, the matrons were "mothers" because, as Sue put it, "whoever took care of you was your mother." But, as she added, you never forgot that "they were there to supervise, they were matrons in every sense of the word. They were policemen, that's what they were, not mothers."

Altogether, this sketch of the ladder of authority in the Jewish Children's Home shows it to be self-contained, a sovereignty as it were. There were, however, external official surveys of the Home. Annually, a commissioner of the New York State Department of Social Welfare appeared to inspect the Home. Hollander and Hart would present the report to the Board and a briefly summarized statement was printed in the *Home Review*. As it turned out, these reports were the only recorded remnants of business between the superintendent and the Board. The reports certainly lack detail and specifics but their positive evaluations of the Rochester Home imply something about the conditions in other New York institutions in that era.

In 1930, the Commissioner expressed appreciation of the good care and training of the children. The next year's report added that the "Home is progressive in its method of child care" and placed in Class I as to administration. In 1936, the Home was commended for carrying out previous recommendations, though no mention was made earlier about what they were. The report went on to say:

> Members of the Board take pride in providing a real home for children rather than just institutional care . . . giving children a thorough religious and moral education as well as academic and vocational training to prepare them for life. . . . Superintendent and Board seem to work in splendid cooperation. . . . President maintains close interest, generally in daily contact . . . also generous contributor. . . . Daily routine satisfactory. Excellent plan for social development of children inside and outside of Home to be commended.

The 1938 report was equally enthusiastic, adding that both Board and superintendent were well informed with regard to modern methods of child care and training and the attempt to have children live as near normal a life as possible.

The theme of patriarchy captures the character, the temperament of the Home. Even if we stretch the symbol, it was not a "family"; noticeably missing, after all, was the key maternal figure—the gentle, loving, caring woman, the nurturing member, the pivot of what family life is all about. In addition, the Home did not offer either the kind of intimacy or the opportunities for privacy that family life is supposed to provide. This is what the "cottage system," established in the more progressive institutions, tried to approximate by creating separate, self-governing residences for small groups of children and their houseparents. As we will continue to see, living in the Home meant that you had to sharpen survival skills usually not required for living within the soft bosom of what family life is supposed to be like.

Still, somewhere within this survival consciousness, the children tried to feel that the capitalized Home was their living home and translated their experience *as if* it were something close to a family. In their own words, "We all helped each other," or "Whoever took care of you was your mother," or for that matter, "Hollander did care about us in his own way."

It can be said again that the *culture* of the Home and its *context*—its place in the religious, cultural, and geographical community—was in some ways analogous to an "extended family." It would not be overly sentimental to say that within this likeness were the gentle, ever-caring "aunties" that made up the Mothers Club, the good and faithful "cousins," in the form of Big Brothers and Sisters, and the mature, emancipated constant siblings, the alumni of the Home.

THE MOTHERS CLUB: THE "AUNTIES"

"Ah, the neighborhood and the women who lived there," was Will's tender recollection that introduced the first chapter. Will is a kind of spiritual fellow behind a face (really, in Yiddish, a *ponim*, a singular countenance) that still retains his youth and makes him, even after fifty years, immediately recognizable. Other alumni also were stirred by sweet memories when talk got to the Mothers Club.

They were memories not only of special events but of special symbols that made a difference: rights of passage, celebrations, the joyful holidays. Sue recalled the kind of bar mitzvah festivity each boy could expect. "I still remember how they made the kiddush (Sabbath ceremony and prayer) after the bar mitzvah service and then lunch. Mrs. Kolko made the sweet and sour pickled fish that I liked. And when the alumni girls married, even long after they left the Home, the Mothers Club made sure they were given a bridal shower." Miriam and Seymour, who together grew up in the Home and shared a marriage of almost a half century, agreed that the Mothers Club "went a long way to make it good for us . . . like a family. A lot of people growing up in their own homes didn't have some of the things that we did." Lil, on another evening, made the point that the seemingly endless Depression had hurt other families but "we didn't know from Depression—we got clothes a couple of times a year, every Chanukah and every Purim from the Mothers Club."

The Mothers Club was the first of the auxiliaries of the Children's Home. The 1921 publication, *The Story of Our Home,* gives this account of the origins of the Mothers Club:

> With the predominating thought that every child needs the care and the guidance of a mother, a handful of Jewish women organized, most informally, on August 6, 1919, the Mothers Club, an auxiliary to the Jewish Children's Home. From a meager handful the Mothers Club increased rapidly in membership and, as it expanded, its members assumed greater and more responsibilities, until anything from sewing clothes for the children to planning Purim parties were included in its categories of activities. . . . Perhaps one thing that the Mothers Club has done which cannot be measured in dollars and cents is the fact that with the inception of this auxiliary other local organizations began to take more than ordinary interest in the Children's Home and vie with each other in their efforts to improve conditions and better equip the Home.

Almost twenty years later, the Mothers Club was again acknowledged, this time in the Home's Silver Anniversary publication.

> Here Jewish Mothers found fertile field for expression of Mother instinct. Our children do not lack those intimate tender ties because Jewish Mothers of Rochester—525 of them—devote hours and hours to our little ones. No holiday or festival goes by but what our Mothers Club has a part in its preparation and celebration. They are concerned with their health, education, and upbringing. It's the Mothers Club that provides the means for Hebrew education, for books, for Tephillum and Tallasim (prayer shawls), for bar mitzvah, for parties, festivities.

The name, *Mothers* Club, was proper, but I believe the term "aunties," or the Yiddish *tante,* better captures their relationship with the children. As Will recalls, there was no shortage of affection bestowed on the children in passing or at special events. But I don't recollect, nor do the former residents, that many of the women spent much time in ongoing personal contacts with the kids in ways that some mother-volunteers now do in schools, day-care centers, or institutions. This cannot be considered a shortcoming, however. In those days the relationship between mother and youngster in the normal home did not resemble the kind of easygoing, egalitarian partnership that is seen in modern times. And the members of the Mothers' Club had their own working-class families to think about. Recalling the daily chores that women faced—particularly in the spotless Jewish home—it remains a source of wonder that they were able to give so much of their lives to charitable work.

They did what "aunties" are supposed to do: dote, indulge, provide for, celebrate, honor, and preserve ritual and tradition. To support all that they lavished on the Home and children, they raised their funds by annual social events that their members would enjoy. The yearly picnic at Seneca, Ontario, or other parks offered the delights of the deli world; a short strip of five-cent tickets would fill a limp paper plate with well-charred, fat-dripping, kosher hot dogs, homemade slaw, and sour dills. Bridge parties at the downtown hotel or Temple

Beth El, perhaps a linen sale at Workmen's Circle, bingo parties, the bazaar, and the well-attended membership luncheon and election of officers rounded out every year's fund-raising activities. A random search through items recorded over the years in the *Home Review* offers a sample of their dedication.

> December 1928: Served supper and gave each child a gift following children's performance of Chanukah plays. Presented alumni with curtains for clubhouse.
> May 1929: Mrs. Goldman entertained at her home in honor of Harriet who became 8. Gave reception for Eddie's confirmation. Presented Henry now at Yeshiva with watch and chain in recognition of his earnest effort to succeed.
> October 1932: Presented gifts to Washington Junior High School grads. Contributed $100 to Camp Fund. Simchat Torah party with bags of fruit, candy, nuts for children.
> July 1940: Purchased silk dresses for girls. Presented Vulcan stove. Shower for Pauline's marriage. Reception for Izzy's confirmation.

In turn, the good works of the ladies of the Mothers Club gave the children the opportunity to reciprocate, to show their gratitude, a response no doubt orchestrated by Mr. Hollander. Annually, the children presented the Club's president with flowers for Mother's Day. Frequently, the children offered entertainment at the annual luncheons. At the August 1941 meeting, for example, it was noted that Izzy spoke on camp life; Don, Jeannette, and Estelle played the piano; and Bobby sang.

THE BIG BROTHERS AND SISTERS: THE "COUSINS"

The Home's Silver Anniversary booklet describes how, in its earliest years, a group of young adults was invited to raise funds for the Home. Because of their success and enthusiasm:

> the late Mr. Alfred Hart became inspired with an idea that was entirely novel in social work involving the care and welfare of orphaned children . . . as a result, the Big Brothers and Sisters Club was born . . . [It] has, for many years past, furnished most of the recreational facilities, indoor games, athletic supplies, and hobby work materials . . . it has helped develop a better understanding between them, and has made the children more conscious of the fact that their "big brothers and sisters" were interested in them in a very real way.

Their interest was shown in many other ways. The library was stocked by the Club and story hours were conducted by members. The Boy Scout troop of the Home was provided for and led by the Big Brothers. "In addition, the entire general membership has frequently joined in furnishing Sunday afternoon entertainment of the children; and whenever talent has become scarce within the organization, arrangements have been made for procuring talented professional performers, local orchestras and bands, minstrel shows and marionettes; and bazaars, contests and picnics have been run so steadily that these affairs have become an accepted part of the recreational routine of the Jewish Children's Home."

This was indeed a local, grassroots phenomenon. Like the Mothers Club, BB&S not only raised its own operating funds but, in so doing, enriched the social life of its young members. The annual banquet at the ritzy Sagamore evolved into an annual dinner and dance and, in the later years, a concert and dance that brought acclaimed concert performers of that period to the entire community—among them, tenor Jan Peerce, soprano Lucille Manners, and the violinist Joseph Szigeti.

Beyond its service to the children of the Home, the story of Big Brothers and Sisters might be studied as an account of the passage of young Jewish men and women into adulthood during that era in Rochester, New York. Its primary devotion to the Home never dwindled, even during the days of the War when its members were drawn into the armed services or defense work. But as these young men and women joined in a formal enterprise, the service club could not help but become a social club in which young Jewish folk would meet new friends, date, and, not infrequently, marry.

The back page of the monthly *Home Review* belonged to the BB&S Club. Beyond announcements and exhortations, its paragraphs ranged from preciousness to sober concern. Over the years, the pages registered the spooniness of boy-girl relations, the pinch of the Depression, the gravity of the second World War. It is worth offering a few excerpts from those pages reflecting the character of the times:

> September 1931: As the New Year approaches we become retrospective and review events of the past, and those of us who are of an inquisitive turn of mind attempt to peer into the future. . . . The entire world is entering upon one of the most trying years in its history. The same may be said about our little organization. . . .
> August 1936: *Doings of People.* Lamont and Lee Kaplan stopped over in Niagara Falls on their way home from vacation. How ducky . . . a second Honeymoon?????
> Who has been writing duck-wucky letters to Pauline Weinberger since she came back from Niagara Falls? The wild man instinct of Irwin Kaltenbacher is coming to the fore. He is spending his vacation in the wilds of New Hampshire.
> January 1945: The energy of our members has been diverted to the war effort. It is with pleasant memories that we can recall the monthly meetings. These gatherings brought together young men and women who were interested in the welfare of our "little brothers and sisters." . . . We all look forward to the time when the members can again resume their active part in the meeting to renew friendships.

The buoyancy that characterized the outlook and activities of the Club and its membership spilled into its activities with the kids of the Home. An accounting of the picnics, hot dog roasts, third Sunday entertainments, gifts, books, ball games, contributions to Camp and Scholarship funds would require a special section or an appendix. The following is a small sample of a few of the *Home Review* entries that capture the sometimes playful spirit of the Club.

February 1928: Showed movies with motion picture machine borrowed from the Talmud Torah. On pioneers building up Jewish homeland. Children thrilled when movie was run backward.

May 1928: Entertainment show given by Mogen Dovid Club. Audience convulsed with laughter at jokes of amateur fun-makers who heaped ridicule and sarcasm on heads of children. Most laughs came from "laughing act" in which audience joined in heartily. Ice cream and cookies served.

January 1929: Dues for married members reduced. This should not be considered an inducement to matrimonial attachments.

February 1929: Comedy skit and piano and violin duo. Suggest that girls should band themselves into a faculty for teaching boy members manly art of dancing. They sure need it.

April 1932: Snappy program. David Harvard, community song leader led children, taught new dances. Hot Billy Gilbert's Band furnished snappy music for dancing. Virginia Reel.

April 1934: Minstrel show. Endmen "Early" Earl Goldstein and "Kalty" Irwin Kaltenbacher. "Weenie" Sam Susswein and "Rappy" Sam Rappaport surprised friends and themselves with ability to entertain. Gales of merriment. Hy Cohen, Interlocutor.

Like the members of the Mothers Club, the Big Brothers and Sisters stepped out of their normal routines to join for a time the institutional world of the dependent child. The significance of both clubs was not only in what they *did for* and *gave to* the children of the Home but what the Clubs *did with* the children on those special Sundays, holidays, roasts, picnics, and other excursions. These events were meaningful breaks in what was the otherwise drab, daily, routinized drills of congregate living.

THE ALUMNI: THE OLDER "SIBS"

The Home was not, of course, another world for the alumni; in the place of blood ties that tend to fasten relationships among family members, the formation of the Alumni Association in 1926, urged by Mr. Hollander, kept alive the feeling of belonging. Participation in the Association meant that "graduates" could preserve their bonds as they left the institution and crossed into the outside community of young adulthood. This strong sense of identity persisted for many even though they returned to live with parents who, as brief entries on discharge forms noted, "had now made a home." As one graduate put it: "Some of the kids could have been my brothers, though you liked some more than you liked others. There was a camaraderie that developed by virtue of our all being—uh, a kinship of some sort. . . . You had a feeling this was my group."

If the graduate didn't know it before, he or she was quick to discover on leaving that the Home had much more to offer in both spirit and substance than was available in the Depression community. Henry remembers:

After my brother and I left the Home, Jewish holidays would come up. My father never was a real active member with a shul, too expensive for him, he didn't earn much as a poor tailor. So what we used to do was go to the Children's Home for the services. We went because of the fact that we were friendly with so many of the kids and spent more time there. Went to alumni meetings there. Became ex-officio members of BB&S, though they didn't ask us to pay the dues. We went along on boat rides to Coburg. Got involved with alumni more and more.

By its thirteenth year, as reported in the Silver Anniversary publication, the Alumni Association regularly included 175 members, 90 living in Rochester. The regular monthly meetings brought the graduates together at the Home, where they could see and take part of the goings-on.

Internal committees served various purposes. The welfare committee helped alumni members find jobs, perhaps one of the most critical functions of the Alumni Association during those economic hard times. The entertainment committee planned programs for the Home's children and parties and outings for Club members. And the publication committee took responsibility for publishing and distributing the *Home Review*. In addition, the Alumni Association felt it had some influence on the operations of the Home since its officers served as representatives on the Board of Directors and on the Big Brothers and Sisters Executive Committee.

For several graduates, sentimental feelings about the Alumni Association persist. Sally, for one, even now, forty years since the Home ceased to be and *sixty* years since she departed, still hoped for some kind of reunion of the alumni. Well into her seventies, she is trim and attractive. She explained she had always "worked with the public where appearances were important." As she talked about the kids who were about her age, the passing of time lost its meaning. It was as if Sally were telling me about how she had just yesterday bumped into a girlfriend at Cohen's deli on Joseph Avenue or at McCurdy's department store, Rochester landmarks long gone. "I knew them all . . . Gert, Henry and his brother, I saw Betty in California. It is always nice to see someone from the Home, like a brother or sister, you always feel so close to every one of them. But it's hard to get in touch with everybody. I wish to God that they would have an alumni here and we could all meet at the Jewish Community Center . . . that would be a beautiful alumni affair. . . . " Since the *Home Review* was a child of the Alumni Association's efforts, there is scarcely an issue that does not report on the doings, the comings and goings, of the membership. Where the reports of the activities of the Mothers Club were properly sober and businesslike, and those of Big Brothers and Sisters often witty, the Alumni items were typically celebratory when achievements of the Association or its members were announced. The Association also deserves its share of excerpts from the newsletter.

In the late twenties, shortly after its birth, the major concern of the Alumni Association was the "Clubhouse Movement," the attempt to get the Board to grant meeting and activity space at the Home. The headline of November 11,

1928 finally announced: "Alumni Gets Clubhouse. Board finally decided to satisfy desire of Alumni. Three rooms turned over to Alumni, two to be used for social life, the third to be editorial and composing room." Three months later the clubhouse was opened with great ceremony and festivity. Alfred Hart and members of Mothers Club and Big Brothers and Sisters attended. There was dancing in the afternoon and evening.

By 1930 there were eighty-eight members in thirteen communities. The number in New York City was large enough to create a branch. A report from the New York Alumni: "Meeting held at Minnie's home, thirteen present. Committee appointed to adopt constitution and by-laws. Bennie moved to have a skating party. No second because no one owned skates."

During the early thirties, monthly meetings were augmented with speakers on a diversity of topics such as "self-engineering" as a means to happiness, appreciating music, chemical warfare, Hitlerism, and Hebrew poets—programs reminiscent of the Chautauqua circuit. Entertainment also was frequent, including a performance by a curious group called "The Depression Nut Club." The Alumni Association was a club in its own right, continuously planning annual picnics, dances, card parties, debates, mock trials, chess and checker tournaments, lectures and discussion groups, the regular monthly meetings, and, of course, the annual ritual or anniversary celebration and selection of new officers.

Clubs, at least up to the second World War, were popular for many young men and women as an opportunity for fellowship, even kinship, while sharing common social activities. Clubs were essential then to every aspect of adolescent development—identity, social learning, discovery of interests, sports, and not the least, dances, parties, and other occasions to meet members of the opposite sex. The many clubs that the Rochester Jewish Young Men and Women's Association made available to us helped me get through my teen years.

By the early forties, the country was at war and the numbers of the alumni entering the armed services multiplied. At the 17th Annual Dinner in 1943, all the officers were women "because men are either in the service or defense work." That year Chanukah gifts were sent to the boys in service, each kit containing a razor, shaving cream, metal mirror, shoe polish, and waterproof matches. Fortunately, Jewish dietary laws prohibited shipment of the cans of Spam and Vienna sausage that were bestowed on other nonkosher serviceman.

As it turned out, over eighty of the boys of the Home and three girls served in the War, virtually everyone eligible for service. At the annual installation dinner in 1945, the president reported that twenty-five of the alumni were serving overseas, nineteen in the European and six in the Pacific theaters. Max Weinstein was the one alumnus who was killed in action, in battle in North Africa during the early stages of the War. Israel Jacobson, only three inches over five feet tall (but also a prizefighter), was wounded twice, received two Purple Hearts, a Bronze Star for gallantry, a Silver Star, and a Croix de Guerre from General DeGaulle's headquarters. Two others received Purple Hearts and

Jake Joffee was awarded the Air Medal and the Distinguished Flying Cross for extraordinary achievement as a turret gunner on a B17 when a shell exploded inside the aircraft.

In 1947 a grand reunion was held at a banquet at the Children's Home, attended by sixty-six former servicemen and women, the Rochester mayor, and other civic officials. Not long after, the New York City and New Jersey alumni held their banquet at the Paramount restaurant in New York.

Five months before the Home closed its doors, the last major event of the alumni, its 22nd Annual Banquet, was held at the Normandie Hotel in Rochester. Unwittingly, it turned out to be a requiem since no one could have anticipated the demise of the Home. The banquet offered tributes to the groups that had shaped and sustained the organization—the Mothers Club, the Board of Directors, Big Brothers and Sisters. The major tribute was granted to Mr. Hollander, who reviewed the life of the Home, emphasizing the successes of the graduates, some of whom had become attorneys, social workers, pharmacists, psychologists, and businessmen.

The last regular monthly meetings were sparsely attended. After the Home closed, Will was president of the Alumni Association. But as he recalled: "I must admit that without the prompting of Jake Hollander, I didn't do anything to keep the organization together. I felt for the other kids . . . like it was good to see them and so forth. But personally, I didn't feel a strong need or desire to keep the alumni going—to call meetings or do anything. But, God forbid, if somebody died or something, I would always go to the house. You know, you always have a sort of family feeling. You know, we all lived together."

OTHER AUXILIARIES

A few other organizations should be commemorated as examples of the community's investment in the Children's Home and their intent to bring pleasure and diversion to the children of the Home.

The Aleph Eien Club, also formed shortly after the opening of the Children's Home, included a group of teen-age boys and girls who had visited the institution and, as the report has it, "visualized a great opportunity to bring a few rays of sunshine into the lives of the parentless and homeless children." The Club helped raise funds for new buildings and a playground. On through the mid-thirties, the Club provided monthly entertainment—movies, a Scottish bagpiper in a kilt, acrobatic dancing, a magician, a talk by a high school teacher, and refreshments and dancing to Pop Ware's orchestra. In addition, annual outings were held at local parks.

The True Pals Club, young men who had gone to school together, invited the children as guests to theatrical plays and sporting events. The boys were special guests of the Monroe County Sporting Club to see the pride of the Jewish community, Ozzie Sussman, in a boxing match. The Elks Sunshine Committee arranged a dance complete with orchestra. The Kiwanis Club used its Joy Car during a few summers to take children to parks and lakes. Children were guests at the Shriner's Circus and virtually every movie theater in town. And there was the Annual Orphans Outing, a citywide event sponsored by the Auto Club, in which the Home's children, as the following bit of 1934 journalese exclaims, joined the public parade of all the city's "orphans." "Annual Orphans' Outing a Sea Breeze. Began with a street parade—sirens of police motorcycles wailed shrill warnings, a half dozen bands blared forth lively tunes, men and women on sidewalks paused in their ordinary pursuits to wave farewell to more than 1,100 laughing, shouting youngsters who were beginning the red letter day of the year. They were given strips of tickets for ice cream, punch and all the concessions."

And not the least was the Jewish Young Men and Women Summer Camp at Conesus or Seneca Lake. Every year there was a Camp Fund drive to support the twenty or thirty boys and girls for two weeks at camp.

Mention of a financial support evokes the importance of the Scholarship Fund. Created in 1926 by Sarah Wynar's bequest of $1,000 in memory of her son, the Fund continued to attract gifts large and small from the auxiliaries and other community benefactors. A few notices in the *Home Review:* Ben Forman pledged $500; Big B Flour, $10; Mrs. Fanny Cohen, $5; Fay Levy, $20 in honor of her son's confirmation; J. Cohen, $25, for speedy recovery of mother. There are many more.

From 1927 onward through the Depression years, the Fund supported post-high school or advanced training for almost fifty of the Home's residents (and there were others who achieved further education on their own). About half this number attended Rochester Business Institute; three went to beauty schools; and two enrolled in the local Mechanics Institute. The remainder matriculated at prominent schools of higher learning—four at the University of Rochester, and the rest at universities as diverse as Cornell, Yeshiva, the Universities of Buffalo, Wyoming, Washington State, Michigan, and Illinois, Columbia College of Pharmacy, and Brooklyn Law School. Such opportunities, as I noted earlier, were not open to most of the other young folk in the local Jewish community, those residing with their own families.

It should be noted, however, that these funds were not dispensed with a generous, unstinting hand. Support had to be earned; these wards of the Home had to be excellent students not only to qualify for support and admission to the educational program but also to surmount the restrictive quotas placed on Jews applying for higher education. Many of the residents literally were at the head of their classes; in 1935 four boys were elected president of their respective classes at Washington High School. The actual subsidies were meager, requiring college students to find other jobs to get by. Jakey, who attended Washington State, recalls how he had to hop freights across the country just to get home once in awhile.

There is something symbolic about the Scholarship Fund that sets up its contrast with the other charities, activities, and gifts. The Fund was just one of the Home's few practices that *individualized* the youngster, paid attention to the particular child's unique merits and achievements. The picnics, gifts, parties, entertainments, and other good things that were provided surely made a critical difference in the otherwise unrelieved lives of the children. But largely, these gems of pleasure, excitement, and diversion were granted not to *a* kid but, without distinction, to *all* the kids. No *one* was invited to an outing; *every one* was required to attend. No *one* was fitted with Passover outfits; *every one* with regimentation and uniformity once a year marched in lines of two by two to the downtown store, The National Clothing Company, where they were sized and given their attire. There was no choice.

A YEAR'S ACTIVITIES

To this point, I have pieced together the mosaic of the Jewish Children's Home, its elements interlocked to shape a structure that was not family-like but nonetheless a *home* as far as its members were concerned. There were predictable differences in how some events were recalled by various alumni, but little disagreement about its stable, predictable characteristics—its people, rules, rituals, discipline, and provisions—that together made up the routines of everyday life. Except for a slight decrease in control and regimentation in the later years and the variations occasioned by people coming and going, changes over time were scarcely discernible. So we do have a sense of the objective composition, order, and arrangement of the Home at 27 Gorham Street. Having the form settled, how can we gain some sense of its operations? I am not speaking at this moment of the dynamics of the home—the give-and-take, the relations, the schemes, means of survival, and the like: such energies are the material of the next chapter. Simply, from an outside view, what was an average year like? The 1933 volume of the *Home Review* offers a memoir of one year.

The selection of 1933 was not entirely arbitrary: for one thing, my memories of that era are quite vivid since I was eleven years old that year and involved almost daily with my friends across the street. Also, 1933 was approximately halfway between the Home's opening and closing and a time in which the world was facing inconceivable changes. At this midpoint, the community that was the Home was, itself, involved in subtle transitions: the majority of the residents still were the dependent children of immigrant families who were now being joined by the first children referred by the court or other community agencies because of behavior or family problems.

To gain some perspective, it is worth saying a bit about that year. The year, 1933, it turned out, anticipated both desperate fear and hope. It marked the rise of Adolf Hitler and the portents of a second world war; everyone wanted to believe that signs might be found that would signal an end to the creeping Depression. New Year's Eve 1933 endures in my mind as symbol of how desperate that hope was, of how we fastened to anything that remotely signified a way out of hard times. Rochester sits in its infamous snow belt, the southern shore of Lake Ontario. Blizzards are never welcome, but the one that struck on that New Year's Eve was considered a momentous omen, an augury of better times ahead. Men who couldn't remember their last job were actually working. In their shabby overcoats, topped by fedoras or caps, they were out in the blizzard in numbers, clearing the downtown streets with hand shovels. In our kitchen, grouped around the old Stromberg Carlson, we were heartened by the announcer who, like an emboldened oracle, dared to predict that perhaps the storm and the work it provided were signs of deliverance. It didn't, of course, and the more lasting and dismal memory of the gray winter is the image of my father alone in our living room-sample shoe store, as always attired in his only suit, playing endless games of one-handed pinochle while he waited for the infrequent customer who might purchase or order a pair of two-dollar shoes.

It was the year that Franklin Delano Roosevelt was inaugurated and with that pivotal event the beginning radical economic programs and the enactment of the National Industrial Recovery Act. Our Jewish community could feel some ties with this Act since it was one of our own, the eminent Jewish Rochesterian, Congressman, Mayor, and Board member of the Home, Meyer Jacobstein, who first proposed the plan to President Roosevelt.[2] The year 1933 is also well-remembered as the end of the Prohibition era with the repeal of the Volstead Act. But only hints of the dark Depression and other disturbing world events found their way into the monthly issues of the *Home Review,* usually in oblique ways as announcements of occasional talks given at alumni meetings about the troubles in Europe or in requests for jobs for unemployed alumni.

THE *HOME REVIEW*

The monthly newsletter was much more than just a basic bulletin board of the Home's activities. Over any year, it was a medium that, in capsule form, captured achievements, rites of passage, literary works, awards, benefactions, and other tributes to and from the Jewish immigrant community.

Honors bestowed on the Home's Board members filled the front page of the January 1933 issue of the *Home Review:* Alfred Hart and Ben Forman were elected trustees of the Rochester Chamber of Commerce; Rabbi Sadowsky had published his second book of a Jewish series. As always, the inside pages reported the marriages, births, and educational achievements of some alumni. And the activities of that winter month for the children were detailed: The Aleph Eien Club sponsored a Sunday afternoon performance by an accordion player and pupils of Marjorie Miller's Dancing School; the children saw the movie *20,000 Years at Sing Sing* at the Capitol Theater; there was a hike by Boy Scout Troop 93 of the Home to Ellison Park and the Home's Girl Scout Troop 37 gave a demonstration of Hebrew folk dancing.

Every issue of the *Home Review* contained a column headed "Contributions" that acknowledged the extent to which the Home depended on the large variety of contributions to the Home from local businesses and families. The contents of this section in the January 1933 issue were typical, expressing gratitude for: ice cream and cake sent by Mr. and Mrs. Cohen in honor of their son's fourth birthday; a crate of oranges from Eber Brothers; four suits for boys from I. M. Forman Co.; ten dozen Rice Flakes from H. J. Heinz; 330 loaves of bread, twenty cakes, fifty dozen rolls, 135 dozen cookies from Hart Food Stores; six talisim (prayer shawls) from three families.

The February edition headlined the 18th Annual Meeting of the Children's Home. Mr. Hollander reported that the Home was rated Class 1 by the State Board of Social Welfare and that fifty children were in residence. He also applauded the children's educational progress, a result of special effort to stimulate interest in their studies.

The February release illustrated the importance of the Children's Home as a catalyst and social center for many of the Jewish community's adult social activities. A sampling of the month's social life included: the Alumni Association's meetings that hosted special speakers; the Mothers Club celebration of the 25th wedding anniversary of one of its families, the Abe Kolkos, which included a surprise dinner party and evening bridge game; the Aleph Eien Club's successful annual affair, complete with orchestra at only fifty cents a ticket; and the Big Brothers and Sisters' annual Dinner and Installation at the Roof Garden of the Sagamore Hotel. The Aleph Eien Club announced its Open House Social at the Home: "JUST LOOK WHAT YOU ARE GETTING FOR 15 CENTS - ENTERTAINMENT - DANCING - BRIDGE PRIZES - REFRESHMENTS!" The ladies of the Mothers Club attended a luncheon and bridge party. Amid these goings-on, it was reported that the children enjoyed a Sunday afternoon dance with music by the Aaron Silverman orchestra.

Notice of the establishment of the A. F. Horowitz Memorial Foundation to benefit the boys of the Children's Home filled the first page of the April 1933 issue. Created to perpetuate the memory of the founder and head of the National Clothing Company, the Foundation pledged that all the boys' clothing needs would be cared for. And so, early in April in anticipation of the Passover holiday, "all the boys, ranging from 3 to 17 years, were taken to the store and completely outfitted with new suits, hats, shirts, ties, shoes, and sox."

The news in the July 1933 issue had to do with gifts and presentations apropos of the summer season. Over $500 was collected to allow nineteen boys and eleven girls to attend the Jewish Young Men and Women's Association camp at Lakeville. The Jacob Robfogel family provided playground equipment in memory of Jacob's wife. A Mrs. Rubin gave a party in honor of her daughter's marriage and the Rosenblatts presented the children with forty free admissions to see the Rochester Red Wings of the International League play baseball. The Aleph Eien Club held its annual children's outing, as did the Big Brothers and Sisters. And it was proudly noted that the children of the Home made the best showing of all in the Flower Day collection for the Jewish National Fund.

The front page of the September 1933 edition offers an interesting but indirect glimpse of patriarchy and its natural place in the system. It is also a tribute to the remarkable literacy and expressiveness of two of the Home's children. This page covered two essays, both titled, "My Idea of a Good Superintendent," one written by Ruth, the other by Harry. The two essays were entries in a contest devised by the Superintendent's Division of the State Conference of Social Work (of which Mr. Hollander was a member of the Executive Committee). The entrants' essays were restricted to one of two topics—the first already noted, the second on "My Idea of a Good Children's Court Judge."

It would appear that the originators of this contest assumed that wards of the state's institutions would be eager to let their personal views be known without the benefits of anonymity. This is an interesting assumption since the superintendent of the contestant's institution was given the responsibility of reading all of his wards' essays on what a good superintendent was supposed to be, select what he judged as the best two, and send them to the Chairman of the Division. Who would question the possibility of bias? Obviously, it was not an issue.

Written with the intelligence, care, and style that modern English teachers would covet for their students, the essays can be considered representative of the quality of schooling of many of the Home's children. The two essays also suggest a certain disparity in the way the men and women graduates of the Home recalled their early experiences: the theme of relationships and interdependence often colored women's vision of life in the Home, whereas the men centered on the uniqueness and character of the individual.[3] And I must add that the words of the two authors remain instructive for present administrators.

Ruth writes about the importance of ideals and obligations in human relationships and roles and apparently leaves it to her contemporaries to judge whether *her* superintendent in any way conforms to her standards. She speaks first of virtues: "An ideal superintendent . . . is one who is an able guide of children . . . kind, broad-minded, cooperative, and impartial. . . . He should study his charges individually, learn the defects of each, then help correct them by patience and understanding." She adds that "to err is human" and therefore punishments should not be delivered hastily. On the other hand, praise for good behavior will also benefit other children who might be envious but "at the same time may be inspired to do good." She uses a charming but apt metaphor, describing the role of the superintendent "as a leader of a choir in which the children are the singers." Then she sums up: "A good superintendent should do his most to *substitute* (my emphasis) a real father. He must be careful in his choice of words, must have self-control, and most important of all, he must always remember that he is the pattern and the children's characters will be molded as his . . . he need not be perfect, but truly human."

I pondered her insights and wisdom, wondering who or what was the inspiration of her convictions. She was, after all, only *fifteen* when she wrote this essay and had already been in the Home for seven years following the deaths of both parents. An opportunity to inquire arose when we met in her gracious home. When I asked, during our conversation, about the source of her ideas, she honestly couldn't recall. She guessed that was just how she had thought about things.

Harry's essay, in contrast, was straightforward in terms of his definition of the good superintendent: "One who is a kind, loveable, sympathetic father with the wisdom of a man who understands his responsibility." Harry added that he must be a "pal" of the boys and girls, but must also be a man of the community, an upright citizen. The ideal of the archetypal father is evident in Harry's belief that "a good superintendent conceals his pain and sorrow, reveals his joy and happiness, instills in the child the spirit of God, love of country . . . and has the responsibility of molding the character and ambitions of his charges." And, if any questions remained about the prototype of these virtues, Harry confided that "I am indeed proud to have for a superintendent a man who measures up to that high standard; a man who fills the vacancy left by the death of my father."

Harry was also fifteen when he wrote this essay and the Home had been his home for five years. His father died of pneumonia when Harry was eight; his mother, almost blind, could not care for the three older children who were placed in the Home. Harry apparently fancied himself as a writer, particularly taken with the theme of male leadership. In the next year, 1934, Harry composed a poetic tribute to President Roosevelt that began with these lines: "My God I must thank you for being so fine / For sending us Roosevelt in this pressing time."

It turned out the poem was acknowledged by a letter from Roosevelt's personal secretary. But as far as the results of the essay contest are concerned, we will never know whether Ruth or Harry won the first or second prize—$5 or $2.

The November 1933 issue announced the forthcoming Chanukah entertainment to be given by the children. The front page of this issue best exemplifies the ambitiousness and variety of the program.

Sunday afternoon, December 17th, the children of the Home will present their Annual Chanukah entertainment in the assembly hall. The program will be as follows:

A play in Jewish, entitled "The Blind Girl", the cast consisting of:

Leah, the blind girl. . . . . Ruth Clifton
Sarah. . . . . Beatrice Goldblatt
Dvorah . . . . Hadassah Hollander
Shoshono. . . . . Irene Tillim
Judith . . . . Harriet Tobin
Anna. . . . . Anna Berman
Hemdah . . . . Judith Hollander
Ziporah. . . . . Hattie Underberg
Rachel. . . . . Lillian Goldblatt

Barnet Bitensky, Coach

* * *

Sketch, entitled "The Chasn"

Isadore Snyder, a plain Jew—Harry Silver, a Chasn

RECITATION,—"The Matchmaker"..... Harry Silver

* * *

Selections by the Hart Mandolin Group—Anna Cohen, accompanist

DANCE PROGRAM

* * *

Russian Dance......... .Lillian Goldblatt, Harriet Tobin
Gypsy Dance. . . . Rebecca Alpert, Judith Hollander, Hattie Underberg,
Pauline Sendus
Dutch Dance. . . . Winifred Benes, Hadassah Hollander
Waltz of the Flowers. . . . Minnie Itkin, Marion Oken, Betty Tillim
"Waltz". . . . Anna Berman, Ruth Clifton, Dorothy Greenberg
"Blue Prelude". . . . Vera Berman, Selma Goldblatt, Anna Maroz, Pearl
Silver

Miss Kay Cohen, Instructress—Anna Cohen, accompanist

The year concluded with a special notice to the children informing them of the plan to reestablish the Honor Roll system in January: children who make the Honor Roll most often will be awarded gifts by Mr. Hart. The Honor Roll was employed intermittently over the life of the Home. How children were selected is not clearly known, although it is safe to say that Mr. Hollander had some say in the choices. Typically, the Honor Roll included five boys and five girls, scarcely representative since boys always outnumbered girls. Some kids, such as Will, were frequently nominated because of their excellent schoolwork, dependability, and good behavior. Others who worked at getting away with what they could were rarely found on the Roll. And mavericks like Phil would consider their selection something less than an honor. Still, children who were active members of the Honor Roll were not always razzed: the Honor Roll was seen as just one more adult invention.

It is worth noting that the December issue shows that the children were not overlooked in any way during the Chanukah gift-giving season. The Home received candy, suckers, and ice cream from several families and organizations; fifty books for the library; dishes from the Liberty Theater; six dozen knicker sox plus other attire from National Clothing; and $15 for the rubber fund. The children were guests of four different movie theaters but also brightened the lives "of the folks at the Home for the Aged." Meanwhile, the auxiliaries continued to maintain a busy social schedule—a raffle for $2.50 by the Aleph Eien Club, a bazaar by the Mothers Club, and planning for the annual concert and dance by the Big Brothers and Sisters.

All told, the view of the Children's Home from the pages of the *Home Re-*

view is at least benign and often running over with harmony and goodwill. The symbiosis of the institution and the community noted previously is wonderfully apparent in these news items: indeed the Home was a magnet in the Jewish community that attracted the community's blessings, beneficence, and most imaginative forms of *tzedekah;* in turn, the Home provided the *raison d'etre* for a good part of the social life and purpose of the young adults, the marrieds, and perhaps most important, for women who otherwise would be restricted to the traditional role of homemaker.

Without humbling their values for the Home, its children, and the community, the structure of the Home, its functions, and the good works discussed in this chapter offer one perspective. The perspective is largely two dimensional, a public view that encompasses space—all that makes up the Children's Home—and time, the Home's chronology. Altogether, a certain objectivity is granted the Children's Home and its culture, a "realness" that everyone could identify with, hold dear, support, and by that ensure its existence.

Having this reality in place, it is finally time to add the third dimension to fill out the portrait—the human quotient, the subjective, more intimate, personal accounts of having lived in and shared that reality. No warning is intended since the reminiscences of the alumni do not disparage or diminish the importance of the people, groups, and events described.

Rather, these conditions in time are kneaded and reshaped by memories that temper the documented facts with personal meanings, that try to make sense of the Home years. The graduates with whom I talked consistently recalled with affection the treats, the parties, the Sunday entertainments and more; these events took on a different shade, however, when they interjected the conjunction, *"but,"* to show, ironically, that fun and sadness went hand-in-hand. "Sure," said one, "life was pretty hard in lots of ways, *but* if it wasn't for the Mothers Club or the Big Sisters . . . " or, another, "There were too many times, I dunno, I was just angry *but* we did have music lessons, and the dances." And one more, "We really enjoyed the free movies downtown *but* I never got used to people watching us march in a line to get there."

Life in the Home
Views from the Inside

Attention now shifts to the themes of living, to personal renditions of "how it was for me," "how it was for us." The narratives that came before and those that will now follow can, of course, be read literally for their interest and the information they offer. But for our purposes, they have more to tell us—often in ambiguous and sometimes hard-to-decipher ways—about "how I grew up," "how I made it," "how I became a person." Whether they spent a few years or an entire childhood as wards of the Home, the children obviously were growing toward something called maturity. In the jargon of modern child psychology and development, we might say they were dealing with certain *developmental tasks*, acquiring *social skills*, undergoing *moral development*, shaping a *self-concept*, forming an *identity*, and so on.

For these children, however, this process was unfolding not within the familiar boundaries of family life, but in the structured and often paradoxical confines of an institution. Ideally, both family and institution might afford (albeit in very different ways) comforting bonds of kinship and a sense of belonging. Whereas if the kind benefits of family life nourish identity and individuality, the price of institutional life—particularly life in the old classic congregate institution—is conformity and assimilation. If the "developmental task" of the Home's children was to achieve a measure of whatever might be called selfhood or independence, this paradoxically had to occur within a patriarchal, restrained climate that demanded docile compliance. And so, these stories offer a curious view of child development—a view from the present twilight years about how these ironies were once met and selfhood was achieved.

Why a curious view? First, the personal accounts of these men and women are scarcely memories of a child's garden of delights, of a childhood suffused with love, caring, comfort. In fact, it would be all too easy to become captivated by the morbid, even pathological, details of institutional life. Taking too seriously the enlightenment freely given by the fields of psychology—theoretical, clinical, and popular—about the tribulations of growing up, we can be persuaded by the thesis that when bad things happen in children's lives, they are bound to result in unhappy outcomes—behavior problems, poor relationships, neurosis, ad nauseam. And if the children in question happen to be unlucky enough to be inmates of an asylum, they are doomed to a more dismal future.[1]

Let us acknowledge that the hardships and hurts experienced by the Home's children can hardly be adequately documented in these pages. Still, the fact that this study is centered not on speculations about "what will happen if" but on consistent, real-life recollections of "what did happen when" gives it undeniable credibility: accounts of, let us say, an atypical childhood are told some sixty and seventy years later by a group of former residents whose worthy lives contradict the simple cause-effect equations that purport to predict how people will turn out. By all accounts, it would be expected that many former wards of the Home would turn up as statistics in the records of correctional, psychiatric, or welfare systems, or in divorce courts. Clearly, this did not occur: in fact, the graduates of the Home in the early or later years were remarkably under-represented on these rolls. Even more to their credit, these elders chose not to use the hurts of childhood past, as is so common, to justify the losses or anguish of the present or to excuse themselves as victims. Instead, their stories suggest—implicitly, to be sure—the strengths they perfected to enable them to grow up, to make it, to become a person. Or, in accord with the highest standards of Yiddishkeit, to become a mensch. Dear Bertha, ailing but still tough, looks back from her seventy-fifth year and offers her philosophy of child development in her time: "You had to have a sense of humor or you'd be creamed. I'm not bitter. What saved me was the tricks I pulled on Hollander. Being able to outwit Hollander made me overlook a lot of stuff."

ISSUES IN SELECTIVITY

Considering the question of credibility as far as the retrospections of these elders are concerned, it is important to say something about the natural role of selectivity in social research and its place in this study. In quantitative studies and surveys, selectivity occurs at the very outset when the researcher determines the sample and the questions that will be asked. In qualitative or ethnographic studies that do not impose such specific boundaries, selectivity occurs as a phenomenon of human nature.

First, the story told by the teller cannot help but be marked by selectivity. How and what people recall and tell about their lives, whether the tale is comic, poignant, despairing, or absurd, the narrator's self is at the center of the story and, more often than not, the self has a stake in what the story intends to convey: our narratives cannot help but express how we want to be seen and understood and to explain our circumstances even within the limits and tricks of memory.

I have mentioned how selectivity was active in my conversations with the Home's alumni because of our recollections of one another. Nonetheless, without imposed constraints, my companions were generally free to respond to my simple queries on their own terms.

The context of our discussions, where and how we were meeting, also made for different shades of response. When it was just the individual alumnus and myself talking, say, in the comfort of Joey's living room or Sally's sunporch, my respondent tended, at least at first, to be cautiously alert to what he or she thought I wanted to know. When a spouse or brother or sister was present, the storyteller sometimes used the opportunity to make a particular point for the benefit of the relative; conversely, the other person at times acted as an editor by correcting certain memories. Then, too, if my wife was joining us, say at dinner with Bert and Dot or at brunch at Sue's apartment, she was warmly received and told what she needed to know so she could feel she was part of the circle.

The spirit and cross fire of memories truly lit up on evening get-togethers of several alumni arranged for my benefit. At these times I was gently assigned the role of audience, there just to listen and enjoy and learn. In the banter of these old-time graduates, memories of particular hurts and angers were duly recorded. But what took center stage were the escapades and pranks, the victories that were relived in their tales.

A more subtle kind of selectivity became evident when voices expressing gender and personality were heard. An example is an excerpt from an afternoon's talk with Lillian (Lill) and her brother. Both are now retired from rewarding life's work. Both resided in the Children's Home at the same time, although they were separated by the division of boys and girls. First, Lill's expansive reply to my "what was it like?" question: "It was a very cold situation. Cold. They fed us. They clothed us. They taught us religion which they thought was all that was necessary. That's it. Nobody ever called us in to say once a week if there was any problems. But still, I don't think any of us ever made it to jail. I'm sure." Then the contrast of her brother's crisp reply after just a moment's thought: "It was just a time you were there and you had to go through it and had no choice."

His rejoinder echoed the concrete, solitary, even perfunctory ways some men tried to compress their memories and experiences. Without exception, all sincerely put forth their impressions as candidly as they could. But when I asked for deeper thoughts, a mild sense of confusion seemed to be stirred as if they were returning to a dark, unvisited attic to search for contents long forgotten. As Joey put it, "A lot of it is a big blur except for a couple of things."

In contrast, most women (even cynical Lill) were attuned to the relational and emotional climate of the Home, exceptionally sensitive to the nuances in the ways people, the children, shared their lives. In a few instances, talking with Anna and Sue for example, they became almost motherly in how they needed to fill me in on the lives of others before I could begin to pose my questions. They brought out the thick, well-worn photo album that occupied a prominent position on a nearby bookshelf. We sat close together, turning pages of old, fuzzy black and whites, snaps of groups at camp or picnics or parties, boys in knickers, young ladies brazenly posing as nifty flappers. A stream of anecdotes informed me about what happened to whom, where, when, why, and so on.

Subtly, a certain moral tone infiltrated the voices of both men and women, almost as subtext of the story being told. Intonations of a personal justice, whether failed or demanded, questions of right and wrong, the importance of special virtues and values—not the least, personal responsibility—and the benefits or defects of religion were sounded here and there within the texts of their reminiscences, all apparently indicative of the place of these ethics in their lives.

Considering the importance of selectivity in any study of human affairs, it would be negligent to overlook the importance of *voices not heard.* Whose voices are these?

The voices I did hear, those of the Children's Home alumni who agreed to share their memories with me were, in the jargon of social research, willingly "self-selected." But there are other voices of other folks associated with the Home I did not hear who, no doubt, could also cast new light on what this inquiry was all about. Some of these voices of course go unnoticed because they were stilled by death. Among the living are prospering old grads that I could not reach because of lack of information or other ordinary reasons. I know of others whose impressions would have added to and enriched this social history: they chose to exclude themselves. To be sure, some may have felt that they had more interesting things to do than dredge up old memories or chat with some stranger from the past. Or perhaps they wished to avoid reviving old hurts or to escape any misgivings about life as it now is. No matter the reason, the voices not heard are surely missed.

THEMES OF INSTITUTIONAL LIFE

Perceptions of life in the Children's Home did not pop out of the stories already ordered and catalogued. With careful inspection and repeated readings of the texts of their recollections, certain recurring themes and melodies became evident. One embraces the routines, rules, and doctrines governing daily life in the Home, all grounded in religious ritual and duty. The second theme concerns the nature of relationships and interdependence that accented the emotional climate of the Home. Stigma is the third theme, the recalled feeling of being conspicuously and painfully different. All three converge in what I will call the themes of patriarchy, permissiveness, Yiddishkeit, and play.

ROUTINES AND REGULATIONS

It was not necessary to ask directly about the firm patterns of everyday life: strong recollections about the many demands of daily life were freely offered. It didn't make much difference whether the respondent had lived in the Home in earlier or later years. Over time, little changed in what made up the ironies and tragicomedy of life in the Home.

Sue and Phil spoke in similar voices in the opening chapter about the burden of the routines of institutional life. Phil recalled his feelings of loss of autonomy that resulted from the average day that was regularly intersected by periods of chores and prayers. His recollection that "there was never time to be a child" echoed Sue's impression that "there was never time to play . . . we were always washing . . . cleaning, sewing."

Other alumni added their memories in Anna's family room after the summer's eve barbecue. Casual talk about the daily menu of work and prayer was interrupted by Arnie, who reminded his comrades that the routines were not always dull, something you found out quickly if you didn't snap to the regulations. Speaking of a boys' supervisor, a recent graduate whom Mr. Hollander had appointed to this position, Arnie recalled that "he would go around the beds. If you didn't get up, you'd get a bucket of cold water. You got up, you got dressed, they'd want you down there for services. Then you'd go and eat. And after breakfast, back upstairs making beds, mopping floors. I used to mop six rooms before I went to school." "Did you just have to take it?" I asked, immediately feeling foolish. "Did anyone ever try to revolt?" "We did revolt," Arnie replied, with a glance that confirmed my foolishness, and added "but our shins were pretty sore after that."

The question of routine arose in my conversation with Joey, but in a startling way. For most of his adult life, Joey had been the owner of a cut-rate jewelry store in Rochester; recently retired, he had turned the business over to his son. Now in his seventies, Joey struck me as an almost militantly independent man who tended to wrap his rather volatile and rebellious childhood in tidy, unemotional bundles and store them away. Brandishing his cigar, he assured me that, as in all things, something really positive could come out of even rotten things. He summed it up in one breathless sentence: "You got up, washed, dressed, did your work, then go to services, eat your breakfast, go to school, come home." So what was positive about that? According to Joey, excellent dental health: "I don't think there was a kid in the Home who had bad teeth. Why? You start to think, you had to brush your teeth every day. You'd line up twice a day with Hollander—he'd give you a piece of gum. For fifteen years you chewed that gum. I got all my teeth, no problems. I think that helped me, just thinking back that far."

Meals and food of course were part of the chain of daily life. Like most graduates, Joey ordained oatmeal as the major symbol of deadly routine: every generation of wards could count on it for daily breakfast fare. But Joey pointed out there were other predictable culinary customs: "Every single Friday after-noon we had hot dogs. I can't remember a lot but I know that much, the menu for all those years. Every Saturday afternoon Hollander would read the Bible, every Saturday after services. You'd get chicken then he'd read it [the Bible] whether you liked it or not. You got it."

Being of the Orthodox Jewish faith that largely excluded women from daily prayer (attendance at Sabbath and holiday services was required, however), the girls had their own routines. In accord with their assigned gender role, their duties included preparing breakfasts and lunches. As Ruth recalled with some bemusement: "OK, the routine was we got up, dressed, and we each had a task to do . . . that sort of thing, probably after breakfast. Boys had religious ser-vices, but we had to go over to the other house, the boys', to make breakfast. To this day I don't like farina because it was lumpy. I'd get water boiling for the cereal."

Lumpy, thick, coarse cereal also sat torpidly at the center of Dot and Bertha's recollection of their life together as sisters in the Home. Now that the sisters—Dot, still slim and stylish, Bertha, well, less so—were in their seven-ties, it might be amiss to call their sharp exchanges sibling rivalry. Still, it seemed to turn out that Bertha always knew better. Dot mentioned that she had to pay Blanche, one of the other kids, ten cents to get her to eat Dot's gummy portion. Bertha, ever the champion, shrugged, saying: "Cost me nothing. I put the scummy stuff in my mouth and waited 'til I got outside and threw it in the garbage. Hollander caught me one day and he gave me a dose of castor oil. D'you know, I can't drink black coffee today because we got castor oil in it (Dot added, 'orange juice, too'). All this because I walked out with the scum off the top of the oatmeal. The cocoa had scum on it too."

It was Bertha's opinion (not shared by all) that "the only time we had a decent meal was when the supervisors from the State came to inspect." But when she was in charge of making lunches that the kids would carry with them to junior high, Bertha didn't always follow the sandwich rules and made sure she made what she liked. "Me, I came up with concoctions. I loved cream cheese so we had cream cheese with raisins and olives. Also egg salad. Tuna was ex-pensive but once a week. Friday was corned beef."

In contrast with the Berthas of the Home who banked on chicanery of some kind to get the best of things, there were others who worked out a style of adjustment that was less assertive and certainly less antic. These men and women recalled their shares of conflict and strife, but these painful memories were tempered by more positive reconstructions of the routines of living. So-phie, who will be remembered as the author of the tribute to Mr. Hart, is a contemporary of Bertha. Not just her words but the tautness of her mouth and brow told of the anguish she had endured in her marriage and later years. Ap-proaching her eightieth year, she dealt with her loneliness by taking writing courses at a nearby community college and tending to a small but charming garden apartment. She offered her guileless counterpoint to Bertha's assertive slant on life: "We all took an interest in each other. We were close, took up for each other. One time they sent Bert and me to the drugstore to get a prescription. And I saw Bert take a tube of lipstick and I said nothing. But then I think the druggist called Mr. Hollander. I think that's what I got hit for because I didn't report it. I don't know what he did with Bert but I know he hit me, he hit me."

Her grimace changed to a fixed smile and, without taking a breath, Sophie hurried on to assure me of more pleasant memories: "But we used to come home from school and go into the kitchen to get a big slab of black bread shmeared with peanut butter . . . oh, that tasted good . . . and then we'd go to Hebrew lessons. We had three good meals a day, we had dancing lessons, piano lessons if you wanted to take it." And then familiar declaration of these Depression children: "We had things there that I never could have in my own home."

Finally, the grand pirouette that executed her need to cling to "good" memories: "But one thing we had, we had a wonderful breakfast. We had either oatmeal or farina with bread and butter and a cup of cocoa." At that moment, Sophie and I were having breakfast at her favorite diner. I noticed she did not order hot cereal.

Morrie, like Sophie, also tried to preserve the wavering balance between the "good" and the "not so good." His modest living room, the setting of our conversation, was filled with the mementoes and photos of a devoted family, the children now grown and gone. The duplex in an older pleasant section of Rochester had been their home for most of their married life. At the moment, it was fragrant with the aroma of Ethel's beet borscht being prepared for the Succoth holiday. Despite suffering bleeding ulcers during most of his adulthood, Morrie supported his family as a factory worker. But his major satisfaction, he proudly announced, came from his years of activity and leadership with the Boy Scouts and, of course, from his children's achievements—among them, two Ph.D.'s, one from MIT, the other from Berkeley. Distress is what he remembered first about his early years in the Home: "I was very young, living in the Baby Cottage. We were playing there and a window broke in front of us. We didn't know how it happened and Mr. Hollander was very angry. He actually never hit me but he put me between his legs like he was going to. 'Who broke the window?' 'I don't know. We were playing and it broke.' I was crying."

After a quiet pause, he relaxed visibly and more lightly recalled certain rituals that other alumni did not recall with as much bliss. Even after he left the Home (he was still quite young when his mother remarried and he returned to her new home): "I loved to go there on Saturdays because after services we'd go into the big dining room in the big house and Mr. Hollander would read us stories from the Bible and he would translate them as he read them. The story about Ruth still brings tears to my eyes whenever I read it. We'd all be sitting around after eating—boys and girls. They had to be there. You couldn't walk out of the room without getting in trouble."

Coming home to the Girls House after school meant homework, supper, perhaps some listening to the radio, and then, another kind of ritual: getting ready for bed while ten girls were trying to use the mirror to set their hair. Bertha remembers the nightly antics as an object lesson in the loss of privacy: "Another thing that would burn my ass, excuse my French, was that there was one bathroom with only two toilets. There were two bathtubs but the way they had it nobody could take a bath with anyone in the other tub. You had to take it alone. We managed twenty in one bathroom. We washed and got out. We had a system there: 'Let me know when you're through.' "

I wondered how, in these circumstances, the girls learned about menstruation. I knew very well that boys received no instructions about anything to do with sexuality: roused by curiosity and unspeakable sensations—and the plainly lecherous flights of fancy about the island of femininity on the other side of the driveway—we picked up fragments of misinformation from guys with "experience." But the young ladies of the Home obviously could not enjoy the luxury of such ignorance; their bodies, the physiological onset of the menarche, insisted on the need for immediately instructive, if not comforting, information. Sophie, an earlier resident, complained: "Nobody told me. When I started to menstruate, I didn't know what it was or what to do. Mrs. D. (the girls' matron) said to go tell Mr. Hollander. That's what she said. In my mind, even though I was only thirteen, I thought, why does he have to know? It's a lady's problem. So I went over and told him, I just told him that I got my period. He didn't say anything."

Things didn't change much in later years. Lill's recollection: "I was never told about periods. I went to school one day and got up to say something. The teacher says, would you go into the bathroom with me and she told me, Lill, you have blood on your dress. She washed the dress—she was my 7th grade teacher at #9 school—and she took me in and told me the facts of life. That's how I learned about it. In the Girls Cottage there was no discussion of sex. Just stay out of the boys' room! Sometimes I think of how it would be if we had a nurse there."

Clearly, taboos of all sorts were in operation, and in this culture of repression one had to also reckon with the Old Testament rules of Leviticus that applied to Jewish women, the biblical proscriptions and the onus placed on the "uncleanliness" of the menstruating woman. Consider Sue's account of the damning rituals of those times:

> The laundry room was equipped with a washing machine and a hand wringer and ironing boards. When the girls had their periods—who ever heard of Kotex?—we used to boil the napkins and hang them outside to bleach. The guys used to walk by and what they didn't call them—rags. The first time I got my period, I wasn't

even twelve. Walked around with toilet tissue until they believed me 'cause I did know something, nobody taught me. Each girl, when she reached her menstrual time, was given birdseye sanitary napkins that had to be washed after each session. To bleach them—you'd change two-three times a day—soak them in a pail with borax, then boil—they had to be hung out on the line outside the Girls Cottage. That's when the smart aleck guys went by, giggling because they knew what they were.

The onset of menstruation stirred many fears, anxieties, and serious misgivings about what it was to become a woman. But as Bertha contended, if that initiation was delayed you had other problems: "Nobody taught us about periods. I got some of it from Fay who was older. But the payoff was that the younger girls, my group, got it earlier than I did and they started to exclude me from female conversations. I kept saying, 'Please God, why don't you give it to me, God? I want to be with the girls.' I didn't get it until I was almost sixteen."

Apart from these bodily problems, Anna offered another slant on what it was like to become a sensual young women in those years when any flicker of passion was crushed as surely as the thought of munching on a ham sandwich during Orthodox Sabbath services. Vestiges of bitter irony, of a confused and undefined guilt, still colored her words.

I was deathly scared of Hollander. Manny and I, y'know, we were kind of lovey-dovey and I would meet him in the basement while I was drying the towels. We did nothing, just talking to each other. Hollander found out. He got hold of me near the dining room. One thing he did was step on your feet so you couldn't move and stick his face in yours. He asked, "Vat vas you doing?" I said, "Nothing." "You vere doing something, vat vere you doing?" I said that Manny brought down the towels and we were talking. He gets me behind the room there and he hits me. He hit me right across the face. I lost my balance and fell against the fireplace. I really didn't know what I did that was so terrible, what he was talking about.

The ending of Anna's direful story is a kind of object lesson in learning how to prevail, how to discover one's strengths and integrity through the power of kinship or, what Sophie meant when she said, "We all took an interest in each other." "I was crying in the washroom and Becky [who was older] asked me what was the matter. I told her Hollander hit me and why. She says, 'The next time he does that to you just look him in the eye and tell him, "If I did anything wrong would I be able to look you in the eye?" ... It's the only way you'll get him off your back—and your foot.' There was a next time and I was petrified. But I said that to him."

Anna's married daughter, who seemed to be the target of this episode, was surely touched by her mother's strength and revelation, particularly when Anna added: "And you know what? He never bothered me again even. It didn't mean that we stopped talking or became more distant. I don't know, maybe he respected me a little."

RELATIONSHIPS: TRUST AND CARING

Anna's touching anecdote begins to tell us how the milieu of the Children's Home encouraged an active awareness of self-worth. The sense of trust and caring that existed among the children and between the different age groups, while it could not entirely compensate for the absence of familial affection and intimacy, offered its own kinds of safety and protection.

Most often, as in Anna's case, guidance, concern, and sympathy were more of what is called, in modern terms, a "safety net." Things had to get rough before such supports came into play. Otherwise, one coped with and got by some of the hard times of daily life. Moving from one conversation to another with the alumni, as folks talked about exploits or events, not much was said spontaneously about the subject of affection or closeness; loving feelings just did not seem to fit with notions of life in the institution. The vocabulary of "love," "caring," "tenderness," "empathy," "warmth," flows easily when there is talk about the bonds of family life. But these terms have a forced or artificial cast when they are applied to the pragmatics of the asylum and the absence of ties that are natural, biological, and affiliative.

Recall how the matrons were remembered. The best the alumni could say is that they "told us what was right and wrong . . . encouraged us to be neat and clean." Will confirms this impression, still remembering his very early years when "there was no hugging stuff in the Baby Cottage. Whatever hugs I got came from elsewhere."

Henry is one of the few who spoke specifically about the emotional sterility of the Home that he endured in the earlier years. His laments are particularly fascinating when those years of deprivation are balanced against the warmth of this elderly widower, who had been married for over a half-century, who is a father of three successful children, and who openly *kvelled* (the Jewish idiom for the pride and pleasure one feels for one's offspring) over his six grandchildren and one great-grandchild. Clearly, the melancholy had not been erased as he recalled the 1920s, when "there was nothing personal there": "No one paid attention, you're a number. My number was 60. Shirts, nightgown, underwear—all numbered. I don't remember pillows. Everything impersonal, one face among the crowd. There was no one to ask you how you're doing. You'd bring your report card to Hollander and he'd put his name on it—that's it unless if you had a bad mark, he'd tell you."

Lill, a wife and parent, had also retired recently from her position as school secretary, held for almost thirty years, and still missed the joy of being with young schoolchildren. Her years in the Home were the late 1930s, but not much had changed: "I feel there was nobody you could be close to there, nobody that you could *tell* anything to, that you could confide in. Nobody to talk to, to explain things to. It was a very cold situation."

And, as Phil reports, the lonely newcomer had special challenges, having to find his place in the pecking order that existed during his days in the Home:

"The first hour I came into the orphans home, I was told that I had to have a fight with another kid . . . got my head split open, but I learned you didn't squeal." Phil's account serves more as a symbol for how each kid had to learn quickly how to find his or her place in the milieu and discover the resources required to deal with routine demands.

Still, I find it hard to explain in modern terms how the harsh, almost unfeeling—at times, in current terms, abusive—way of life was intertwined with protection, care, and trust. Again, it is necessary to look back at time and context to make sense of these conditions and ask the question, Was life in the Home markedly out of line with life in the community as a whole? One might even ask, for the moment, whether the adversities of life in the Children's Home are markedly out of line with what we see in too many present-day families. I will consider this question at the close of this book.

In no way do I want to depreciate the warm rewards and joys of growing up in a family where parents were entirely devoted to the *kinder* (children). Still, as far as I could see, and from what has been documented in the extensive literature on Jewish immigrant life in America,[2] parents were not expected to be involved with—or for that matter, even understand—our Americanized games, sports, hurts, or disappointments. What Yiddish father would, say, play ball with his child? And Jews didn't go fishing. Our parents were "old": they worked, cooked, cleaned, tried to scrape out a few dollars and, if they had leisure moments, fathers would play pinochle and mothers would visit neighbors. We were their *kinder* who were nourished, cared for. We were expected to obey and do good, get good marks at school, and, above all, be good Jews. Our family was, well, *family*, in its most fundamental sense; my only recollection of "doing something" with my parents is a long walk once with my father on a wintry Thanksgiving day while the bird was cooking and a trip to see the movie, *Fantasia*, with my mother.

With some variations, of course, these were the norms for Jewish family life. Any child would be bereaved by the loss of a parent, but the homes that many of the residents had to leave were marked by more severe strains and deprivations. Certainly it was not a matter of a full trade-off or substitute for a close family but, as Sophie and others observed, "We had things in the Home that I could never have in my own home."

By necessity and carried on by tradition, children who were deposited in the Home had to create and discover kindred relationships that made a difference. Phil spoke earlier of an ambience "of camaraderie . . . of this being my group." In lieu of a biological parent, there were others, older perhaps by a few years, who cared and helped. As Phil affirmed: "I'll tell you what saved me. People like Manny Hirsch, people like my gym teacher saved me." Then, falling back on the lingo of his social work profession, he added: "Through them, I developed ego ideals that helped me erase a lot of negative feelings I was developing."

Morrie, another beneficiary of the kindness of his seniors, put it this way: "I remember one feeling, that the older kids were affectionate to you." I asked him what he meant by "affectionate." His answer: "That somebody was there caring for you. *That someone cared what happened to you.* Somebody had sympathy when something went wrong. There was no physical contact, but you knew, you sensed, that the older ones were worried about you being all right. I was sick one day and had to take castor oil. It wasn't one of the matrons who brought it up to me, it was one of the kids. He gave me a spoonful. You felt they were brothers and sisters." Clearly, Morrie and his partners didn't ask for much; even a dose of castor oil delivered and administered by someone who cared could be taken as an expression of affection.

Indeed, there were older kids who did care, who deliberately assumed a protective, if not parental, role for the children, some who were just a few years younger. I doubt that Jake, ever stoic and matter-of-fact about his many years growing up in the Home, would define himself as paternal or even big-brother-like as far as his relations with the other children were concerned. As if he were seen by the other kids as a kind of young rabbi (he was a serious student and one of the first to go to college), he said: "Other kids used to come to me if there was a conflict. They would take my opinion—they would ask me who was right about something and they would take my decision. Whether I liked the person or not, if I felt he was right I would say he was right. That was being honest."

Sophie was another of the older kids whose devotion was warmly recalled by a few of the other graduates. I mentioned this to her, saying that they still are touched by the love and caring she gave. Almost apologetic, as if she had to explain, she said: "By my rules, I never put myself first. I was always good to the children. I used to comb Ruthie's hair and braid it. And every Thursday I gave the little kids a bath." She went on to list her other deeds, doing the laundry for an older boy with heart trouble for fifty cents a week and tutoring another girl for thirty-five cents. "So I was a very rich girl with eighty-five cents a week. It was *my* money. I didn't have to give it to Hollander."

Her sister Suzie was less diffident about her role:

> I adapted myself. I figured, I've got to be here, I might as well. I was the mother of my four siblings. I had to fight for them. I had to do well because they looked up to me and I wasn't even the oldest—the middle one. Responsibility just fell on my shoulders, I guess. If anybody touched my sisters, I'd kill. Everybody took care of one another. I was the tough one. I had to plan for them. My sister Dorry ran away, my brother Manny ran away, I had to go look for them.

Many others spoke of these protective bonds. As I moved between and among the old graduates, I sensed the presence of a quiet wellspring of devotion, an enduring concern for the well-being of their childhood comrades. The passing of time, geographical distance, or the fact that their respective lives and relationships had spun off in separate spheres, made no difference. That I could locate many of the alumni who speak from these pages was a result of how the graduates kept tabs on the whereabouts and well-being of their comrades. Since I traveled to visit with various alumni, I was used as a clearing house, as my respondents checked on how others were doing in Fort Lauderdale or elsewhere.

Although the alumni had no pressing need to cling to old affiliations, there was a special quality in their relations (evident in my evening with Will and Phil described in the first chapter) that I tried to capture in my field notes after an evening get-together.

> Without being maudlin and with no obvious obligation, they truly like each other. Teasing and joking seem to be part of how they get along. Certainly they are not "traumatized" or in any way stand out as "orphans" or as having been institutionalized. In some ways, this circle cherishes something special among themselves that others who had a more "normal" childhood cannot share. Their common roots, their shared sense of having "made it" together allows them to review and reconstruct their early lives with humor, with bittersweetness, or even with plain bitterness meanwhile getting feedback and confirmation. Every story told that evening was the product of an ensemble performance—a combination of improvisational theater and theater of the absurd.

STIGMA

Along with the other stereotypes of institutional life is the burden of *stigma*. Some alumni dismissed this as a problem; others were quite eloquent in expressing their feelings, even into the present, of "being different."

"Being different" is perhaps the most accurate term since we were unaware of such terms as "stigma" and "stereotype"—and besides, "being different" in a section of Rochester that, like other urban areas, was almost balkanized by nationalities representing most of Europe seemed to be the way life was. In our time, almost everyone bore a label of one kind or another. To start with, *we* were *Jews:* that was our own identity. Depending on the circumstances, *they* might call us "Jew-boys," "yids," "kikes," or "Christ-killers." Conversely, *they* were first of all "goyim." When precision was required, they could also be known as "dagos" or, more affectionately, *lockshen* (Yiddish for noodles, applied to Italians because of their fondness for spaghetti); others earned such choice epithets as "polacks" or *schvartzes.* At any rate, these labels didn't necessarily call for ethnic warfare; they were, as I remember, social artifacts, the basis for differentiating the unit one did or did not belong to.

Even among the members of the same group, there were always some kids who were branded with nicknames that classified them and set them apart from the rest. It was supposed to be good fun, of course—malice was not intended; still, the difference was there. As was natural in those days, some children, for obvious reasons, were stuck with simple, unimaginative monikers: "four eyes," "goggles," "fatso," "stork," for example. For part of my young life, I had friends whose given names I never knew. Because of his father's business I know why one was called "Fishy"; I don't know why another was called "Cueball." Some of the Home's kids seemed to earn a pet name, particularly the dedicated bed-wetters. One boy got the literal Yiddish title (needing no translation) of "Pisher." There was also "Crisco" (fat in the can); "Chink," so named because he was born in China during his parents' escape from Russia; the "Fink," a less than honorific title assigned to whomever squealed about some exploit; and some unforgivable names that mocked the child with a speech defect.

Surely, feeling and being treated as "different" was a natural, even inevitable, part of growing and being. But what made the children feel "more different," even humiliated, was not so much the attitude of unfriendly outsiders but, ironically, the cost of well-intentioned benevolence.

Another authoritative, though less benign, imprint was Jacob Hollander's presence that was felt in most activities—leisure and entertainment as well as religion, discipline, and routine. Given Mr. Hollander's need for all of his wards to be visible to the public, the occurrence of stigma, the feeling of being different, becomes more understandable.

Henry, with his eye for detail, spoke gratefully about the amusements furnished by the community, for example, how Mr. Fennevesy who owned the Strand Theater used to come down and show movies from time to time. Henry added the qualifier: "He would invite the children to come to his theater, but those times Hollander would want to show off the children, how nice we were. He had us march down Clinton Street in strict order, two by two, down the sidewalk, then we would walk down Main Street to give us full exposure to everybody. We'd do this both ways."

There was a price to be paid by some children for the pleasures and diversions they enjoyed, especially when benefactors wanted their good deeds known and appreciated. It was not unusual for the Home's children to find themselves on display, the pinnacle of this exhibition in Rochester (and, no doubt, in other cities) being the annual Orphan Outing, sponsored by the Auto Club, for all of the city's institutionalized children. The headlines of the *Rochester Herald* proclaimed "Everyone Happy and Gay . . . Rochester's Orphans are Royally Entertained," and the text (reflecting normal ethnic attitudes of the time) began with: "Mary and Sally, Jack and Billie, Pat and Mike, Maggie and Agnes, Ikey and Izzie, Beckie and Sarah, Sambo and Rastus, Dinah and Pansy—all were there and were there in style."

Other settings of misplaced goodwill also held the risk of being seen as "different." In the first chapter Will talked about school where "everyone knew who we were" because "*we* got free milk and *they* paid two cents." For many graduates, just knowing they were dependents was a source of humiliation, as this bit of dialogue between Lil and Anna tells us:

Lil: Today we laugh, but in those days we cried. Some of the kids are ashamed of having been in the Home.

Anna: Talk about being ashamed, I would never admit I was in the Home when

Orphans' Day Parade, Downtown Rochester, circa 1927 (Courtesy Stone Negative Collection, Rochester Museum & Science Center, Rochester, New York)

I was in high school. When someone asked, "Where do you live?" I'd say, "Oh, on Gorham Street." I wouldn't admit I was in an orphan asylum, never would admit.
Lil: There was a stigma at the time.
Anna: I'm just getting now where I can loosen up and admit that I was brought up there. I was in high school, nursing school, worked with people in their own homes. Never said a word about it.

Sue also felt that the blight of being an "orphan" in public school was deeply ingrained.

Oh yes, we were embarrassed. *"All the kids from the Home rise! You get free books!"* Only the kids get free books. We weren't allowed to sing Christmas songs—well, neither did the other Jews. But then when they used to go through your hair looking for nits—and there was plenty of that going around in the Home. The kids had ringworm or nits or bugs. Maybe other kids had them too, but there was a message. But "free books, you're from the Home?" Like they were giving us charity. You felt like a . . . I don't know what. Now I'm such a big shot. . . . That's why I think I had an inferiority complex for many years, that's one thing I was left with coming from the Home. I was shy, self-conscious, with people who I thought knew I was in the Home. But I overcame that.

Ruth, always moderate and gently in control of her life, was hardly calm while recalling the onus of being a ward of the Home. "I think that I just felt kind of like an outsider while I was there at the Home. We used to go to the Camp, the JY Camp. Somehow it was always known that we were the kids from the Home. At least I felt that way. Not that people were not friendly. If you achieved you became something. For the girl camper the ultimate was you became a squaw. . . . I'm telling you it was one of the highlights of my life. People were friendly, but I sensed there was this little thing or that." Then the paradoxical trade-off: "Yet, by being in the Home I was able to go to college. It was just one of those things—it was done for me but not for other people."

Sometimes commonplace events of no real concern to ordinary children might escalate feelings of being the odd, peculiar child. One of the women never forgot how degrading it was when, on Memorial Day, other children would bring pennies for the poppies. The kids from the Home didn't have any money so they used to mark an *X* after their names.

Being clothed, that is, favored with free suits for boys, dresses for girls, plus all the other accessories from bare skin outward, should be an event celebrated and free of embarrassment. Recall that National Clothing Company pledged to care for all the boys' clothing needs—from hats to shoes—annually at Passover. To get outfitted meant that the boys would have to march, two by two, led by Mr. Hollander, down St. Paul Street to the big store on Main Street, usually after the store closed. But for Phil and a few other boys, it was another event "that made me different from anyone else." Another added, "I stood there like a waif waiting for my handout. At the same time I knew that old man Horowitz was a wonderful man." And a third acknowledged, "OK, it was in my mind, I just felt that way. I walked to National Clothing with a whole bunch. I was treated nicely, got a nice outfit—'course they wouldn't let me have long pants. But I just felt everybody had to be looking." If one could just feel like a "waif" and deal with that, that would be enough. But they knew they were obligated to appreciate the heartfelt goodness of their benefactors, especially when they were well aware that the best that kids with families had were hand-me-downs. As Will ruminated, "We were not treated as individuals and I hated it. But I shouldn't complain. I got a suit." You just couldn't be plain indignant without feeling the sting of guilt.

The girls of the Home were not beneficiaries of an annual clothing endowment, but they too were set apart and too visible as a result of others' desire to help out the "orphans." As one woman remembered: "I know it's a small thing, silly, thinking about when Kroll's Dress Shop wanted to donate the dresses they couldn't sell. So they marched us over there to fit us up with some clothes. When you came out you had such an inferiority complex. I fought it for years."

And fight it they did; not in major battles, in hard fought clashes of will, but often, as will be evident, in comic strokes of craftiness. As Bertha proved, if they had to be different, at least they didn't have to *look* different. "We had high-top shoes and I took my shoes and threw them in the furnace. Well, you want to talk about being killed? Then there was the lumpy long underwear we had to wear under our stockings. Our stockings were like bagels. To go to school in the morning, Hollander would walk us two by two down the block. But as soon as he left we'd roll our stockings down, roll up the underwear, pull our stockings up. Then when we got farther away we would roll our stockings down." Then, victoriously: "We did that and no one was the wiser for it."

DISCIPLINE AND CONTROL

It is safe to say that few of the children really *invited* punishment; there were hardships enough without having to pay more penance. Still, those who dared, like Bertha, Lil, and Phil, took chances, and therefore put themselves at risk. Bertha's lumpy underwear story shows that it was not so much *defiance* or rebellion that moved them as it was *audacity*, a kind of playfulness mixed with assertiveness that had as its purpose the child's need for mastery. Others were not exactly conformists; they tended to be cautious, even wary, as they dealt with the pitfalls of congregate living and autocratic control. Abe, who spent most of his youth in the Home and went on to become an attorney, expressed this cautious outlook, making the point that "as long as you lived up to the rules there was no trouble." He went on to explain that "everyone knew there was discipline. For example, you couldn't go in the Girls House. The rules were clear and we abided by them. I don't know if it was out of fear or what or we didn't want to cross Hollander. He would fight with some of the kids even though he was as big as he was. He kept them in their place."

Then he offered some thoughts about how you learned the rules to avoid getting punished:

Big kids told us what to do. When they gave you a towel and told you to hang it up, each one had his own little box and if you let it hang out instead of tucking it in, they would tell you where to put it. You did it. I'll tell you, after I left the Home, nobody could tell me what to do. When I was there and even after I got out, there was still a great deal of respect for Mr. Hollander as well as the feeling that everybody there better do what they were supposed to do. I remember Mr. Hollander would question you if you skipped a meal. Where did you eat? He was always there watching the table. He knew what was going on. And his family was there, too and they kept a finger on things. I suppose his children told him this one was fighting, that one was out of line.

Other, more audacious graduates who didn't entirely subscribe to the "as long as you lived up to the rules" precept were somewhat less sanguine about the way discipline and control were dispensed. It is not that they were particularly shocked by the use of physical punishment, since it was an inescapable part of one's childhood, but they didn't approve of unfairness or certain punitive methods. As Joey commented on the times: "It wasn't a place where they beat you and all that stuff, put you in solitary. I never heard too much of that.

Dining Room, Children's Home. Mr. Hollander as overseer. (Courtesy Jewish Family Service of Rochester, New York, Inc.)

I saw kids do a lot of things. They got punished—Hollander would whack them, this and that, but it was part of growing up, right?"

In the way Joey describes punishment, it was indeed a part of growing up, for that time and that culture and in accord with the prevalent "psychology" of the times. In my own home, like those of other friends, there were moments when wills were tested, when parents would not look kindly on anything that disputed what they firmly believed "was best for the *kinder* (children)." I learned very early what happened when you broke the rules, but I temper my wish to offer examples, knowing that in the present mood and opinion, my dear parents would be defined as "abusers." They weren't: "it was part of growing up, right?"

It was this simple, as Irv said: if you broke a rule *and got caught,* then you got punished. The trick was in not getting caught; if you did, you had better improve your technique to reduce the odds for the next caper. Recalling a Sabbath afternoon when, as everyone knew, quiet and rest are the regulations of the day and Hollander was supposed to be taking his nap, the boys got some sticks and were throwing them up in the pear tree hoping to knock one down:

"All of a sudden, there is Hollander watching us. He looked at everybody and got their names in his mind and said, 'I want you all to see me after supper.' We all went and were told to line up and gave each one a large dose of castor oil. I suppose to a certain extent he was right."

Arnie didn't necessarily agree that "he was right" but to get by you had to know how he operated: "He was that kind of person. Sometimes he would hide behind the door or even if it was open he'd stand where you couldn't see him and he'd listen. If someone said something wrong, he'd walk in. 'Vat did you say?' He had a way of doing it. But I really wasn't frightened of him—well, up to a point—but we had him figured out."

Bertha told how she made the most of his "behind the door" tactic. With much zest, she recalled a Friday night when she and four other girls tried not only to skip religious services but really compound the sin by going to the movies. She forgot her hankie and hurried back to the Girls Cottage, where she ran into Mr. Hollander, who was lurking around. She tried to signal her accomplices, but with no luck. Bertha wound up being called a "snitch." She went on to add:

My punishment? He gave me the job of dishes THREE TIMES A DAY—no dishwashers, no nothing. The first couple of days I cried through it. The next day I'm washing the dishes and I hear him in his bathroom which was right off the kitchen. So I says real loud so he can hear to one of the kids going by, "Hollander thinks he's punishing me? He's teaching me how to do dishes and everything and when I get married, boy will I know how to keep a house!!!" He came out and said "OUT!!" and I didn't have to do dishes anymore. Hah!

Bertha then told her side of the purloined lipstick episode; perhaps, when she reads these pages, the mystery of "who snitched?" will finally be solved for her. "We were disciplined! We had such a fear of God put into us that when I stole the lipstick, I looked around to see if God was behind me. Somebody snitched, who I'll never know. He called me in his office. He said, 'Where's the lipstick?' I said, 'What lipstick?' 'What you took from the store.' " On second thought, however, "fear of God" didn't slow her down as she added, "You had to mind your p's and q's. But if you looked around and saw it was clear, then chance it. But if you missed, punishment."

I do not want to imply that all reminiscences were recounted with Bertha's zest. Some alumni preferred to leave some painful memories untold. Others had dutifully plied their way through those years of regimentation, doing what was expected of them; as a result, they had less to say about first-hand encounters with humiliation or pain. And there were not a few alumni who not only truly suffered punishment but bore the pain and humiliation into their later years. In one conversation, a venerable gentleman lapsed into what he called his old habit of stuttering when he tried to talk about being hit. The wife of another alumnus remembered with evident sorrow the many nights during the first years of their marriage when she was awakened by her husband's weeping.

PATRIARCHY, PERMISSIVENESS, YIDDISHKEIT, AND PLAY

Why this odd assortment of ideas? A preliminary answer might be that human affairs and developments are more often concatenations of the unexpected or the coincidence of events that Carl Jung called "synchronicity." A more explicit explanation is forthcoming.

Throughout the life of this study, I was ever alert to the nature and quality of life in the Children's Home that enabled the children to realize more than just survival. The first realization, expressed in the opening chapter, was a richer appreciation of something that I had taken as a given in my childhood: the Jewish community and how it protectively enveloped its children in a heartfelt, almost classically maternal manner. There was a similar ethos within the culture of the Home itself; despite fights, pecking orders, and other rivalries typical of congregate living, there was a brotherly or sisterly protective warmth of one child for others. The Alumni Association was the formal embodiment of this filial commitment; even after one graduated, the Association was the medium by which alumni could continue to show their care and concern for the younger children.

Now we have considered the harmonics and the dissonances that filter through the "what life was like" narratives, the incongruent memories that play off one another. On one hand, there were the deadly routines that made every day like the last; yet within that brittle structure there was room for variation and deviation that kept a spirit of irony and paradox in the forefront. Call this something the spirit, the imagination, the will—perhaps what was previously called identity and self-concept—or whatever the energy is that shapes what might be called the personal hardiness, the resiliency, of the child.

Are these not the basic materials of a story like Lil's that tells about breaking the fast on the highest of High holy days, the Day of Atonement for past sins, within the strictest, most rigid Orthodox institutions? "We'd get really hungry on Yom Kippur. So where was the best place to go? We'd sneak into Hollander's house. His refrigerator was full of all kinds of great food for the big meal to break the fast. We'd rob the food."

This was not an act of delinquency but an outrageous dare, a spoof on authority. Here, the intent is something more than just slipping something past God without incurring his wrath, but to slip something past Mr. Hollander whose wrath was far more proximate on this, the holiest of holy days—in effect, invading the castle to delight in the monarch's feast. An otherwise dependent youngster gives new meaning to self-assertiveness. Then there is Anna's gleeful memory of the time: "We would get out of Friday night services by telling Hollander we girls were going to Temple Beth El instead. Only one of us would go because we knew he would quiz us on what the sermon was just to check up. Me, I would go to the Zionist Club meeting."

Another alumna laughed, saying "the rest of us went to the Lyric Theater. We scrounged up the money and if we didn't have enough, one of us would go in and open the side door from the inside."

Implicit in the two tales are the interconnected issues of *patriarchy, permissiveness,* the essence of *Yiddishkeit,* and *play* that help explain how, in this one institution, resilience was inspired.

PATRIARCHY AND PERMISSIVENESS: INTERCHANGES

To reiterate, the first and most obvious earmark of the Children's Home was the intrusion of patriarchal control and regimentation into most every routine of living. By itself, autocratic rule called for the children to hone their basic adaptive skills—the simplest, the ability to stay out of reach if not out of sight—and to acquire more advanced techniques such as that exemplified in Anna's learning how to confront Mr. Hollander. During my early years, Mr. Hollander was known as "The Boss." This explicit, categorical role by itself defined the child's reciprocal role—that is, how he or she was supposed to respond in specific situations. It also aroused the need for unity and mutuality among the wards. It must be said again that it was not simple, unvarnished malice that the children felt about their superintendent: some did define him as their perennial adversary; others as a role model whose virtues deserved to be emulated; and many accepted his virtues but were not blind to his faults.

As thoroughly patriarchal and regulated as the Home was, its granite-like facade seemed to be marked, if one looked, by almost visible cracks and fissures; an indefinable permissiveness, a quiet laxness virtually invited the children to test the limits. In its benign form, it allowed the children to pursue self-made activities and adventures such as raising turtles, white rats, and pigeons, as well as the traditional dog or cat; taking part in informal sports; hiking to distant parks; and taking trolley rides to the beach. These activities were as rewarding in their own ways as were the grand picnics and other entertainments. Joey, for example, described busy summer days when buses would come two or three times a week to take kids to Caledonia or Lake Ontario for picnics, or the "highlight" of marching to a downtown movie. But the rest of the time "you'd play ball, run across the street to the 'priest's house' [an abandoned, crumbling cottage overgrown with vines and weeds], go over the back fence to Hand Street—you did what you wanted. If you weren't there for dinner you just didn't eat."

Appetites were whetted in the story told about the "nice Italian family" that lived next door to the Girls Cottage: "The mother used to sneak us some spaghetti and meatballs over the fence. If we got caught, God bless us. Meat mixed with cheese? *That isn't kosher.* I can still smell the aroma of the sauce cooking."

There was usually enough to eat at the Home; getting *what you wanted to eat* when you wanted it was another challenge. In response to Will's legitimate way of getting extra food by working in the kitchen, Phil said he managed it in a different way: "Friday night, after they made all the kugel (a sweet pudding of noodles, potatoes, or rice) for Saturday when you weren't supposed to cook, I used to cross over the roof in my nightgown and climb down into the kitchen like a sleepwalker fixated on kugel. I'd bring it back to the dormitory, enough kugel to feed twenty kids." He further advised that "you could get in the storeroom if you knew how to use a sardine can key. I'd get a half dozen onions and some rye bread and take it into the dorm. We'd camp out, crawl under the bed and put sheets over it."

The stories are told with zest and pride. They are not simply about "beating the system"; more so, the joy of self-discovery, finding the creative talents to take advantage of the cracks and loopholes in the system is what counted.

Needless to say, the refinement of these talents should not have to depend on oppressive or forbidding environments. And as I want to show now, it is not the environment itself that energizes one's boldness and self-esteem; in fact, the harsh, insensitive atmosphere may provoke only hostile retaliation that defeats the self. Something must be apparent in value, tradition, ideal, or belief that serves the spirit of the self.

YIDDISHKEIT

In the case of this one institution, it wasn't just the beliefs of Yiddishkeit that made the difference but its obliging and somewhat quixotic paradoxes that created an inviting culture of defiance. I spoke to this in the first chapter, referring to a frame of mind that grants authority or patriarchy its proper respect but at the same time, deflates anything pompous or overbearing in the position of authority that is granted. It is a view that, in response to status and officialdom, allows for frivolity as well as soberness, lightness as well as seriousness. Recall Hartman's[3] thoughts noted in that chapter about how the Jew is ever aware of the presence and power of his God; his consciousness of this power, however, is also an invitation to probe its limits, to test one's strength and mastery against the threshold of the master. But this invitation raises one's consciousness, since God gave each man a conscience, by which he had to make his own decision; reason, to analyze everything under the sun; and free will, which allows error, sin, or blasphemy (and their consequences).[4] And so, short of being sacrilegious, the Jew in his approach to God can at once be devout and critical, reverent and resentful. A visual example is Tevye the milkman wrangling with the Almighty in *Fiddler on the Roof*. Might we suppose, if only metaphorically, that this delightful covenant or archetype of Jewishness found a place in the culture of the Children's Home that encouraged imaginative, creative, at times, outrageous ways of pressing the limits of imposed control? If this is too exorbitant a prospect, let us examine the notion of pressing the limits from a more sober, secular standpoint.

PLAY

Except for the occasional lipstick lifted from a drugstore counter, some smokes that were sneaked (including, from my father's store, the sulfurous bamboo shoe sticks that we used to light up), and some filching of candy at the corner store when Mr. Berger wasn't looking, it is safe to say that most of the kids' exploits were innocent of vice. More accurately, their escapades seemed to fall within the broadest meanings of the word, *play*.

By "play" I mean something more than children just enjoying games, toys, sports, or other amusements. I use "play," in Erik Erikson's terms, as a noun that is linked to the theater, to the stage, to acting. Erikson speaks of the function of play or playfulness as "the restoration and creation of a *leeway of mastery* [his emphasis] in a set of developments and circumstances."[5] Putting this another way, children usually find themselves enveloped by circumstances created by adults, most commonly, in the home and classroom; in our area of interest, we add the institution. As Erikson sees it, the child's play is not far removed from the natural outcome of the work of the dramatist or playwright. When the child finds himself boxed-in by the adult-created scenario with its script, cast of characters, and roles, he can find a way out. Using intuition and imagination, the child is free to recreate, act out the scene by creating his own comic or tragic "play." It may seem a childish drama, but on some level achieves growth and mastery when the youngster works out *his* own script and persona in contraposition to the adult scenario.

Where is there a better setting for the child to dramatize his circumstances than the orphanage, asylum, or institution? Its stock characters, its obvious scripts and routines, its austere backdrop offer the creative inmate rich material for dramatic play. Consider how the following "skits," excerpted from the recollections of several graduates, fit this notion of "play" and "playfulness":

> The Home used to get its milk in those big twenty gallon cans. That was before homogenized milk so the cream was at the top. Working in the kitchen, we used to see "Shaindel" (Mrs. Hollander) sneak in early and scoop out the cream for her own family. Know what we did? We used to take turns in the morning getting up even earlier to run down to the kitchen and give the can of milk a quick stir. No cream.
>
> At religious services, Hollander used to ask who was going to *daven*, lead the prayers. We'd always get Lenny to volunteer because we knew we'd get finished ten minutes earlier. Hollander would holler at him, "Slow down, slow down," but Lenny knew how to rush through it and still cover all the prayers. Hollander couldn't do a thing and we had to try to keep from laughing.

In contrast with that of their modern cousins, the children whom mental health people call the "actor outers," the "play" of the children of the Home most often was governed by a fundamental respect for legitimate authority. By any standards, these were "good kids," rarely in any serious trouble in the com-

Choir, High Holy Days, 1939 (Silver Anniversary publication)

munity and at least tractable students in school. This is not to paint a utopian picture of the members of the Home as a bunch of compliant "goody-goodies." Particularly in the last years of the Home's existence, when problem children referred by the court increasingly began to replace dependent children, there were, occasionally, serious incidents. Joey offers himself as an illustration: "I was one of the problem kids more or less with Hollander. He sent me over to Oswego for a few months with some lady and her family. ('Why?') He had problems with me, I used to give him a hard time all the time. Do this, do that, defy him and all that type of stuff. Finally he couldn't take it no more, couldn't handle me and he farmed me out. ('To a foster home?') Yeah, that's what it was. Then I came back to Rochester, finished up in the Home and that was it." And Joey added, "I don't know anybody who hasn't done well, that's down and out. I don't know anybody that's got problems."

The regard for authority seemed to have flourished throughout adulthood for the typical graduate; by no means did this kind of citizenship connote timidity or obeisance. In fact, if we take stock of the adult lives of many alumni, they seemed to have come to terms with authority—whether in interpersonal relations, in professions, or with their families—in ways that abstained from the misuse or abuse of power. And for many, judging the way they reviewed their lives, their intrigue with playfulness has not lessened. I, too, was affected by involvement with the kids and the Home. Playfulness, a wariness about the absurdities of adulthood, and an aversion to the abuses of authority have been abiding themes of my lifetime. This theme may be part of my own Yiddishkeit, an outgrowth of the chicanery I shared with the kids or some other combination. No matter, after a half-century absence, I was pleased to discover that the affinity remains.

There is much that shows that "playfulness" and challenge to authority apparently nurtured the children's well-being and didn't harm the intimacy of their relationships. Will, as a social worker and administrator of a Jewish home for the aging, was a strong but gentle leader who created a climate of helpful warmth and interdependence in his institution. Phil's exterior, even in his seventies, is that of a warrior; as he said, "I went through life with my fists doubled up." But he did so as a social worker, "ready to start swinging—but mostly for other people, not for me." Ben, who became a prominent attorney, devoted much of his profession to legal aid work. Ruth, after college graduation, worked for the Red Cross and the rights of veterans. The richest part of Roz's adulthood was her work at the welfare department and pleasure she gave to the elderly. For that matter, Mr. Hollander's two sons, who were as much a part of life in the Home as the wards themselves, also chose the helping professions.

Let me try to sum up the relationships among the four seemingly various concepts of *patriarchy, permissiveness, Yiddishkeit,* and *play* as forces in combination creating an environment for growth, resilience, and self-determination. Among the four, the vitality and ubiquity of Yiddishkeit created the pattern for life in the Children's Home. And so patriarchy might have defined certain roles and boundaries, but within the folkways of Judaism also subtly inspired creative, good-natured defiance. How this was accomplished was through play, the child's need to redefine his or her environment and role within it.

But Bertha's own words express this conclusion in more vigorous and lusty terms. Bertha did not become a professional in her lifetime. Within her own adulthood, one marked by hardship and the pursuit of security, her loving courage and remarkable strengths served as the mainstay of her extended family. As she and I sat side by side, with great, almost tumultuous pride she turned the pages of her stout scrapbook that documented not only a lifetime of her extensive volunteer work with Jewish organizations and the mentally retarded but her own written reflections on her life and countless letters of commendation. Able to strike the actress's attitude, Bertha, without bitterness and with gratitude that havens such as the Children's Home were available, summed up the kind of role one had to adopt to be more than a survivor:

I would never have been a victim. I think I was born with a chip on my shoulder. To think that my mother had to leave us, and we were taken and put in that place. Now I understand it was a matter of necessity, my father couldn't help himself. So in a way it was a mitzvah that there was a place to go because I had aunts who had their own kids and you know goddam well that they cater to their kids before they cater to you. So in a way it was a Godsend and it was what you made of it. You could either be a sniveling little nothing or you could be mischievous and upset people around you. You had to have a sense of humor or you'd be creamed. I'm not bitter. What saved me were the tricks I pulled on Hollander. If I could outwit Hollander that made me overlook a lot of other stuff.

SEVEN

Lives and Meanings

When it comes to life's experiences, each individual decides within himself
what their meanings are and how these experiences are going to affect him.
If we are going to preserve our identity, we have to decide within ourselves
what these experiences should mean. Will they cripple us or will we gain
greater strength that evolves from our own determination? . . . Therefore,
the Home could hardly be the same environment for each of us who grew
up there.

—Phil, in personal letter, 1992

Phil's thoughts were included in his response to my drafts of completed chapters sent to him and Will for their critical comments. At times, Phil's replies
hinted at the journey he also was making back to Gorham Street; he seemed to
be burrowing his way through seven decades of life. His letters often were
reflections on his life and the lives of his comrades and friends and the young
and old he served as a social worker for almost a half century. His words that
introduce this chapter make for a good enough explanation of how, as humans,
we make sense of life and thus try to get on with it. They also shape the theme
of this chapter concerned with how the alumni of the Children's Home found
meaning in their lives and moved forward.

Many allusions to and exclamations by the graduates about growing up have
already been rendered; this chapter, in effect, gathers them into certain meanings and implications. It is the culmination of the grand tour that began within
the Home's community and culture.

The intent to draw together into one coherent frame the diverse impressions,
reminiscences, and beliefs of people of different eras and various experiences
was, of course, most demanding of discretion and sensitivity. The stories, as
we have seen, were shot through with contradictions and ironies that had to be

characterized: tragedy and victory, disability and strength, grief and joy, dependence and self-reliance, honesty and chicanery, hopelessness and faith, and more.

I am fond of a hopeful metaphor that applies to the challenges of this interpretive stage of ethnographic inquiry: if you study the data long enough they will begin to reveal themselves to you—talk to you. In reality, of course, analytic and synthetic talents are the skills required to translate a conglomeration of narratives into a reasonably reliable account of lives. At any rate, a format for this chapter did emerge.

Let us begin with the unspoken accounts of lives of a few former wards who have passed on, the testament of their years in the Children's Home left in scraps of official forms, reports, and other bits of data. They are the handful of kids who for many reasons—some physical, others inexplicable—may not have enjoyed the quality of life of most survivors. Still, they traveled a fair distance because of the Home's safekeeping and protection. A second group of three is tragedic but at the same time heroic in how they approached life as combatants, as risk takers. The center of the chapter will detail the lives of six ordinary men and women and the valuable meanings these graduates attributed to their uncommon experiences. Then, an account of Phil and Will's sagas will yield two major themes of resilience and strength that realize more than just survival. By the close of the chapter, it will be possible to venture some ideas about outcomes usually not considered within the league of institutional child care: fulfillment in marriage and parenthood.

THE TROUBLED ONES

Nowadays, people whose attitudes and action are considered alarming by society typically come to the attention of a court, clinic, hospital, or welfare agency. Here these "deviants" are classified and labeled according to a standard policy or manual and often are officially tendered a particular label and role. Prior to the second World War, however, communities had not yet "progressed" to that level of bureaucratic efficiency. The few children's agencies and child guidance clinics used simple intelligence testing—Stanford Binet, for example—to classify the occasionally referred "problem child"; even so, few people were sophisticated enough to understand the professional appraisal, as was the case when the test results of several of the Home's children were tucked into the child's records without further comment.

I have described how acting strange or being "different" was, paradoxically, pretty "normal," especially in a culture and community that looked after its own. And, in looking after its own, the Rochester Jewish community, like most others, had its own way of defining its members, including those who were in some ways variant—among others, the *mishugene* (any and all variations on bring crazy), *nafkes* (loose women), the *gonifs* (thieves), the *shikkers* (drunkards), the *kaylekeh* (cripples). Although not kindly or correct by current standards, these designations—the traditions of the Old Country—did not necessarily intend to degrade the person and, in fact, were part of the everyday vernacular: for example, "You have to be a *mishugene* if you disagree," or "Watch out when you buy tires from that *gonif.*"

These traditions were no less common in the Children's Home. A few odd kids were "our deviants," who held a firm and good-humored place in the memories of many of the alumni. To be sure, these hapless youngsters did indeed suffer the gibes and taunts of looking and being different; still, they could always count on other members of their tribe to protect them. There was a special place for these children.

PAYSHE

The name "Payshe" was known to and remembered by all; in some minds "Payshe" became an eponym for others who mean well but wind up fumbling and muddling. I am sure that many "Payshes" reside in many contemporary child-care settings. But his modern counterpart surely has been "processed"— studied and classified—by specialists who make such fine discriminations in how they apply the label of learning disabled, neurologically handicapped, exceptional, or mentally retarded, to name a few. Payshe was also subjected to examination. A Stanford Binet intelligence test administered at age ten placed him in the "borderline range." Doubtful that Mr. Hollander or, for that matter, the principal at Number Twenty School was aware of whatever these "borders" were, it is improbable these results got much attention. Aside from being the butt of a passing jibe or chant, Payshe was simply "Payshe," the aggregation of all those characteristics that were associated with his name. He never wearied in trying to make himself part of whatever was going on; characteristically, his efforts were ungainly, foolish in ways that invited teasing. I remember him always a bit oversized for his age. He was homely, to be sure, but in a way that fitted his being Payshe. Chronic skin problems and a generally unkempt exterior also went along with his personage.

Payshe's entry into the Home when he was five (father died, mother herself was weak and dependent) marked the beginning of what in current jargon might be called a lifelong protective network. Payshe and trouble were synonymous terms: never quite sure of what was going on, he was an easy mark, sometimes a willing clown. But there were other kids, like Phil, who were champions of boys like Payshe and who would quickly slap down any of the other boys who got too tormenting.

Payshe wanted his own identity and tried to be helpful and as much a part of the activities as anyone else. The *Home Review* reported that Payshe, at age twelve, played Sambo in a Purim minstrel show. He was on the Honor Roll many times. At his bar mitzvah, Payshe read his portion of the Torah and made his confirmation speech. How fulfilling it must have been for him to complete his rite of passage before a full synagogue and then be given a reception after the service by the Mothers Club. He received awards at summer camp, played on the Home's basketball team, and when he was seventeen, graduated from vocational high school.

He quickly was offered another sanctuary by the Kolko Paper Company, where he worked until he died over thirty years later. Payshe married in his early twenties, had children and grandchildren, but suffered many hardships and the deaths of two children. But the guidance and caring of his immediate community—his employer and the Home's alumni—were ever present. With a tolerant shrug, one alumnus recalled when Payshe needed tires, he "sold" a set to him, knowing Payshe would never return to pay; another remembered having to set aside precious time to talk with Payshe when he made his deliveries. Commenting on her father's commitment to the Home's children, Ruth, Mr. Kolko's daughter, recalls: "Payshe constantly needed supervision and I don't think anyplace else would have taken him and his set of problems and guided him through his life until the end. He had a wife who got him into debt and when the debts came to my father's attention they had a system for garnishing his salary."

While the "amiably deviant" such as Payshe are frequently remembered with a certain fondness, the few others whose troubles were more profound were accorded silence; they were perhaps the few not considered part of the "most of us" who many alumni proudly exclaimed "turned out pretty well." There was at least one resident, Solly, who at one time became a "famous criminal," though he was scarcely in the same league as the notorious Jewish gangsters of that era, Legs Diamond and Arnold Rothstein. In fact, in his entry into the world of crime, it was not Solly who made the headlines of page three of the *Rochester Evening Journal* (January 30, 1932), but the rookie policeman whose "quick thinking and fast revolver draw" resulted in the arrest of "youthful burglars breaking into Flickinger's grocery on Chili Avenue." As far as some graduates knew, Sol married a woman bearing another man's child "to give it a name," divorced, entered the Army, and was "kicked out with a dishonorable discharge."

The lives of two other unfortunate graduates of the Home ended prematurely as patients in the state mental hospital. The accounts of these troubled lives necessarily lead to some observations on the Home's philosophy of child care, a philosophy that at once was practical and ironic. The ironic element in the case of these two boys is that it was the *absence* of a mental health or psychiatric program that sustained the two boys (and many other residents); in the end, when mental health services and hospitalization were called on, it turned out to be an act of final failure.

If indeed there was a philosophy of child care, it was not documented but most evident in the ordinary routines of daily happenings. The roots were, of course, commonly shared religious precepts that embraced sets of consistent and discernible rules and expectations, all tied to explicit virtues—among them, industry, achievement, courtesy, and, of course being a good Jew. It must be understood that these imperatives provided troubled kids with a safe and watchful haven, a set of roles, an identity—a way of being—all within known boundaries that would not be relaxed by even the most inventive excuse. For the fearful or confused child these rules simplified life and made expectations clear and certain. Not the least, the nonpsychological perspective meant that troubled children were accepted as they were. There was no expert groping for underlying causes or disturbances and, most important, the youngster did not bear the stigma of a psychiatric label; nor did they ever need to ask the question, "What was wrong with me? Why was I treated so differently from other kids?," as was the lament in a follow-up study on adults' views of their early experience with psychotherapy.[1]

One of the two graduates was five years old when he was admitted to the Children's Home after his mother's death. He was found to have, along with his two siblings, hereditary syphilis. The other boy was admitted at age eleven as an orphan. There are few details recorded about their lives in the Home. To be sure, they presented problems—the first boy seemed to be continually involved in pilfering one thing or another, the other would get unreasonably angry. Still, they were not only tolerated within the community of the Home but even gained some recognition and esteem. The first youngster was honored with a wristwatch by the synagogue's congregation for his leadership and musical talents and made the Honor Roll a number of times. Along the way, the second youngster won an essay contest sponsored by the Big Brothers and Sisters.

Only after their discharge as young adults, when they left the protective confines and controls of the Home, did their behaviors finally result in commitment to the state hospital. The young man diagnosed as having hereditary syphilis could not hold a job and was allowed to return as a young adult to the Home, where room and board were earned by a few hours of daily household duties. For months, Mr. Hollander struggled futilely to break the string of meaningless petty thefts. The boy would weep bitterly when he was caught because he just didn't know why he stole.

Commitment to the state hospital in those times was tantamount to the final act. State hospitals then were not temporary centers of treatment and cure. They were truly the last resort, the final disposal center for people whose deportment could no longer be tolerated.

THE TRAGIC ONES

These are stories that lend themselves better to drama or the novel than to the stolidly sober nature of the behavioral sciences. To be sure, all the Home's children were struck by some tragedy—death, loss, abandonment. But they did not define themselves as victims: as shown frequently, dark humor, play, and artfulness outweighed not only tragedy but the ironies of institutional life and the travesties of patriarchal control.

Tragedy, after all, is a familiar companion to Jews and, in some ways, reflects something about the spirit and identity of Yiddishkeit. Tragedy and suffering fuel the writings of Jewish authors, past and present. Sorin mentions that Yiddish, borrowing freely from almost every other European language, developed innumerable words for adversity. "A Yiddish thesaurus needs nineteen columns of fine print for all the synonyms of *misfortune; good fortune* needs only five."[2]

The lives of three of the Home's children were tinged with shades of tragedy in the classic tradition, where serious themes and a person of high worth are inescapably flawed in some way. Two lives involved despair and suicide, the third, heroism and its sorrowful aftermath. Their lives are all the more dramatic since the tragedic elements were interwoven with virtues of excellence and achievement, with joy and victory, and with heroism. One wonders: would these lives have been more forgettable had these virtues not been pursued?

Uncomfortably, I take certain license in telling these stories. The tragedic life defies explanation, even by those intimately tied to the individual—mates, children, dear friends—since, almost by definition, tragedy and the anguish one suffers are deeply personal, known only to that individual. Not rarely, even the sufferer cannot give voice to the pain: what marks tragedy is its profound sense of isolation.

My discomfort also stems from the absence of personal knowledge about the adulthood and circumstances leading to the lamentable turning points in these lives. I was able to locate only a spotty assortment of details; other graduates could tell me, in affectionate terms, about the *lives* of their former comrades but little was said about their deaths. And so, these chronicles are necessarily incomplete, perhaps in some parts, apocryphal, the stuff of legends. Still, taking account of these reservations, these lives deserve commemoration both because of their intrinsic value and how *their* stories add to the knowledge and understanding of the lives of all children of the institution.

GOLDEN BOY

As a youngster, I did know the three children. But because of age differences they remain as wee figures passing across my field of recollection. The imprint that Isidore left is quick to recall: a slight, little blond fellow with a pleasant but earnest smile, quietly and gracefully playing table tennis. There is important symbolism in that scene: as trite as it may sound, *how* he played that game of ping-pong anticipated how he played, up to a critical point, his game of life.

As far as Jewish kids were concerned, ping-pong or table tennis (along with basketball) was a world class sport, one of the major attractions of every Jewish community center. So, Isidore (or Izzy as we knew him) had plenty of able challengers, but few who could beat him. A typical match: his adversary, al-

Ping-Pong Tournament, 1939. Isidore, front row, third from right, waiting turn. (Silver Anniversary publication)

ways a bigger guy, is poised for attack, bobbing and shifting; Isidore stands loosely, almost disinterestedly, but with his paddle at the ready. The opponent serves a crushing drive with forward English spin. Isidore taps it back. With flourishes and motions the other boy tries cuts, chops, spins, lobs, drives; Isidore, with graceful wrist motion, easily taps them all back. The opponent gets flustered; Isidore remains calm and wins the tournament. That's how Izzy was.

At five years old, Isidore, along with his ten-year-old sister and two brothers, seven and four, respectively, was deposited in the Jewish Children's Home in 1932 by an uncle. In the summer of that year, his forty-year-old father, a tailor who had left Russia nine years before, died of cancer. A few months later, his mother, despondent because of the loss, committed suicide by hanging. Described as a tall, beautiful woman, she was found dead by the oldest sister.

There are no accounts of how or if the Home addressed the double loss these children endured other than the following notation found in the sister's records: "She was only ten years of age when her mother committed suicide, and she saw the body of her mother hanging, which seemed to have some queer effect on her, although she said at the time she was not frightened, but she could not understand why her mother did this. For some time . . . she was nervous, and she could not seem to clearly understand what was being said to her." More concerned with behavior than feelings, the record turns to something apparently more important than "nervousness": "She is very neat in her personal appearance. She had a very bad habit of nail-biting, but during the past year has managed to overcome it."

Isidore's reactions to his orphaned state are equally obscure. His serene exterior, unruffled even in the heat of competition, betrayed nothing. But the litany of his achievements over the course of his thirteen years in the Home, his entire youth, is one of almost flawless distinction. He was on the Honor Roll virtually every month and was awarded the Alfred Hart Award for scholarship and conduct. Isidore gave piano recitals, acted in many holiday plays, conducted religious services, was the flag bearer, and was elected to offices in public school. He was a worthy orator and prolific and exceptionally literate essayist. A few selections show his talents.

From an essay on "Unity in Judaism" at age fourteen: "With Europe and Asia in flames, it becomes necessary for Jews throughout the world to work with unity and cooperation. . . . Who can foretell, but perhaps in the near future we shall see a democratic world with equal liberties for all as well as an established homeland in Palestine."

From a speech, "Jewish Survival," delivered at graduation exercises of Rochester Hebrew School, also at age fourteen: "A problem which has troubled my mind for some time and whose solution I found in the Talmud Torah. Why have we Jews survived as a people notwithstanding dispersion, persecution, exile, and a hostile world? . . . In learning Jewish history and particularly the Torah, I find two factors—one, Judaism, Jewish religion or, as others may call it, Jewish culture, the other, Jewish solidarity."

From an address he gave to the New York Yeshiva when he was fifteen: "Besides giving one a keen mind and a fine character, Torah as it is taught in Yeshivas furnishes an answer to all problems of mankind. The present conflict [World War II] is entirely due to the lack of understanding of the Torah. Nations do not realize the presence of a higher power."

Frequently, Isidore was referred to by various alumni as "Hollander's fair-haired boy," or his "golden boy." This was an admiring truth, not a statement that in any way discredited and disparaged Isidore. All the "kids" respected him; many were awed by his natural qualities. Being the "fair-haired boy," however, meant that he was first choice to represent the Home at special events. But what must have been most profound to Isidore, already too familiar with death and loss (but not yet as familiar as he was destined to become), was that he was the one called on at funerals and memorial services to deliver the kaddish, the mourner's prayer, always recited in a deeply sorrowful chant. Ordinarily, this prayer is said by a surviving son. In the absence of this survivor, Isidore was chosen to serve as surrogate. And so, when he was but nine, he said kaddish at the death of Alfred Hart and did so for the succeeding anniversaries. At sixteen he recited kaddish at the memorial services for Max, the Home's sole casualty of the second World War. A year or so later, he gave the prayer at the memorial services for the venerable matron, Anna Daugherty.

Isidore's life seems to fit the genre of the bildungsroman, the classic novel of the sensitive, talented youngster who presses on to find himself amidst the conflicts and struggles of the big world. But the full story itself was sealed in Isidore's sorrowful passing; all I can do as the collector of "facts" is offer the available data and my impressions that may suggest something about plot and meaning.

Even Isidore's departure from the Home had the attributes of a novel about young aspiration and hope. His graduation portrait presents a remarkably handsome young man who returns your gaze with personable confidence. He graduated with honors, and among other achievements he was president of the Social Science Forum and a member of the National Honor Society. With the support of the scholarship fund, he entered Cornell University where, as he wrote in a letter to Mr. Hollander, "I am impressed with the atmosphere of college life, the beauty of the campus . . . peaceful, tranquil, fresh rapid creeks." His studies were interrupted by a brief tour of duty in the Air Force and the golden story continues as he returns to his studies in psychology. In his senior year he attended two summer college sessions in Israel.

The next sequence of his life now becomes uncertain, the details even murkier. With plain sadness, one woman who confided her memories of Isidore recalls her affection for him years ago: "It was really a terribly bitter situation because we really—as young people—we were really in love. Who knows, I might have gone on to marry him." But her father, a Board member of the Home, interceded "with a heavy hand . . . because he knew of Isidore's 'psychiatric problems' while in the Service." She did not know what these "problems" were.

According to one his relatives, Isidore subsequently married a nurse, "someone who was really good for him." They went to Israel, where his wife became pregnant but shortly thereafter miscarried. Two months later, still in Israel, Isidore's wife was severely burned by an overturned kerosene heater. He nursed her for six weeks but could not prevent her death. It is important to mention that, as I garnered impressions and recollections from the few who talked about Isidore, I sensed a certain circumspection, a lasting ache, a growing tragedic tone that made for a reluctance to probe, to ask too much.

Somewhere along the way, Isidore returned to America and enrolled in graduate school. That he earned a degree in social work says much about his intent, further shown in how he was drawn to helping unfortunate and abused children for many years, as was the case for many other alumni. Beyond his training, Isidore, like Phil and others, had little difficulty understanding and identifying with a child's pain. But costly it must have been for Isidore; another relative mentioned that he was frequently shaken when he heard his own suffering retold in the tales of his young clients.

Isidore later remarried and soon fathered a son, now a successful attorney. But as I was told, again in a manner that did not invite further question, the "marriage was brief and stormy," marked by frequent separations.

The golden story, already pocked and worn, ended in 1964. Death, from early on at every corner of Isidore's existence, at last took center stage. At thirty-seven years of age, Isidore took his life, alone in a motel, by means of an overdose of pills.

THE TAP DANCER

Jeannette's life story begins and ends with tragic overtones all too similar to Isidore's; the space between, however, is an account of a very different battle by still another kind of person—as both child and adult.

The image of Jeannette as a little eight- or nine-year-old also owns a special corner of my mind. It is not the image of quietude and composure that shaped memories of Isidore. Jeannette was all motion, vivacity, excitement, bustle—a little carrot-topped girl, usually in high spirits, swiftly hopping, but barely balanced, across the yard. For Jeannette wore a prosthetic device on one leg. She was born without toes on her right foot, and subsequent operations during her early childhood left her with a stump at mid-calf. Little girls grow but artificial legs don't; and so her gait was lopsided with hops and skips keeping her moving without too many falls.

Six-year-old Jeannette, along with her brother, a bit older, had been admitted to the Children's Home by the Department of Public Welfare in 1936. Previously, she had been placed in a non-Jewish home by the Society for the Prevention of Cruelty to Children. Her mother, thirty-four, had been in the general hospital for some time; a month after her children entered the Home she died of pneumonia and other complications. Two years before, Jeannette's father, thirty-five, had deserted the family and according to her records, returned after the death of his wife. There is nothing in Jeannette's record, however, that suggests any regular involvement of this man with his children.

It turns out that with the timing of Jeannette's admission we are introduced to a new voice—in effect, one more perspective on life in the Home. Now the words of the *caseworker* can be heard, words that offer an "authorized" point of view of the child. Jeannette entered the Children's Home at the start of the last decade of the Home's existence, about the same time that a full- or part-time caseworker was added to the small staff. Since there are no remaining records of the proceedings of the Board of Directors, the rationale for this addition is unknown.

The addition of the professional's recorded impressions lodged in the official case record raises a problem: whose version should be considered dependable if we wish to re-create a reasonable sketch of elfin Jeannette during her years at the Home? The spontaneous recollections of her former companions? The chronology of a few of her activities recorded in the *Home Review?* Or the no-nonsense judgments of the expert caseworker? All three need to be heard if only to show the various impressions Jeannette could provoke.

Jeannette's trademark of chatter, jokes, and hustle assured that she would leave a sharp and caring imprint in others' memories. Lila, who shared the dormitory rooms with Jeannette, laughed as she remembered how her friend was always the clown, sometimes hopping around, waving her artificial leg. "She was the greatest—so well adjusted about her leg that you wouldn't know." Lil, already an adult when Jeannette was in the Home, cherished the memory of the little girl sneaking into the sacred churchyard of St. Bridget's and

Children at Sabbath Services. Jeannette, right corner. (Courtesy Jewish Family Service of Rochester, New York, Inc.)

stealthily cutting *"one hundred tulips* so I'd have flowers when the Mothers Club held a wedding shower for me." Phil recalled an incident at summer camp when, after Jeanette had undergone yet another operation on her leg, a counselor tried to "help" her, offering the advice that she should be less self-conscious about her prosthesis. Her response was graphic: "Don't try that psychology crap on me!"

Items in the *Home Review,* starting when Jeannette was nine or ten, recorded her eager and nonstop participation in many of the Home's programs and holiday plays. As well, she gave a piano recital at a few Mothers Club annual luncheons. And despite her spirited and saucy demeanor, Jeannette even succeeded in making the Honor Roll on occasion.

Now the caseworker's records. If you take the starkly impersonal record literally, you could easily assume that Jeannette was being seen not by one, but by a horde of caseworkers since *"we"* was as personal as the pronoun got. Other times, a state of depersonalization was implied when, in the entries, the writer referred to herself as "the worker." Still, Jeannette's spirit was not deterred.

From an early interview when Jeannette was eight:

Jeannette said that she was born in Indianapolis or India. "I know it was not Rochester." She laughed as if this were a huge joke. . . . She announced abruptly, "I don't have a leg like other people have. I was born that way, without any toes." Worker asked if Jeannette played games with other children. . . . She said she could run and jump as fast as anybody else. "The only time my leg bothers me is in tap dancing." She said she had at least twenty friends in the Home . . . she likes to act in plays . . . she hoped she could come back another time and hugged the worker as she was helped on with her coat.

Later, the caseworker is troubled about twelve-year-old Jeannette's "volatility, sensitivity, and expressions of a fantastic nature." The prescription seems to be a return to down-to-earth reality. After Jeannette explained that it was her red hair that caused her bad temper, "*We* attempted to point out to her the fallacy of her notion that hair color determines temper. . . . It is *our* feeling that she is unwilling to see any point other than her own."

Soon after, Jeannette complained about her painful leg and cried about how her teacher and other children were treating her—no one liked her. This compelled the worker to record that "we felt Jeannette was using tears as an attention-getting device . . . she had received some sympathy from us at a previous time through tears and may have felt it would work again."

A year later the continuing discomfort led to a surgeon's examination of her leg, recommending "a mid-calf operation and new extensible artificial leg. Two week's hospitalization. Surgeon's fee $100."

A year or so later, in her fourteenth year, surgery was completed and Jeannette was fitted with a new leg. She was pleased with the new limb and excited about how wonderful everyone was when she returned to school—"they think her leg is beautiful." From this point on, the entries in her record reflected the "worker's" conditional response to Jeannette: pleasure when Jeannette showed progress; frustration when she didn't curb her "volatility." Her school work was erratic and her high school advisor strongly recommended that she *not* be encouraged to go to college since "she was not intellectually fitted." Almost as an afterthought, the worker commented on Jeannette's relations with the other kids: "She meets the needs of other children . . . has a high status in the Girls House, and other children often take her advice."

In the same spirit, just prior to the Home's closing, entries in her record commended Jeannette for how capable and efficient she was in her responsibilities for organizing, chairing, and supervising a girls social club at the Home. Her accomplishments at school were also noted. Nonetheless, another caseworker (her third) for the first time began to describe Jeannette in psychiatric terms. Jeannette was being escorted into the grave estates of psychiatry: "she seems less able to accept her handicap . . . manifested a number of hysterical symptoms—headaches, indigestion . . . she has quite an insight into the situation and realizes that she requires professional psychiatric treatment."

And so, she came to be evaluated by a psychiatrist at Rochester Child Guidance Center who intoned that Jeannette indeed "presents a wide variety of symptoms with periods of depression being prominent more recently. Her chief defense consisted of dominating the other girls at the Home. These defenses cracked last year when the older girls grew away from her, developing heterosexual interest which she could not countenance."

He recommended a private school with psychiatric treatment. In her seventeenth year, 1947, and coincident with the closing of the Jewish Children's Home, Jeannette was admitted to Grove School in Connecticut, her stay financed jointly by the Children's Home and Jewish Social Service Bureau.

It is now 1951. I am eight years (since 1943) and almost 3,000 miles distant from Rochester. I have seen the other side of the world and weathered a sundry assortment of ordeals: the invasion of the Philippines and Japan as a combat photographer; a befuddled return to civilian life in California; and an introduction to bankruptcy proceedings—our (my brother, brother-in-law, and me) business partnership predictably failed.

Having survived these troubles, I was now diligently trying to find my way toward a more confident new life. It was that rousing, post-war time when young men, even veterans like myself already with families and mortgages, believed they could, with determination, virtue, and hard work, create a better life. I was halfway through college, driving a Yellow Cab on weekends to supplement what the GI Bill provided and, when I was not too exhausted, enjoying the adventures of a Los Angeles cabby. Just the right setting for Jeannette's sudden and unexpected reentry into my life.

On an evening like any other, my cab was parked at the stand in suburban Westwood, a good spot to pick up passengers going to UCLA or the fine estates up the hill. My taxi moved to the head of the line where a young woman was waiting. She entered the cab and gave me the nearby destination. I drove off, my mind on negotiating the traffic. After a moment, a soft but, as I remember, teasing voice from the back of the cab said, "Hello, Howie." I was at loss until, with a great grin, my passenger said, "Jeannette." It was all of a moment and as she exited my cab, she caught my instinctive glance at her right leg. Her grin widened: "Looks great, right? No one can tell."

Trite to be sure, but it was a better ugly duckling story than the original. Jeannette was so comely, so smartly dressed, poised and clearly enjoying her encounter with this dolt, this clumsy relic of her past. I was indeed awkward: I wanted to hug her, to say something caring about the magic of her reappearance in my life. Not just the appearance of this unfamiliar young woman, but the image of the little Jeannette that she personified, the child who, on this pastel, palm-lined Los Angeles boulevard, reawakened the vision of gray Gorham Street. She touched my hand, explained she was out here as a student at UCLA studying child development; she planned one day to help kids with disabilities. I could only mumble a few words about the miracle of our meeting, perhaps said something about seeing each other again. We wished one another well, and went on with our lives. But for me it was a bungled episode, unfinished, dreamlike, one of the many intangible memories that, after so many years, inspired this study.

As this study took form almost forty years later, the idea of finding Jeannette was compelling. Only the traces of her that I have just documented were found. One of her former Home roommates, a graduate I talked with, recalled that, yes, Jeannette had returned to Rochester some years ago and, strangely, apologized for the times she had hit her friend with her fake leg.

I called and wrote to the UCLA registrar and alumni association but there were no records. Finally an impulsive search through California phone books located a Maxine with the same uncommon surname as Jeannette's who, to my astonishment, turned out to be Jeannette's sister-in-law, a widow for over twenty-five years.

Maxine was of course bewildered by this strange phone call but after I could offer some persuasive reassurance, she gave me a short synopsis of Jeannette's brief life. Jeannette (who soon shortened her name to Janet) had followed her oldest brother, Garson, to California and for a while lived with him and Maxine, his wife. Yes, Maxine recalled, she did graduate from UCLA with a degree in psychology "but never did anything with it." She married soon after graduation and had one son. Then another void in time, empty of event and meaning, eclipsed, in Maxine's terse conclusion, by tragedy.

Jeannette committed suicide in 1968 (she was thirty-eight) with an overdose of sleeping pills after her husband asked for a divorce. Maxine seemed obliged to explain this sorrowful episode. But the rise in her voice suggested that she wasn't all that sure about her reason. "It was another woman," she said, adding with even less conviction that after Jeannette's deprived early life maybe another rejection was just too much. A silent pause. Then she punctuated this uneasy conversation with *her* tragedy. Her husband, Garson, terribly shaken by his sorrow and loss, died of a heart attack the same year.

WAR HERO

Israel is the third player in this set of extraordinary trials. One alumnus, on remembering his young friend, Israel, advised me rather grimly that "you got something to write about if you want to talk about human drama." Thinking about themes, Isidore and Jeannette's lives were twisted in the web of personal, existential ordeals. Israel's, in contrast, is the warrior's story, the battler beaten by fate.

Israel was one the last batch of kids, one of many "behavior problems," admitted in the years prior to the Home's closing. He was considered a delinquent by the Children's Court and was committed to the Children's Home as an alternative to more corrective placements. I was surprised to find that he was already fifteen years old when he entered the Home in 1936; he was a "little kid" as I remembered him. Little he was for he never grew beyond a few inches over five feet. Compact, muscular, and quick, he was a ready-made bantamweight boxer, but always good-natured.

Israel was born in Poland and, as an infant, was brought to the United States by his parents. His thick case record notes that his father was a *shochet*, the ritual slaughterer of animals who ensures the meat is kosher (somehow, in later reports of Israel's achievements, his father came to be described as a rabbi). Apparently his father had some difficulty in keeping a job and, at the time of Israel's admittance, the family was receiving relief.

A year or so prior to his entry in the Home, Israel was caught stealing from downtown stores and was placed on probation. Investigation revealed his father as "harsh and unbending . . . would whip the boy mercilessly when Israel refused to follow fanatical religious practices." He ran away from home and asked to be kept away from his father. Placed in a foster home, Israel did well for a few months and then ran away after stealing $33 from his foster mother. He was picked up in Brooklyn and placed in another foster home. Israel was studied by the SPCC and institutionalization was recommended "because of the serious nature of his delinquency."

As a commentary on present definitions, acts such as running away from home, petty thievery, and brawling amounted to "serious delinquency" in those pre–World War II years. Serious as these behaviors were, violence was generally uncommon. Consider Hermie's (who had been a pal of Israel) account of his own transgressions, which also led to the Children's Court placing him in the Jewish Children's Home. As "a lesson in not covering your tracks," Hermie recalls that "I hung around with all the Italian kids. It wasn't so strange that they caught us. We saw some boxcars sitting out there so we just broke into one, grabbed a box that we didn't know what was in it, and when we got home I saw what they were—all Parker pen and pencil sets. Every kid in my school, #18, got a Parker pen and pencil set. Boy, what happened when they got home? It didn't take long before the school jumped on us, me, Patsy Russo, and Charlie Argento. . . . *Where did you get it from?*"

In Israel's case, confinement didn't decrease his misdemeanors. In less than two weeks, the caseworker recorded that: "the children reported that they had seen him smoking and, when spoken to, promised not to do it again. He likes to get into fights . . . he had a fight with a boy regarding which radio station to have tuned in . . . two windows were broken and sashes smashed." A more serious episode occurred three months later when Israel left after supper without permission. When he returned: "A search of his pockets revealed a package of cigarettes *and a condom.* Mr. Hollander did not say anything about this article as he preferred to have him questioned by the probation officer. . . . He was brought to the probation office. Although the boy was later questioned about two hours, he insisted he found the condom in #9 School playground." Believing Israel was lying, "no threats or coaxing" could make him change his story. With this catastrophic problem still unsettled, sixteen-year-old Israel was later seen by a clinical psychologist at the SPCC. His report:

> Boy referred because a condom had been found in his possession and there was some question as to the possibility of his developing interests in sexual activity. Israel indicated he had obtained it from another boy. . . . This was confirmed by his indefinite knowledge regarding the price. He admitted most of the boys at Wash-

ington High had them; most of them like him carried them for the sake of reputation, rather than use. [I can confirm his statement; I was one "of the boys" whose wallet was embellished with the imprint of a perfect circle.]

Although "considerable progress" was recorded, in the next months Israel was occasionally tardy at school, would hang around Lapides' Pool Room on Herman Street, and in one instance, was inveigled by another boy into breaking into Braverman's Junk Shop to take some junk and sell it. A neighbor spotted them and called the police.

His career as a delinquent apparently ended when, according to newspaper articles that later eulogized his remarkable deeds, he quit school and became an amateur bantamweight boxer. He went to New York, turned professional, and won his first eight fights. In 1941, immediately after this country's entry into World War II, Israel enlisted in the U.S. Army, an act that would have legendary dimensions.

Israel's letters from the battlefield are telling in how they reveal what character and literacy meant in those days. Even as a high school drop-out and an adjudged delinquent, his correspondence, reprinted in the *Home Review*, like those of other graduates, represent a rhetorical style and grasp of language not prevalent nowadays. An excerpt from a letter to Mr. Hollander (that casts Mr. Hollander in yet another light) after the invasion of North Africa:

> I want to impress on you that not for one moment have I had the Home, that particular phase of my environment out of my mind since I have been on foreign soil. I now take the opportunity to write an open letter through you, Mr. Hollander, the most understanding person I have known. . . . I am writing to all the boys and girls of the Home . . . you cannot realize an iota of the great personal interest Mr. Hollander has in each and every one of you. If one of the boys was unhappy and crying, you could spot a suspicion of moisture in Mr. Hollander's eyes.

Israel concludes almost offhandedly with "can't say much about North Africa because of censorship. I was cited by the Commanding General and decorated with a Silver Star for gallantry in action."

A few months later, this letter came from Italy:

> It's not the fighting that's tough, it's moving over these mountains, the biggest in Sicily. The most beautiful is Mt. Etna that reigns majestic over the surrounding mountains, its peak rimmed by clouds, a column of smoke spirals slowly up into the sky, a white cloud. . . . When we take a town, civilians rush out, overwhelmed with joy that the Americans are here. I hope this letter finds you in the best of health.
>
> One of the Boys, Israel

If Israel was not, as many alumni claim he was, the most decorated Jewish soldier, he was not far from the top of the list. Immediately after his discharge from the Army he was honored at a ceremony arranged by the Jewish War Veterans at New York's Waldorf-Astoria. He was awarded medals for his bravery on behalf of New York State by Governor Dewey, former governor Herbert Lehman, and Mrs. Theodore Roosevelt. A year later, he married Rose at the synagogue of the Children's Home. Mr. Hollander officiated.

The three-columned article in the March 21, 1966, issue of the *Rochester Democrat and Chronicle* sums up Israel's fabled wartime exploits and his remaining, less dazzling, post-war years. Headlined, *In Memoriam: Ex-Boxer Loses Toughest Fight*, the article did not mention his troubled teen years or his residence in the Children's Home but detailed how, in the army's First Division, Israel spent 570 days in the front lines in French Morocco, Sicily, France, Germany, and Austria. He won the Silver Star and Purple Heart fighting to save a wounded officer from German machine-gun fire. Wounded a second time, he received the Oak Leaf Cluster for the Purple Heart, a Bronze Star for gallantry, and the croix de guerre from General de Gaulle for saving a French platoon.

Israel was chosen to attend officers training school, but elected to remain on the battlefield. Later, after a week of fighting in Sicily, he was told his fine war record qualified him to be sent home. Instead, he joined the Sixty-fifth Division to fight in France and Germany. He was chosen for a battlefield commission but was disqualified because of his injuries and remained a platoon sergeant.

The article notes that after the war, Israel returned to New York and his former career of prizefighting. Later he returned to Rochester, first driving trucks, later operating parking lots until cancer struck.

In July 1965, after eight months of treatment at the Buffalo Veteran's Hospital, he was allowed to return to Rochester briefly for a testimonial dinner. More than 500 of his former army buddies and friends honored him. At the dinner he was given seven army medals he had won but had not yet received. In addition, he was awarded the Conspicuous Service Cross of the State of New York for gallantry, a citation signed by Governor Rockefeller, the key to the City of Rochester from Mayor Lamb, and a certificate of merit from the David Kauffman Post, Jewish War Veterans.

The 1966 newspaper article concluded with: "Yesterday morning, March 20th, 1966, he lost his toughest fight of all, against cancer. Survivors include his widow, Rose, three sons, and one daughter."

THREE LIVES

The intensity of these abbreviated lives tempts one to reshape them into classic dramatic forms, to reveal deeper existential meanings, or disclose a universal truth. Resisting this appeal, there is still something worth saying about the worn term, "human spirit," as it is revived in the examples set by Isidore, Jeannette, and Israel. I speak of their compulsion to retain a measure of self-esteem, purpose, caring, and hope in the face of travail. By the highest of society's standards, all three dignified themselves and their lives and left an unmistakable signature. Isidore, only five years old and orphaned, entered the Home and became, as many of his comrades saw him, a "star," a leader, an achiever, and as everyone, including myself, remember him, as a kind, warm, decent human being. He cared, he drew from the meaning of his own pain to help other children. Jeannette, born a "cripple," as the term was then so commonly used, symbolically fought to be able to "stand on her own two feet"—as a young clown, as a hoyden, and in her young adulthood, as a lovely, poised, educated, and altruistic woman. Symbolism didn't count for much in Israel's exploits; his was straightforward, unmistakable courage and heroism. Within the stories of the three lives, the subtext of playfulness, even mischief, that I explored earlier, seemed to be a major motif, even a life force, in their sagas: Isidore's more subtle and inward; Jeannette's as the joker, the cut-up; Israel's impulsive and defiant. Lives of irony—comic, dark, sad; death, a loss, and a tragedy.

CONTEMPORARIES: THE ALUMNI

The themes of resiliency, irony, and often, playfulness are found as well in the stories of the surviving graduates who shared their wisdom, their perceptions, and, often in oblique and suggestive terms, the meanings they found in their lives. The stories and their plots also are marked by a literary, even a romantic flavor, often involving acts of will and critical choice. The spice of Yiddish whimsicalities carries over from the recollected episodes depicted in previous chapters. Their narratives at times mirrored the ironies, humor, and compassion of the stories typical of Jewish life written in the years before and after the turn of the century by authors such as Sholem Aleichem.[3]

The stories of the graduates of the Home of course were not deliberately developed tales: some alumni did feel compelled to offer a carefully worked-out chronological sequence of events; some waited for my questions; others enjoyed the adventurous trip back in time and reported recollections met along the way; a few wanted to make sure I was impressed with a particular point of view. Certain recurring themes found expression in these narratives.[4]

From the rich bounty of reminiscences the alumni favored me with, I select eight lives much less exceptional in dramatic qualities than the preceding. Still, we will see that the "ordinariness" that represents the majority of the graduates' lives also demanded courage, resilience, and self-esteem.

Selection of three men and three women was based first on gender considerations. The burden of having been an "orphan"—and Jewish at that—during the Great Depression was heavy enough for men; the price women had to pay for their independence and achievement was more punitive. Other themes are covered in these stories: marriage and parenting; play and chicanery within the ethos of Yiddishkeit; and variations on the goal of self-reliance. The mean and painful temper of life in the Children's Home was not recalled with equanimity or indifference. My companions were surely bitter about some of the ways they were treated, yet felt no need to assign blame nor to lose respect for legitimate authority. Their assertive and independent approaches to their lives were in some ways tied to work, to vocations or careers that, for each of them, held purpose, worth, and identity: "I became something." Ordinarily not uncommon motives, they must be considered remarkable for these "kids" who had little preparation and even less parental encouragement as well as every excuse to give up or find an easy way out.

For a few, these achievements came later rather than earlier. Some goals were reached by plan, others by wandering and searching. One or two appeared to be accidental or the result of good fortune; even so, a radical choice still had to be made at the right moment.

I start with Stan's account because this study started with Stan when he phoned me to ask if I was the Howie who once owned a dog that understood Yiddish.

STAN

My relatives were sure I'd wind up in jail. I said to myself, "I fooled them."

Stan and his wife, Alice, greeted me warmly. Their modest home, bought many years ago as part of their plan to settle in an established Jewish neighborhood, was neatly arranged and full of traditional symbols of family life. Despite signs of weariness lining Stan's face (I learned about his battle with cancer that he felt he was winning, but, soon after, lost), he was eager to display his incredible memory. Like an animated version of Trivial Pursuit, he filled the space between us with forgotten vestiges of our past—people I couldn't remember, juicy details of our past years, a panorama of Gorham Street history. Then he pronounced his personal pride of *naches* (parental gratification): His daughter is married to a rabbi, his son is a lawyer. And he proudly let me know that he was planning to retire after years as a purchasing agent with the United States Coast Guard; we both agreed that indeed that was an unusual career for a Jewish boy.

Now after a half century, two old Jewish Rochestarians shared lifestyles and achievements that couldn't be imagined by us as children of immigrants during the Depression era. Over the evening, Stan wove variations on the theme of success throughout his reflections on his job, his marriage, and what his kids were up to. It was the good fortune that Stan had never even looked for, never mind felt he deserved.

The young Stan that he summoned up was a "rebel among rebels, a lousy kid" who didn't want to conform, to be restricted, to be forced into religious rituals. His rebellion had nothing to do with being Jewish; he pointed out, in fact, that he now belonged to and was active in *two* congregations. But as a kid, he wanted to be left alone, to work at fairs or at the ballpark with Joey where they made three bucks a day. "My interest was baseball which I instilled in my son who is an avid sports fan. I coached Little League." If there was anything good about the Home it was that it was open, "we could be part of society . . . I was able to adjust to society." He added, speaking of Mr. Hollander, that "we survived in spite of him. Very few of the kids who left there ever got into any kind of trouble." Stan didn't suggest there was any kind of formula that either he or the other kids learned as far as surviving was concerned. But how he thought of himself as a "rebel" who had room to rebel within the "open" institution speaks again to a setting that tacitly allowed for attempts to "beat the system, to challenge authority."

But his assertiveness and rebelliousness began to evaporate once Stan left the Home, was on his own, and didn't have the familiar adversaries to battle with. It must be remembered that he was but eighteen, unprepared for any trade or occupation, entering a world caught between the last stages of the Depression and the entry of the United States into the second World War. Despite the actuality of these handicaps, the older Stan of the present was not at all forgiving about the idle, unproductive years of his younger self: "I was a nasty character—put myself in the wrong direction, always on the minus side," or "I wasn't polished, I didn't know my true value and I didn't put it in the right direction."

But a good story—especially one that dramatizes the narrator's grit and tenacity—is burnished by irony, crisis, choice, and eventually, winning determination. At first, nothing much worked out for Stan in the years after he left the Home. He moved back to his mother's home, they couldn't get along, so he took a room at the Y. He planned to go to college out west with a neighborhood friend, but "I didn't have the confidence." He enlisted in the army, but when it came time for his tank unit to go overseas, he was discharged because of bad eyes and worse knees. With "Gabby," one of his buddies in the Home, he went to Florida but found nothing worthwhile there.

Finally, a turning point, some direction. In his later twenties, Stan became a shoe salesman in a Rochester chain shoe store. With the prospect of actually becoming a manager, he was transferred to Cleveland where he met Alice and, in a few years, they began a marriage that lasted over forty years. He finally became a store manager, returned to school for some courses and, just by chance and because he was tired of working nights, let himself get talked into taking a civil service exam: "Actually, I was the one who did it." He admitted he was astounded, not only that he passed the exam but that he was hired by the Coast Guard, where he worked for almost twenty-five years: "Best move I ever made even though I had to take a cut in wages. Gave me an outlook on life, a little more self-esteem, a little more independence. It took years for my mental capacity to come out in me. . . . There I had to make decisions, money decisions, work independently."

Stan proudly spoke of awards, admiral's commendations, his ability to supervise his staff, and not least, that he was again part of an institution in which *we* were responsible for foreign embassies, oil spills, buoys, and other essential duties. "It was the best thing that ever happened to me. My wife went to work and we were able to build up our resources and savings. Now I'm able to retire anytime I want, to travel. I just got evaluated. Excellent. It's nice to have that feeling."

We finished the last cup of coffee and both Stan and Alice were signaling something about early mornings. I said, "After all, Stan, what really made the difference? How come it worked out this way?" Very matter-of-factly, he replied: "All I had when I left the Home was pride. That's all I had. Someone else like me would have gotten incarcerated. I was headed the other way. After all these years, when I got back to Rochester some of my relatives looked at me and said, 'You got a *family?*' 'Yes,' I said, 'I have two young children.' They thought I'd end up in jail. I said to myself, 'I fooled them.' "

With this compelling response in mind, I left for home feeling pensive, looking at this study in unexpected ways. Now I had at last conversed with, not an abstract "respondent," but from out of the past, one of the real "kids" I'd been seeking. I thought: was there anything truly remarkable about Stan's chronicle of his life? Was it really worthy of study and analysis? His narrative was not as inspired as those of the previous three lives. Altogether, all he and Alice achieved was to take something from life and to repay by becoming part of his community, by bringing up children of value, and by living with civility. That's *all* he and most other graduates did. And Stan introduced yet another theme that recurred in many life stories: the realization that life could have turned out badly since "if it wasn't for the Home I would have become."

JOEY

I always did things on my own, ever since I was a kid.

Now almost seventy, Joey, as I noted in the previous chapter, impressed me with his determined independence, intensified by his brandishing his ever-present cigar to drive home an argument. Joey's hubris was never in doubt. His practiced independence ensured that pride of some kind always remained intact: "As far back as I can remember, I kept to myself a lot, minded my own business. Even on dates I wouldn't double date. I always did everything myself. If I wanted to get a job I'd say to myself, c'mon let's go get a job. I'd have to make my own money, I couldn't get it no place. I couldn't say, 'Ma give me some money,' because no one was there to give it to me."

His first job while in high school was hustling pop at the Red Wing ball park ("I must have been fourteen, fifteen"). Joey didn't wait for clothing handouts from National Clothing: "I used to make thirty-five, sometimes forty bucks. I'd run down to National and buy a pair of peg pants and a sport coat. I was the sharpest guy going to Washington High. 'Goldpiece' is what they called me." He admitted that he was helped once. When someone stole the saxophone the school lent him, his mother bought him one, paid a dollar a week from her slim earnings from her job at the shoe factory.

Draped in his sharp suit and gray suede shoes, he played with lots of bands at dances and churches. Still in high school, Joey fought as an amateur boxer at the Elks Club. "I won my first fight and they gave me a big watch. What do I do with this? I took it upstairs and a guy gave me a five-dollar bill. I weighed 112."

Joey hung around the storefront gym owned by a guy named Tony. "I had an old beat-up bicycle and he used to give me a quarter to deliver to the *nafke* (whore) house. What I'm delivering is whiskey, hooch, that he was making in the back. The girls gave you another quarter, so you got yourself half a buck."

Joey's zeal and ambition didn't slip when he left the Home at sixteen and lived with his mother and aunt a few blocks away. After a year or so, his mother died. His aunt and grandmother would have taken care of him, but "I didn't want to be obligated. I got to a point where I was on my own. So I said, to hell with it and joined the CCC.[5] I was freezing up there in the hills of Albany or someplace." Hoping that by joining the army he would be sent to Hawaii, he enlisted in the regular army where he received $18 a month, and wound up being stationed in an equally chilly army base still in New York state.

Although the Children's Home offered little preparation for the world of work, the experience of institutional life itself adapted its residents to cope with the demands of other large systems. Joey spoke about his wartime exploits: "The discipline in the Home really helped me a lot . . . always learned how to take care of yourself so when I got into the Service it didn't mean nothing. For people who didn't have that, it was harder."

With pride spelled out in the language of valor, Joey boasted about being in the toughest company of the First Division, the first to hit the beaches on North Africa. "I was in front of it all, the first. I had strong determination and I was right in the pit of it, believe me." His words were backed with deeds, for Joey was wounded twice and in addition to his Purple Heart, he was awarded a Silver Star for carrying a wounded officer three miles under enemy fire. He repeated his sentiment that the Home helped him learn to take orders and listen to people. But when he claimed that he had no problems in the Home because of what he learned, I recalled for him one or two episodes we had shared that proved otherwise. "Well," he admitted, "I had problems, a kid y'know, wild here, wild there, like that. I was a strong guy, I was wild there. But after I got out."

After he got out, Joey made the transition from war hero (in a special ceremony, he was honored by then Governor Dewey) to shoe salesman. College wasn't an option: "I wasn't college material and nobody went unless your parents had money. I had to work and that's it." His first job was a "shoe dog," a salesman at a chain store. There he met Rose, sold her some shoes, talked her into a date, and over a year later married her. His prior nemesis, Mr. Hollander, officiated. Rose's father took Joey into his jewelry business where, for ten years, he learned the trade. "Then I went in for myself. I used to go into the country every Sunday to those migrant camps. Load up my car with jewelry and clothes to sell to the peons out there. For years I did that, seven days a week." More confident, he opened his own jewelry business. Now that his son has taken over, "I enjoy going to the store, hanging around, talk to people, make a few bucks. It's a good life."

Joey, like most of the other graduates, had little question about the kind of parent he was. He felt that he and Rose did good for their six children. "Got the four boys bar mitzvahed. Three went to college, the rest wanted to work. I wasn't tough or anything like that. They listened to me. They're all doing OK, so I can't complain."

I asked him to sum up what he thought made things work for him. Joey, the consummate practical realist, responded: "Hustling all my life, that's just about what it is. I made sure I always had money in my pockets—buy this, sell that, make a dollar. No complaints, everything going good for me and Rose. Like I always say to my kids, people with plain common sense, they got more brains. College education is a good thing, but you still have to think out straight what you want to do and do it. That's my theory of life anyway."

NORM

What made me survive is my attitude because I never had any-
thing, nobody gave me anything, and I didn't care one way or the
other. I wanted to be independent. I thank the Good Lord.

I felt the touch of irony in his declaration, since caring Annette, Norm's wife, sat close enough to cuddle him during our entire conversation. She was sometimes protective, anticipating pain at the edges of his recollections; other times she supplied him with the right word or event he was searching for, particularly when strain led to his stuttering.

Norm's account of his struggle to come to terms with his early years was perhaps less dramatic than Stan or Joey's, but offered its own poignancy. Annette set this tone with her tender presence and by ensuring that Norm's massive heart attack five years ago got proper regard. As she attested, "He is a living miracle." Norm's story, unlike Stan's, contained few critical turning points nor could he color his years with the verve, the zeal, the heroism of Joey's tale. His wistful account, however, betrayed something unfulfilled—a life with a bit too many frustrations.

Norm was the youngest of four brothers, one of the three placed in the Home after their parents separated and foster care proved unsuccessful. His records show that there wasn't much to give him a feeling of worth: he was even slighted by the clinical psychologist at the Guidance Center who evaluated young Norm and his brother, David, after they were admitted to the Home. "David is engaging, direct, and friendly," reported the psychologist. But "Norman suffers by comparison."

In many ways, the seeming randomness of his early life appeared to be a consequence of so many events having sunk into oblivion. Norm rationalized this was a result of "just taking one day at a time," or, "being a softie, always forgive, live and let live." Despite the many blanks in his memory, he remembered—even still felt the physical presence—of being "pushed *all* the time" by Mr. Hollander. "I don't remember everything, but I had a bad fight with him, just to keep him away from me." A glib psychologist might call this, "identifying with the aggressor." But for whatever reason there emerged a pattern by which Norm began to push himself. Stuttering, he explained: "I was always pushing myself. I pushed myself for everything. I used to be the top one in basketball with the kids, and I used to push them along. I always tried to make things better. Something about me, I can't quit, I have that instinct, I can't sit around and do nothing."

Like other young men, Norm was called into the armed services after the War broke out but was discharged early because his brother Max was killed in action in North Africa. Most of the male wards of the Children's Home, and a few women, served in the War; Max was the single casualty. In the ceremonies and newspaper articles that followed, Norm's brother was declared not only a true hero, but a true Jewish hero.

Norm and Annette smiled as they talked about their great romantic adventure: They had joined in marriage after they had been "pen pals" for some time. Brother Max, after being shipped to England, met Annette and encouraged her to write to Norm. After corresponding for a few years, Norm phoned her, proposed, and then sent her a ticket on the *Queen Elizabeth* ("I tried to make her feel like a queen"). They were married in the Children's Home just before it closed.

I wondered about the perils of this plan: not only had they never met, but Annette's commitment to Judaism was far more uncompromising, more Orthodox, than Norm's. Norm's response: "I had such a bad life, how could I go wrong, what could I miss? I gotta take chances. To me it was a challenge." The marriage endured the challenge along with disagreements and hardships for forty years. They spoke with pride about their daughter, an independent professional in California.

As to his life's work, Norm's principle was doing the best he could, no matter the job. "College? I wasn't bright. Wish I was. But I made ends meet; we don't need much to be happy." He worked as a baker for twenty years and then, because of an allergy to flour, had to quit and found a job with Xerox ("gradually liked it after awhile"). Twenty years later he was forced to retire after suffering an almost fatal heart attack.

It was difficult to come away from the afternoon conversation with real clarity about the meanings Norm gave to his life. Early on, I felt his vulnerability and cautiously tried to temper my questions. Just my presence seemed to compel Norm to grapple with confounding memories and thoughts that often defied expression. At one moment he suddenly wept with anguish when he spoke of the deaths of so many kids with whom he identified his childhood.

"They're gone, they're gone!" he cried, as if he were speaking of his child-hood. His memories of Hollander were torn; the pain he felt conflicting with his having to acknowledge that "yes, Hollander did help me get a job." I cannot really know how life had been for this guileless and, I think, lonely couple. But they had made it, they were together, devoted one to the other. I asked, How? "We Jews are fighters," he said straight out. "Like I said before, attitude. You could get what you want if you put your mind to it. The hardest part was being honest."

From their stories, for these men to make their way, to gain a measure of pride, achievement, and security was less a decision than a compulsion, a drive to prove they had character and worth. Variations on "no one gave me any-thing" could have been exploited as justification for giving up; for Stan and the others it was an emblem worn proudly—to the extreme of forgetting for the moment the help, support, and guidance given generously by their wives.

Now as we hear the women graduates' accounts, the theme of making it, of independence (of being a "mensch" as Sally will say) becomes more agitated and perplexed. By many decades, they foretold the modern conflicts and strains of the working wife and parent, but with no role models, no one to offer sup-port, no one to guide their struggle. For them, "making it alone" posed unre-lenting problems. Interestingly, their mates also earn little credit.

SALLY

You had to be a mensch. In the Home you learned to stand on your own feet. You learned to take care of things that a lot of people don't.

Sally's use of the symbol, "mensch," stirs several discordant thoughts and feelings shared by other alumnae. "Mensch" is supposed to be an androgynous title referring to a *person* who is upright, decent, responsible. But in practice it suggests and is often used to describe the masculine character; thus, it might seem a bit awkward to refer to a woman as a "mensch." Beyond the title itself, this awkwardness, if not strain and conflict, was apparent when many women tried to reconcile the differences between certain female and male roles. Clearly, Sally and the other women were as ruggedly independent as Joey, Stan, or Norm; at the same time they would not avoid their obligation to or responsibility for others who depended on them. This is not to say that male graduates were indifferent to needs of others. But for Sally and other alumnae, caring and regard were deeply ingrained, part of what a woman was then sup-posed to be. How, then, to fulfill this expectation while coping with the need to be tough and self-sufficient brought about by the demands of institutional life? This question shapes the themes of these stories.

If the maxim, "It wasn't family but it was home," applied to anyone, it would be Sally. The few scraps of information in her record show that she was born in Eastern Europe and came with her father to America; earlier her mother had died of starvation.

Sally's recollections of her life in the Home had almost too much of a cosmetic tone; in a facile way she coated almost everything and everyone with praise: "They were very good to me and everybody." "They take an interest in you, which is a wonderful thing." "You were living with boys and girls and they were like your brothers and sisters, very, very nice." Then, the casual statement that offers some perspective on why the Home was seen in such a pleasant glow: "You know, you appreciate the Home when you leave it because then you're on your own . . . you have nobody."

Her generous acclamations were, at moments, punctured by a heavy-hearted recollection. Her reply to my question about her age when she entered the Home: "I was a kid. I didn't want to go, I'll never forget this, I didn't want to go so I don't know how I got in there. How they dragged me and everything to get in. Then my father would come to see me and I didn't want to see him, on a Sunday, but I would you know. Oh yes, it was a tough life all the way through. . . . Your whole life flies away."

Sally did not graduate from high school. When it was time to leave the Home, she moved in with another family. Her father had remarried, "but I couldn't live with him and his wife. I never wanted to." As it turned out, in later years she felt obligated to look after him. "After his wife passed away he pestered me all the time, drove me nuts, every night he would call me for this or that." She married when she was quite young ("You know when you get out of the Home you're alone"), but in the midst of the Depression she had to go to work to provide for her four-year-old daughter and unemployed husband.

Sally's employment seemed to intensify the never-ending strain between her irreconcilable needs for independence and dependence. Even when her husband was making a living "I wanted to work, I didn't want to be home. Once I got the taste of it, I wanted to work, to be with people, earn money." And she apparently succeeded in her work in selling home furnishings and real estate. With undisguised pride she recalled how she worked long hours, maintained excellent customer relations, and always dressed tastefully and made an attractive appearance. "I can't have a man push me around and tell me what to do and how to live and spend. My husband was wonderful. Whatever I wanted to do was OK with him." But I didn't learn until close to the end of our conversation that she had been widowed just two months before we met; for the past six years she had to work and support the family while caring for her husband who had suffered a stroke. "I almost put him in the Jewish Home before he died . . . I couldn't do it, didn't have the heart even though it was such hard work to clean him, to do everything for him."

Pride, personal responsibility, taking charge, the undercurrent of the need to control life "because if you don't nobody else will, it's yours and don't expect anything from anybody." These explanations expressed one side of Sally. That's the way it was, there were no alternatives or options like turning to a father or anyone else for help.

Still, Sally's sad and lonely self reluctantly was perched on the other side. As I prepared to leave, she wondered softly if her life might have been different if there had been someone stronger to depend on, someone who did not allow her to be so independent. She said that she gets along with her daughter but her daughter complains that "you listen but then you do what you want." She added, "That's a terrible thing. It's not good to be too sure of yourself all the time. You feel very lonely. A lot of people respect me for what I've done. But! It's a terrible thing (with tears). No one wants to hear a complainer."

SUE

Some fell by the wayside. I made a life for myself.

Sue will be remembered (chapter 5) as the author of "27 Gorham Street," her brief but sprawling composition on life in the Home. There she warned that "if you couldn't cope with it, it would ruin you." Sue made sure she always made it to the head of the line (real and imagined) as "the survivor, the tough one."

In this most gracious lady whose comeliness belied her seventy-odd years, her toughness and self-confidence had aged well. Sue had chosen the strong-willed path early on, but as with Sally, certain regrets about her choice surfaced on occasion.

Sue wanted to say that it wasn't all that important, but still made the point that she and her sisters and brother landed in the Children's Home because her father's second wife, twenty years younger, was more attentive to her own children ("Want me to write a book about stepmothers?"). When it was time to leave the Home, she had seen other kids get scholarship money for college. "When I wanted to go, they said, 'Let your father send you.' " She wanted to be a social worker, "but my father had seven kids, including the two stepchildren. I finished high school and went to work for my father in his shoe store. I met an attorney, and I gave him the air. Then I met my husband when I was twenty-one—he sold shoes at another store. What a guy he was—he loved life, a dancer, a singer, looked like Clark Gable. But he was not much of a *fardinner* (wage earner) so I had to go to work."

Sue was devoted to her daughter who, when she was three years old, had amassed twenty-five dolls in her bedroom. "Maybe in the back of my mind, because I never had one." She spoke of a warm and lasting bond she enjoyed with her daughter, now independent and successful in her own right.

From her weighty scrapbook she proudly drew newspaper clippings about her business ("*fashions for SophistiKids*"). She paused for a few moments and with a catch in her voice said: "Whatever I have is through sweat and tears. My husband has been gone eighteen years. He died of a heart attack, a big guy, vital. But listen, y'know what? I was busy in the business to make money so that I can take care of my sisters, which I still do. I tried to help my brother but he died miserable and poor. I'm the survivor and I gotta see them all through. My daughter says, 'Why don't you think of yourself?' You think of yourself when you're doing what you have to."

After the lox, bagels, and other delights of our brunch, Sue, my wife, and I quietly walked together to the elevator of her elegant, shoreline high-rise condominium, in an expensive Florida retirement community. We were pensive about the morning's conversation. Sue glanced at the ornate decor around us and broke the silence. She spoke first about feeling out of place living with people her age who had settled for simple retirement. Then in words that recalled Sally's misgivings, she mused: "Maybe going to work, into business was the wrong thing to do. When you're in business you become aggressive. It was a tough life with him but, after eighteen years alone, I'd give anything to have him back."

RUTH

I think that I was always able to cope. I remember worrying when I was younger, how will I manage without a close family behind me to help? One way or another I got a sense of independence, learning that you have to rely on yourself.

For Ruth, balancing two roles—one in pursuit of achievement, the other, caring and being cared for—seemed more deliberate, planned, and in the best sense of the term, opportunistic. In a previous chapter, Ruth already summed up her outlook, even as a youngster: "I felt like an outsider, but if you achieved you became something." Little of the ambivalence that marked other life accounts seemed to trouble Ruth. From early on she had a clear sense of direction; despite the few alternatives available to ambitious women in the prewar years, Ruth had some idea how to get there.

Ruth was one of the few true orphans in the Home and the youngest of six children. Her father, a healthy man, died of a surgical error in a routine hernia operation. Her sickly mother died soon after from kidney disease. "We were kind of scattered, lived with one aunt and another . . . these were difficult years for everybody, the Depression and everything." And so, young enough to be sheltered in the Baby Cottage, she and her brother were placed in the Home by an older sister. As she has already recalled, life in the Home was manageable.

It was college that gave Ruth "my sense of accomplishment or whatever I wouldn't have had. I was very timid and shy as a little girl and college helped me become more assured . . . much more forward and able to talk with people." It was not the rigors of higher education that daunted her; she had always been a superior learner, an achievement that was a source of embarrassment when Hollander would openly use her as the paragon other children should emulate. There was something to be overcome in college. "It was not a time that I look back on with great joy. . . . I was told in no uncertain terms when I applied that they didn't take many Jews . . . socially, I felt like an outsider looking in."

One has to appreciate the nature of the alienation Ruth and others like us experienced. Many private colleges in the 1930s and 1940s had de facto quota systems as far as Jews and blacks were concerned; the University of Rochester was no exception. But more than just the exclusionary regulations, those who did gain entry to higher education tended to feel an uneasy self-consciousness as far as poise and appearance were concerned. Hand-me-down clothing and barber school haircuts didn't quite compare with the fashion and demeanor of the gentiles.

Although Ruth didn't allow these symbols to block her path, she did discover among the inventory of prejudices that, because she was a woman, her career choices were restricted. And so, it was recommended that she take the four-month college secretarial course if she planned to find a job following graduation from the University of Rochester. With this course and her B.A., she found work as a stenographer ($1,500 a year) until she heard of an upcoming civil service exam for welfare workers for the city, which she passed. When, after a few years, the economy improved as a result of the war, she was fired. "Then, like other single girls, I wanted to go to New York. Also I had a couple of boyfriends, one I'd see in the afternoon and the other at night, and I was going mad because each one wanted a commitment."

Attracted to social work, Ruth located a position in the Brooklyn chapter of the Red Cross. There she befriended an army recruit. "We hit it off right away and in a few months we were married." Ruth returned to Rochester and, with the end of the war and her husband's return, "I stayed home, had two children and was content to be a housewife. . . . I didn't feel any great need to make my mark as a career woman." Still, she said she was interested in learning. "Perhaps I should have done a little more . . . but circumstances in my life, my husband's illness, prevented me from getting another degree."

A middle-aged successful businessman, he suffered a stroke. "He was sick for almost six years before he died, could no longer work . . . and my daughter, she's also brilliant, was born hearing impaired." He was partially paralyzed, but regained his speech, and his mind was unimpaired. "It was a very traumatic experience. There are some people that fall apart a little bit. But, for me, there was no question about the way it was going to be, and that meant not crying on the kids' shoulders. Meanwhile my son graduated, got his doctorate in chemistry from Chicago and is now a professor. My daughter attended Vassar, Yale, then went to Syracuse to study law." A few years later, Ruth met and married her present spouse, with whom she shares a comfortable and rewarding retirement.

Ruth agreed that her Jewishness became very important "though I never observed kashruth. When my son called to say he met a girl and her name is Christine, I said, 'Oh!' and raised some questions until he laughed and told me her last name was Cohen." She added that she was a very doting mother but always on the lookout for trouble. "Whether that has anything to do with growing up in the Home, I don't know," then, with warm laughter, "but believe me, I know how to relate. The Home didn't hurt me that way." Ruminating about her life, she tried to sum it up:

> I don't dwell on the fact that I didn't have a regular family to live with. Naturally I would have preferred that my parents hadn't died and that I was able to live in a regular house. I think sometimes I would feel a feeling of lonesomeness, but everybody gets lonesome—I felt that even when I was happily married. That's just the way my life happened, that I lost my parents when I was very young. I think I always kinda knew I'm responsible for me. I sometimes, uh, get annoyed with people who explain their problems because of the way life was dealt to them . . . my feeling is that when you grow up you should be able to overcome . . . and be responsible for what you do.

PHIL AND WILL: WAR AND PEACE

Starting with the first page of this book, Phil and Will have been our companions. Their stories, exchanged over the dinner table, offered the first insights into the color, the tensions, the often comedic ironies, the very many forces that animated and personified the Rochester Jewish Children's Home and its immediate community. And, as this document unfolded, the two wise alumni served as guides and commentators, offering keen estimates of the Home, its life and conditions. Now they help place these stories in an instructive perspective.

When I first recorded their voices, I could not anticipate that their respective viewpoints would serve as a medium for understanding, making sense of how—generally, to be sure—the residents of the Children's Home perceived and struggled with the ordeals and trials of institutional life.

Phil put it this way: "I made up my mind that I was not going to be a victim . . . and was always ready to fight, mostly for other people not me." Life in the Children's Home for Phil was a challenge to survival. "It was a tough struggle but I did it." Joey and Sue and others who shared their thoughts in these last pages tend to echo Phil's precept.

Will, on the other hand, would say that his experience in the Home was equally crushing. "But there were good things that happened. We had opportunities." Life in the Children's Home for Will provided the opportunities for survival, allowing him "to make it." He affirmed, "I had to be somebody." Ruth would, I think, agree with this definition of the experience: with care and wise choice—and a minimum of bloody confrontation—one could make one's way through the rigors of institutional life, exploiting the few advantages it offered.

These two basic (but not always mutually exclusive) frames of mind seem to characterize how the "realities" of growing up in an institutional world are defined and, consequently, affect how one goes about coping with, surviving, and outlasting the perils of institutional life. One attitude meets challenges to survival in combative ways: the other actively attempts to discover and capitalize on opportunities to surmount and survive. To be sure, it would be misleading to delineate these patterns in fixed or categorical (never mind universal) terms, as theories applicable to any similar set of circumstances. The point that must be emphasized is that the patterns in question derive from *this* study of the narratives of *this* group of people who occupied a special place during specific times. The value of such findings is not insignificant, however: although I assume that some similarities will be found, they encourage *each* group-care setting to explore the manifest patterns of persistence and growth *of its own* members. Let me say more about the two patterns.

Gender alone doesn't account for the differences in patterns: Sue or Bertha could stand toe to toe with Phil or Joey; Will could be as gentle and caring as Ruth or Sue. It was also not a matter of personality, at least according to conventional psychological definitions: no one fell into such neat categories as *passive* or *aggressive* or *reactive* or *adaptive*. Nor would it do justice to these uncommon men and women to simplistically relegate these patterns to an inventory of *defense mechanisms*.

Let us start with what they had in common. The fundamental wish to become a mensch—a person of some worth and character—was what Phil and Will and the other residents desired. The goal of menschkeit (personhood) itself did not necessarily take the form of wealth, fame, or triumph: as we have seen, gaining a civil service job, comforting the distressed, sustaining a child's education, overcoming hardship, and becoming financially self-reliant were equally meritorious signs of self-worth.

It is not unexpected that Phil and Will, as "surrogate brothers," are committed to similar values, world views, even careers. But, in important ways, they contrast and complement one another.

"I could just as easily have been a hit man," Phil reckons: his recollections are marked off by punches and fights. He was deposited in the Home when he was seven—"I'd been a street kid even before then." But he had also been a very young patient at the local sanitarium because "I had a spot on my lungs like my sick mother." His rigidly Orthodox grandfather wanted him removed from the sanitarium because it was lacking in Judaic ritual and belief. Also, "I was becoming a ne'er-do-well kid": his mother was unable to impose control. And so the Children's Home (Phil still calls it the "orphan asylum") took custody.

Recalling the "pecking order," he quickly became "the best fighter in the Home," remembering with visible vigor, and a few jabs, how he "punched out the guy who taught us Hebrew." "One day he came and took a swing at me. That was the wrong thing to do. I punched him in the jaw and knocked him over two rows of benches. I ran away from the orphans home and holed up in a garage. Must have been twelve or thirteen. We used to make a ring out of our beds. Terrible, knock down, drag out fights. Blood all over the floor we used to mop up with towels."

But Phil assured me that he also used his combative skills to protect "little kids who couldn't handle it." Later, when we were talking about his work, I asked when he decided to be a social worker. He grinned and replied, "probably when I was ten, when I was looking out for the other kids . . . sometimes I had to do it with my fists, and sometimes I just had to show up." How much he meant to the little kids was evident when it was time for him to leave the Home: the younger kids put together a petition requesting that he stay on as boys' supervisor. "I didn't want to stay in the institution, but when the kids kept coming to my house telling me about the kids who were being hit, I'd go back and I would knock the crap out of kids that were beating on the little guys. I was only sixteen, seventeen. Then I became their assistant scoutmaster. So I was always with them for a period of time."

More subdued in tone, Phil recalled how inferior, how naive, he felt when it was time to go forth. "We were institutional creatures with social deficits" who did not know about what clothes to wear, how to hold a fork properly, or how to deal with getting aroused when dancing with a girl. "There was a kind of social retardation when you tried not to be an institutional personality."

Still, Phil was scarcely shy or retiring; he met the new world head on. "Once I came out I was always combative . . . it was an innate sense of pride which at times became a problem in my confrontations with other people. I began to wonder, why was I so angry, why was I always ready to start swinging?" But he added again, "When I fought it was mostly for other people, not me."

It was not by chance that Phil became a camp counselor. As he recalled previously, Manny Hirsch, the head counselor, was his model, his ideal, "such a magnificent guy." Becoming Manny's assistant gave Phil someone "I could try to emulate. Manny kept pushing me and I became a head village leader and then program director. I had every conceivable job at that camp and, at first my idea was to become a camp director. . . . It all started with group work . . . with people who had social work training at the Jewish community center and the camp . . . but then the idea of working with individuals sounded more professional."

Phil's camp work naturally drew him into contact with "these rich Jewish kids, from middle-class families." "When I went down to camp each summer I started to hobnob with these kids. And here I was, a *schlep* with a pair of Li'l Abner shoes and no socks. And I was a counselor and began to see that these kids saw something in me they admired . . . they came from families where there were a lot of advantages and I realized that if you wanted anything in life you had to strive for that and I saw how tough it was."

And so Phil was well past his twentieth birthday when he started college, working afternoons, evenings, and weekends at the Jewish Community Center to support himself. He graduated in 1941 and with the entry of United States in the second World War, Phil enlisted and spent three years in the European theater. After his discharge, he took whatever job he could find—"it was bad times."

A period of illness and a lengthy recuperation gave him time to think and decide about his career choice to become a clinical social worker. He entered graduate school and though he had the help of the GI Bill, "I still had to work forty-eight hours a week."

Phil spoke of his long marriage to Iris with deep gratitude: "I don't think anybody else than Iris would have been able to survive a marriage with me during the time I was as combative and angry as I was." Still, he could laugh at his own doubts and fears, recalling that he was afraid to trust any of his relationships with other women. He wasn't sure he even trusted Iris when, at their wedding, "she threw her flowers up in the air and caught them herself. I said there is something wrong here." He grinned: "Now, here we are, married over forty years." And forty years that counted two children now more than grown—long past their graduate degrees, well settled into independent lives and careers.

The name "The Society for the Prevention of Cruelty to Children," Phil's first place of employment, could serve as a caption for his long and varied career as a social worker: caring for, helping, and protecting troubled, delinquent, retarded children was what he did. His anger, his readiness to fight for the little kid that "began when I was ten" crystallized into a vocation that made a difference in others' lives: "My capacity to identify with the delinquent was incredible. They felt comfort with me. Yes, I overidentified at times with some of the kids. But I also had tremendous relationships with the kids. I guess it takes one to know one. The other social workers couldn't understand how I was able to relate to these kids."

From learning how to survive as an angry kid to helping angry kids survive, helping them, in his words, "preserve their identity" as he preserved his own: that is Phil's story.

Will's account, in contrast, confirms the hardships and stigmas of institutional life, but tells not of battles but of what he learned and what he gained. Balanced somewhere between satire and irony is his lifelong and personal truism, stated earlier: "If I got nothing else from the Home, I learned how to daven (pray)." Satirically, his statement is a commentary on how the rigors of Orthodoxy backfired; the pious rituals of dogmatic Judaism became something to deflate, but always in a benevolent but humorous spirit. Ironically, however, from their forced immersion in Orthodoxy, Will and many kids discovered the symbols of Yiddishkeit that allowed for the bond of identity and place in adult life. Not surprisingly, he became an active and lasting participant in the communities of the temple and synagogue. Will said this in simpler terms: "Even though I could daven, I had to prove that I was somebody."

As was true of many of his contemporaries, the reason for Will and his sisters' arrival at the Children's Home got scant notice in their records: "mother in hospital; father feels he can't provide care." It was with irony again that, after that delectable dinner at Iris and Phil's home, Will recalled the wretched meal that marked his first day in the Home: "You know what we had? We had farfel (grains of dough) and milk soup. It was very salty and part of the salt were my tears . . . I will never forget that, I was almost seven, I will never forget that salty farfel soup."

Just as Will could invent the metaphor for his early grief—"salty farfel soup"—he also searched out other creative modes of humor or bittersweet irony to redefine the many hardships and to make the most of his life in the Home. The May 1930 issue of the newsletter reprinted ten-year-old Will's essay that earned an honorable mention and one dollar. "What the Concert Meant to Me," the newsletter reported, shows "a very imaginative mind," as the following excerpts prove.

> I will tell you some stories about music. Number 1 is the Overture of the Bartered Bride. It was a nice story about people having a good time. I know because it sounded like it. . . . The second was Hyman and Cecile. The violin solo was played so sweet that I saw St. Cecile sitting on the grass. She was a shepherdess. The grass was so green and pure and the music so sweet. The 3rd was My Heart is in the Weary . . . well, the story was a poor woman singing for a husband which has died long ago, and for a son. She tried to make him stop crying but he could not. He had a fever and the poor lady didn't have no money to pay doctor bills and she cried too.

Across the years, Will partook in the full and varied array of children's activities, except for sports: "I was no athlete," he assured me. Among other activities he acted in many religious plays, served as master of ceremonies and sang "Walking My Baby Back Home," participated in mock trials, and was a member of the Home Choir. He received highest honors at JYMA summer camp and was elected president of his high school class every year.

Still, his achievements within the community of the Home didn't lessen the feelings of stigma, of differentness, that came, he felt, with being known as an inmate of that asylum. Consciously, Will chose not to allow that blemish to retard his ambitions or pride: "In those years, thinking as a kid, that feeling of stigma was significant to me. I might have been over sensitive but it didn't close doors for me. If it did, it would be doors I closed myself because of feeling that I wasn't as good as somebody else who wasn't in the Home."

Will was president of his graduating class at Washington High and, with the assistance of the Home's Scholarship Fund (which I found was available to more tractable graduates—Will, Ruth, and Jake, for example—but not to combatants like Phil and Sue), went on to the University of Buffalo where he majored in sociology and anthropology. Still, he did not slight his involvement with the Home and especially the Alumni Association. In 1942 he earned his bachelor's degree with honors from the University of Buffalo.

By all accounts, Will's relationship with Mr. Hollander during his ten years at the Home was cautious and respectful; in turn, the superintendent bestowed his patriarchal benevolence on Will. It was to Will's credit that his contemporaries did not ostracize him as a result of his privileged relationship with Hollander; Will earned his respect from all by his earnestness, his honesty, his good humor, and mostly, his lack of guile. At the same time, Will was well aware of the risks in a relationship with someone as commanding and powerful as the superintendent. It took no time for this risk to intrude itself once Will's affections for Mim and their wedding plans became known.

Will said that he and Mim had "gone together for five years, all through high school." Squeezing Mim's arm, he added that he was drawn to her because she was pretty and "she made me feel like somebody." Then, ever playful, he added, "and not only that, she voted for me when I ran for president even though I lost." Will's previous comments about his feelings of stigma prompted me to ask whether Mim's family had any feelings about her marrying anyone from the Home. "That I know was not significant," she replied, "because everybody loved Will." Turning to Will, she asked if he had told me about Jake Hollander since "he didn't think we should even be going steady because Will had a scholarship at stake, we were too young, and he wasn't in college yet."

When Will said that he had been sneaking out to see Mim, I assumed that he was then still living in the Home. That was not the case; Hollander's dominion extended beyond graduation. "Even though I was out of the Home," said Will, "I tried to avoid Jake." Mim wasn't intimidated by the patriarch: "Jake said no and I said yes. Y'know, Will came over one day like a pussycat and said that we can't see each other because Jake doesn't want it. I didn't accept that but, just to be safe, we just didn't walk together on Joseph Avenue 'cause we could have run into Jake." Will shrugged and acknowledged that he should have told him to go to hell. "But I needed the money for school."

They were wed in late summer 1942 and soon after he was inducted into the army. The newlyweds were able to live together while Will received his military training as a medical assistant. In their letters to the Home they emphasized that even though they lived on the edge of army bases they didn't compromise their Yiddishkeit and even "built our own chapel in our off hours . . . small but full of spirit." Will served in the South Pacific and was honorably discharged as a sergeant after Japan's surrender.

Will was twenty-seven, married, and a college graduate when he returned to Rochester, but unsure about what to do next. Somehow he felt that getting a master's degree in social work was the right path to take. When I pressed him for the reason, he could only say that he didn't know where he learned about the profession but that his choice must have had something to do with his thoughts about his invalid mother. "I tried to figure, can I be of some use in this world? I wanted to go to school and figured I didn't have the makings of a doctor and I didn't want to be a lawyer. I wanted to try social work and liked what I was getting." In 1947, Will earned his master's degree and he and Mim became parents to their first child.

With deliberation and compassion, Will blended professional training with what he knew so intimately about the hard-edged penalties of institutional life to ensure that the lives of the dependent denizens of the Old Age Home would be as humane, as close to normal life as possible. In his words:

> When I first went to work at the Jewish Home it was a good place for "everybody but me." In other words, yes, that's a good place to take *your* mother or father but not mine. I wanted it to be the best place for people who could no longer manage at home. We knew people would rather be home but if they needed the supportive services of the Jewish Home, it was the best place to be. We took the strangeness out of living there. I remember how when I was a kid we marched down to the National for clothes. How we were marched to school and back. I didn't want that kind of regimentation for the folks in the Home.

Will spoke with great pride and authority, with the assurance of a fortunate individual who had already proven his worth and purpose. He told of his efforts with staff and community to make sure that responsibility and care for the elder residents in some ways involved family members. He made sure that everyone knew his door was always open to family, residents, and staff. Even as his obligations multiplied with the growth of the institution, he insisted on being available to make the death calls, to make sure the contact with the family was personal, sensitive, and caring. "I didn't want it to be like a hospital, y'know, 'Mrs. So-and-so, your husband died.' I tried to get my staff to understand that people are not crates, that if it has to be an institution at least make the *i* a small one." Will's legacy remains.

Even now, a few years after his retirement, Will still spends many days each week as a volunteer at the Home for the Aged, sharing his talents and skills. In the warm and delightful hours I enjoyed with Will and Mim, I was well aware that although a lifetime had passed by, they were still the "kids" I remembered. Will never lost his droll and perceptive humor; Mim, her tenderness and special insights. And, at the root of their closeness was their joy in being able to *kvell* (another Yiddishism) or beam with pride and *naches* about their thriving children and their even more outstanding grandchildren.

LIVES AND THE MEANINGS OF BEING A PARENT

This chronicle of critical portions of Will and Phil's lives marks the end of this biographical journey across a panorama of lives that, at once, can be considered ordinary and exceptional. Ordinary is the range of human experiences encountered—problems both physical and emotional, tragedy, wins and losses, highs and lows, events altogether something less than sensational. Had I not sought out my old friends, most of these lives would have gone unnoticed, unrecorded, except, of course, in memories kept dear by families and friends. But, paradoxically, the ordinariness of their lives is, by any standard, exceptional, given the adversities that marked not only their childhoods but often anticipated their birth.

Perhaps most exceptional in this social history is that these institutionalized children ultimately defied conventional wisdom and foiled the deterministic ideas of child development theorists. As adults they proved that they could be devoted and caring men and women and, despite the absence of (using current jargon) functional families and adequate role models in their early years, they became pretty good parents of pretty good children.

Some thoughts on how things turned out this way on closing this biography of lives and their meanings. I recapitulate two pervasive and far-reaching themes: one, the influence of the traditions of Yiddishkeit; the other, the corresponding folkways of trust and expectation. Ordinarily, we tend to search for roots and causes only when lives turn sour, when children wind up in serious trouble. It is harder to figure out how families thrive and children succeed. Familiar with the conventional wisdom about the dire outcomes of asylum life, I put these ideas to the test by encouraging whenever possible my companions' reflections on what, if any, influence growing up in the Home had on family life and raising children.

I half expected the alumni to be a bit defensive about their roles as parents since it is so hard to escape popularized notions about the dreadful effects of childhood separation and institutionalization on adulthood. Freud's proclamation that the personality of the individual is permanently shaped during the first five or so years is generally accepted as gospel. John Bowlby, the acknowledged authority on separation, focused on the lasting penalties of a child's loss of affectional relationships: "Intimate relationships . . . are the hub around which a person's life revolves . . . on into old age."[6] And William Goldfarb, who is recognized for his research on institutional and foster care children, was even more forbidding when he concluded that the deprivation experience of institution children results in their being fixated on the most primitive levels of conceptual and emotional behavior.[7]

In fact, many colleagues predicted that I would quickly discover the price of institutional life when it came to interpersonal relationships. While quite the contrary was proved, this misgiving was expressed at one point by Sharon, Anna's daughter-in-law, at one of our gatherings. After our barbecue dinner, Sharon sat on the floor in our circle, resting against Anna's legs, captivated by the discussion among the alumni. The elders, some already grandparents of college-aged young adults, were in harmony that they were "plenty equipped" to be parents when Sharon broke in: "Coming from an environment where your emotional needs were not met, didn't it influence the way you treated your own children? There's something about the way you all are. You expect a higher level of emotional commitment than maybe other people—and maybe sooner." The rest of the group didn't appear to find her charge peculiar. "That's the way we are," they shrugged and agreed, "Sure, I guess we do expect more."

Let me speak for the alumni to explain this phenomenon in relation to my earlier argument that the Children's Home was home for its wards despite the absence of the intimacies of normal family life. In this safe haven, the native relationships that were marked by trust and caring offered not an alternative exactly but its own encouragement for the shaping of a stable self. As so many of the alumni recalled, there was a sense of groupness, unity—even if it was sometimes only a common bulwark against patriarchal control and oppression. Amid the squabbles and conflicts of congregate living, a child might feel a measure of acceptance even if it took the form, as Morrie remembered, of another kid bringing a spoonful of castor oil.

Caring and trust affected, of course, not only how they interacted but what they expected of one another: to put it simply, my trust in you is predicated on my confidence that you have some trust in me and therefore I expect you to respond in like manner. More important, this trust will be tested and molded over time, shaping how we are with one another. Are these the kinds of high expectations that Sharon sensed in what she called, "a higher level of emotional commitment than maybe other people?" In various ways, some former residents confirmed this in their response to my question, "Having missed the experience of family life, how come you turned out to be such good parents?"

One graduate's—Jake's—expectations had a moral center. He thought that as you grow up "you look around and get to know what you'd like as a family, especially what is right and wrong." For him, Mr. Hollander was a dominant figure "who had some effect on my ideas." Jake didn't think that he was too strict as a father: "I would stand my son in the corner, I wouldn't hit him ever, but I had to make him understand when he did something wrong. Both Reva and I felt that way." Reva, with tender pride, added that their son looks and sounds like his father. "He's a research chemist. Went to MIT and got his doctorate at Brandeis. Then a year of postgrad work at Hebrew University in Jerusalem. And three wonderful grandchildren."

Bertha responded in her direct and terse style. She advised me that although "my feeling when I got out of there was that my kids aren't going to want for nothing," they were still supposed to be responsible for what they got. Bertha bought her two little girls a little toy table and two chairs. "Paid 50 cents a week. I'll never forget." The kids left them out in the rain and they were ruined "and I was still paying on it." She remembered how mad she was but "I got them to understand that if you don't take care of things you shouldn't have them."

Miriam agreed that she and Sy raised good children. "Maybe what we didn't have as children we wanted our children to have." At the same time, she saw herself as a strict mother who expected a great deal from her children: "You know, the discipline we were raised with wasn't all that bad. In fact, maybe we should turn back the pages a little bit to how it was."

Before Morrie and Ethel replied, they made known that two sons had earned doctorates, one at MIT, the other at Berkeley. A third son was completing college and working for the government. Morrie felt that he learned something from the Home, from being with the kids who became his family, his world. As he mentioned earlier, helping others, volunteering, was his philosophy and their boys shared this commitment. He agreed with Ethel's portrayal of him as a strict father who demanded quite a bit from their sons: "Maybe too strict, I don't know. But we played a lot, we all went camping for years. They knew they would have to set up a kitchen for their mother before they could play. We had to have organization." How did they make it through school? "On their own," Morrie replied, "by work, scholarships, and grants. I told them they would either work with their heads or their hands."

"Terrific!" was Lill's response to my question about how she raised her children. She, too, spoke in accord with Yiddish standards for achievement: "One of my sons is a medical doctor, the other a teacher. Both doing real well." But she always expected they would get a good education and do well. "Living in an institution made me realize that kids have to know they can talk with somebody. Because I never got it then, we never were and still aren't ashamed to say, 'I love you.' I would never allow my children to go through anything like I went through. They had to do something with their lives. That's all there was to it."

Other alumni added their variations on how they judged themselves as parents, but within a basic framework: all graduates felt the imprint of the coarse regimentation of the Children's Home, the stigma and the separation; still, that imprint, with maturity, was refashioned into earnest values and expectations that molded how they were as parents. Paraphrasing Phil's words, the graduates chose meanings that strengthened rather than excused their identities as parents.

It is not surprising that, as parents, many alumni tended to fall back on what they knew best, the patriarchal and matriarchal structure and rules once imposed on them as children. Not many graduates even hinted at an inclination to be overly permissive, lenient, or indulgent parents. But, to be sure, within these expectations their children were treated with compassion, care, trust, and affection—sentiments their parents missed in their institutional years.

The spirit of trust and expectation, the standards of the parental role, and the like are, of course, grounded in the beliefs, the culture, the ancestral traditions of Yiddishkeit: while these beliefs predominated in this setting, they could, if it were another institution, be grounded in other ideologies. Being a Jew—perhaps more so then than now—was an active way of life: how you were, what you were, what you did as a Jew are what counted, with or without formal creeds and rites. No one thought of Jewishness as something you acquired; many would not be surprised if it were discovered that it was genetic, an inherited characteristic. Such beliefs, in natural and instinctive ways, ordered the quality and character of one's life—not overlooking gastronomic pleasures, politics, opinions, charities, relations with gentiles, and so on. Yiddishkeit embraced folks who pray three times a day—at early morning *shachris,* afternoon *mincha,* and evening *maariv*—and those who observe only the High Holidays; it accommodated believers who were Orthodox, or Conservative, or Reformed in persuasion; it included families living on or around the aromatic commerce of shabby Joseph Avenue or residents of the shady, quiet, fancy Brighton areas of Rochester; and it didn't differentiate between children who got their religious training every day after school at the musty Talmud Torah on Baden Street or in the luminous Sunday school classrooms of the modern Reformed temple.

Talking with Morrie amid the savory odors of simmering borscht, there was no question that his family also shared these lineaments of Yiddishkeit. But for Morrie and his wife, and for his two thriving sons as well, it was something more: "So much of the Jewish religion has pointed the way for the rest of the world. It's not so much the ritual as the moral teaching . . . and you can't profit from the moral teaching unless you follow some of the precepts. That's been our way of life, in my volunteer work, in my work with the Scouts, and in how we raised our sons. Then there is the *shabbes* (Sabbath). It is a pleasure for us. We can relax. It is like being a king for one day."

Most alumni were, of course, considerably less doctrinaire, recalling the exacting religious routines with far more disaffection. As one put it, "There was enough religion to almost make me convert to Christianity afterwards." Or as Will protested: "To this day I will not sing *ʒmires* (Sabbath psalms or songs) whether at Temple Beth El or even in Israel. I don't care—because *I had to do it!* After every meal. God knows I am thankful for that meal. But *I will not do it now!*" Where Judaism in its Orthodox form was something that was imposed, Yiddishkeit, more gently, was something that you were, that you lived, that gave you a sense of citizenship among your own people.

In chapter 2 I cited Charles Silberman's observations based on his fine study of American Jewry. He underscored the distinctive nature of Jewish parent-child relationships in which parents see their children as extensions of themselves: the child's success becomes the parents' success; the child's failure, the parents' failure. A striking finding of my study is the remarkable achievements and success of the alumni's children—the extraordinary number of Ph.D.'s, doctors, professors, and other professionals.

Silberman explains that Jewish parents doted on their children "but not in the sense of being free to follow their own whims. On the contrary, indulgence was accompanied by high expectations and rigorous standards, for parents were anything but modest in their ambitions for their children. . . . Every child-rearing practice entails some risk . . . but the risk of too much love and nurture are smaller than those of too little."[8] The graduates of the Rochester Jewish

Children's Home would, from their experience, readily claim this statement as of their own making.

Our search for meanings narrows down to a fine point: no matter how we explain or try to put these stories and accounts in some perspective, no matter the realities of deprivation or hardships, what counts in any group or culture is its commitment to the value of a wholesome family and the ability to nourish a succeeding generation of worthwhile, contributing citizens. The kids, the graduates of the Jewish Children's Home, came through.

EIGHT

Closings

The years prior to the opening of the Rochester Jewish Children's Home were not periods particularly concerned with statistics or reports about problems and needs, especially in the immigrant Jewish community. The many charities of that community, some duplicating and overlapping others, tried to be independent of the German-Jewish charities as they did their best to relieve suffering, provide medical care, housing, free Hebrew education, and financial aid for the "deserving Jewish poor."[1] Thus, we cannot know how extensive was the plight of children in the community that begged the elders, the grand benefactors, to found the Children's Home, "our" orphanage, an institution where Jewish children would be subject to proper Orthodox upbringing.

The increase in numbers—from the first six waifs who came through the doors of 27 Gorham Street in June 1914 to the 140 children admitted in the next ten years—proved the wisdom of their plan. Thirty-four years later, on July 1, 1948, the Home was closed. The number of resident children who departed through the doors of 27 Gorham Street in that year was not much greater than the six who entered in 1914.

In this final chapter, I will comment on the significance of those thirty-four institutional years. The inferences that can be drawn about the Children's Home and the lives it sheltered and sustained are intriguing in relation to Rochester and the local immigrant Jewish community. What can be learned from this study also allows for wider generalizations about institutional life since the Rochester enterprise was very similar to children's institutions in Cleveland, New York, and other urban areas. And so, although this study is of historical interest, what it has to say about the benefits and losses of this form of child care also can usefully be extrapolated to issues in the institutional care of current young victims of abuse, of family collapse, and other problems peculiar to our times.

Before these concluding matters are considered, it is important that we close the circle of this account by taking note of the circumstances involved in the closing of the Children's Home. By 1948, it was five years since my departure and I was many miles distant from Rochester: thus, I had no first-hand knowledge about the final act of this drama. Even in my last years in Rochester my involvement in the goings-on at the Home across the street had already faded. In this time I had discovered other pleasures afforded by the Jewish Center, the Jewish Young Men and Women's Association—fraternal clubs, sports, dances, and most of all, the occasion to meet girls. I also detected, sadly enough, that although the routines and patterns of the Home were the same, its spirit and ethos had dwindled, become flat.

As is the case when the life of an established organization is in a critical state, personal needs, egos, and, in this instance, the temperaments of patriarchs, are aroused. And so the event produces more than one story. There is, first, the cool official study and recommendations of the Board of Directors; I was fortunate to find this one surviving record of the Board's deliberations. The second, more impassioned, is Will's recollection of himself as a protagonist in the intrigue and drama that led to the closing of the Jewish Children's Home. He was at the time a graduate social worker.

THE BOARD'S STRATEGY

Although no mention can be found, evidence must have been mounting in the last five years of the Home's life that serious changes were occurring. Nothing in the *Home Review*—even up to the last months of the Home's lifetime— gave any sign of the impending closing. The auxiliaries, the Mothers Club, and Big Brothers and Sisters, whose existences were tied to the Home's durability, appeared to be unaware of the inevitable end and its implication for their futures. The *Home Review* in 1948 carried frequent articles of tribute to the returning servicemen, almost seventy in number, virtually all the residents fit for service. And from the burgeoning alumni, the newsletter published the bountiful letters to Mr. Hollander, many of them nostalgic and teary, recalling the good days in the Home and the superintendent's generosities. But no mention of the ending that would soon occur.

It is all the more ironic that the administration of the Jewish Children's Home insisted on marching in its fixed lockstep to such an abrupt end, apparently oblivious or indifferent to the important changes occurring in the field of child care. And the irony grows as we recall that superintendent Hollander had been active for over twenty years as a leader, consultant, and chairman in the State Conference of Social Work. Up to the time of the Home's closing he participated in annual meetings of the National Conference on Jewish Social Welfare.

· In that time, the role of institutions in child care and child welfare was subject to careful study.[2] In one camp were specialists who argued for the closing of these institutions, proposing that children be placed in foster care or returned to their own homes with adequate allowances from federal-state programs of Aid to Dependent Children. The second camp included growing numbers of child-care experts who supported the institution as a favorable method of care for certain children. They showed that many traditional, "orphanage"-type programs had already converted to more progressive community centers, cottage plans, and children's villages over the previous decade. But the conditions weighed in chapter 4, the "dictates of Talmudic teaching," the rigid doctrines of Orthodox Judaism, persevered and justified the Rochester Home's reliance on prescribed customs and procedures. That they had become as outdated and outmoded as the Home's stern, quasi-Victorian buildings and its meager, patriarchally driven staff was undeniable. One had only to consider the progressive changes occurring in other Jewish institutions of that same period that included professional staffs of caseworkers, teachers, recreation workers, and psychiatrists who served the children.

There was a second conspicuous state of affairs that, if heeded, would predict the finish of the Children's Home. Not only was the resident population shrinking but, of greater consequence, the nature of the children's problems and the reasons for their admittance also were changing in radical ways. The original mission of the Jewish Children's Home, created to shelter dependent children of immigrant families, had already been bent to respond to the problems of children of second generation families. In its final years, the Home declined into a catchall of sorts, admitting children for various and uncertain reasons apparently in the vain attempt to stay open. Only thirty-four children entered in the last eight years, half for reasons of parental neglect, marital conflict and divorce, predelinquency, and habitual truancy. For the balance, the Children's Home was a temporary shelter—from two weeks to a few months—for young children whose mothers were hospitalized for medical or surgical reasons.

In early 1947, the Executive Committee of the Home's Board of Directors appointed a subcommittee, chaired by the Board's President, Hyman Kolko. Its charge, circumspectly stated, was "to consider questions which had been presented with relation to the operations of the Home." The committee report perfunctorily referred to "trends in child care throughout the nation" and shifted its attention to the population size of the Home and costs of operation. The principal findings: in the last ten-year span, the population of the Children's Home had dwindled by over one-half to twenty children; the proportion of "other than normal children" had increased; and the annual cost of maintenance for each child had doubled, from $570 in 1937 to $1,125 in 1946. In the most recent year, two children had been admitted and twelve had been discharged. Without comment, a table was appended showing that progressive Jewish institutions continued to flourish in major urban areas.

Included in the committee's report was a carefully phrased letter from David Crystal, then Executive Director of the Jewish Social Service Bureau of Rochester. After offering a statistical accounting of the success of foster care services provided by the Bureau, Mr. Crystal suggested it might be helpful if he could discuss the whole problem "with the group who see an institution as the only and best resource for foster care." A memorandum from the executive secretary of the Council of Social Agencies called attention to the obsolescence of the conventional children's institution, a result of the support of Aid to Dependent Children, the efforts of social agencies to keep children in their own homes, the raising of the admission age level, and the elimination of long-term care. The committee's report concluded with a series of questions: (1) Has "our Home" outlived its usefulness?; (2) Should it be preserved as a state-wide Home for Jewish Children?; (3) Shall the Home be closed?

In the last issue of the *Home Review* (in its twenty-second year) that carried many tributes to Mr. Hollander, Hy Kolko's statement formally answered these questions. After announcing the official closing, he added: "The decision to close was made by the Board after a long study made by the Board of Directors. The population of the Home has been on the decrease for a number of years due primarily to the fact that the tendency in social service work has been to rehabilitate homes and to keep children wherever possible within their own family circles and to give adequate support to these families for such purposes."

This was the objectively framed decision based on an impersonal, solemn document of the kind that only a committee can beget. At variance is a more turbulent story of the person who, standing alone, was shoved onto mid-stage in the melodrama that was the undoing of the Home. It was, of course, worthy Will, the Will who had been the beneficiary of what few goods the Children's Home could offer. Because he had made the most of these benefits he was now in the absurd position of "the expert" who could influence the demise of the Home that, for his lifetime, had been *his* home.

At the time that these currents were shifting toward the ultimate closing of the Children's Home, Will was completing the second and final year of his master's in social work program at the University of Buffalo. I know that interval of professional education intimately: my own experiences as a student and teacher remind me that it is a time of sudden and often outraged awakening to society's ills, to the needs of the young, the old, the deprived. Will could not help but be an impassioned critic of this anachronism called The Home.

Will knew nothing of the inquiries and report of Hy Kolko's committee. But since he knew and admired David Crystal, personally and professionally, Will knew full well that Crystal's antipathy toward the institution was considerably stronger than what Crystal had stated in his prudent letter. As Will recalled, there was a fight going on in the community about keeping the Home alive; Will was drawn in as an expert speaking for the "closers."

As he remembered, he didn't know what started the movement, whether it was recommendations by the Community Chest or Department of Social Services. It made no difference because, "It's what *I* saw, the kids who were there, really troubled kids!" He added that it was too late, "it was over Jake's head.

He got by when I was there, when the Home was a place for 'orphans' and we were family. But these kids were different, troubled."

He was called by a member of the Board of Directors, a successful lawyer, all "blood and guts." "He says, 'Willie, you social workers do right. We are having a meeting at the Home and I would like you to be there.' That's how I got in."

Will paused, sighed deeply, and went on:

> They called me in. I don't remember who was there—Hy Kolko I suppose. I didn't bring new ideas, what I learned at the School. I just said what I felt. Later, one of the other members took me aside and said, 'What an ingrate.' Oy, what a splitting headache I had on the drive home. Remember, I was a favorite son, went to school, president of my class and then I come in and says as a second year student in the School of Social Work that the Home is no longer serving the needs of the community.

And so, the ironies of having to adapt to such disparate roles—resident, alumnus, and now the one who would help decide the Home's existence—were immense. Will's summation: "Jake Hollander did such a good job of making me a moral person that I couldn't stand to see what was happening to these kids in that place. If I didn't feel that way then I should have been kicked out of the School of Social Work. So I had to do it. It was like testifying against your father."

That "father," the patriarch of the Home was, at the closing of *his* institution, still a few years shy of sixty, vigorous and persistent in how he resisted the inevitable final event. That the Home had already outlived its original mission and that he was serving either as a temporary caretaker of transient children or as a custodian of delinquents were not persuasive enough reasons for the superintendent to voluntarily give up his domain.

Certainly the tributes, praise, and acclamations that immediately followed the end of his office must have eased his loss. The Board of Directors was first to "tender Mr. Hollander a testimonial banquet where leaders of the Jewish and non-Jewish circles paid tribute." There he was given a gold pen and pencil set and Mrs. Hollander a wristwatch.

At a JYM-WA banquet, "many of his 350 'children' came to honor him . . . Mayor Dicker bore the greetings of the city." Station WHEC saluted Jacob S. Hollander as Citizen of the Day, citing him as "one of the best loved citizens . . . Rochester's best and most useful Community Chest campaigner . . . one of the best story tellers . . . a contributor to interfaith understanding." Other tributes appeared in Rochester's newspapers.

Jacob Hollander continued to preside over religious services at the Hart Synagogue on the grounds of the Home. He remained an advisor to the Alumni Association, and was elected to the Board of Directors that carried on (even into the present) to provide scholarships. The tribute to Hollander in the

Hillel School yearbook of 1973 following his death at eighty-one observed that when he refused to retire following the Home's closing, he was offered positions with "leading institutions in other cities." He chose, however, to pursue his interest in Jewish education. He headed the Rochester Talmud Torah and became founder and vice president of Hillel School, oddly enough, a modern progressive program that, as the yearbook stated, offered children "a comprehensive knowledge of the language and history of our people . . . fundamental learning in Judaism as a guide for life . . . a warm feeling of belonging . . . an understanding of one's self."

AN OVERVIEW

I mentioned earlier that my original plan for this study was rather unassuming: there was a recurring itch to learn something about the lives of my old friends, the kids who grew up across Gorham Street. Thus, the casual rhetorical question, "What became of Gabby, Mike, and the other guys?" got translated into its more researchable form.

Why expend so much energy, time, and resources studying this bunch? I am not sure that I can offer a rational answer; part of it, it seems to me, has something to do with the mysteries of life after youth. With the momentous event of graduation from George Washington or Ben Franklin High behind us, Sol, Jack, Eugene, and others like myself, who had our own homes and parents, made the expected transition: most of us got jobs; only one or two, like Eugene, went to college; all of us soon were invited to join in the second World War. We thought of ourselves as adults—well, sort of. We had a few dollars in our pockets, enough for dates and some clothes, but we continued to live at home with parents who learned not to ask too many questions.

That isn't how it was with the kids from the Home. Not by their own choice, they were expected to become instant, full-fledged adults. Some returned to live with parents or relatives for a short time. Others scraped by as shoe salesmen. The Home provided a fair number with very modest scholarships to attend college. All, however, dropped out of my young man's world as I knew it then. With time passing, I continued to wonder about their fate.

And so, my first proposal for funding had reasonable but modest ambitions: as I first put it, "to derive respondents' impressions and perceptions of growing up in custodial care . . . how acquired beliefs shaped their subsequent lives." The opening chapters of this book tell how I discovered just how narrow was my original intent. To be sure, the memories, thoughts, stories of the Home's kids are at the heart of this work; but they are inchoate when removed from the encompassing values and customs of community, culture, and religion and the regulations and routines of institutional life.

The study of human lives and systems, their complexities and irregularities, cannot help but produce results that echo these ambiguous characteristics. In these last pages, I will try to round out this study and strive for a few degrees more of coherence. Because of the unpredictable nature of ethnography, the research plan deserves a few comments. I will then draw together some thoughts about the Jewish Children's Home as the milieu for the children's early years and go on to take up the pressing question, Why did lives rooted early in the ordeals of institutional life turn out ahead of the game? Or in the way I was often asked, Why didn't the expected occur? Why didn't deprivation and loss turn into disorder or calamity? Last, I will consider how the results of this inquiry might be instructive, assuming that children's institutions offer certain remedies for children suffering the catastrophes of present day society.

RETHINKING THE STUDY AND ITS METHODS

I have said at various points in this book that this study is an exercise in interpretation, a deliberate and disciplined use of subjective and reflective talents. The intent in joining the methods of ethnography, a well-proven anthropological research device, with the use of social history was, in the words of an eminent anthropologist, to reveal "the symbolic forms—words, images, institutions, behaviors—in terms of which, in each place, people actually represent themselves to themselves and to one another."[3] These methods included interviewing, gathering life histories of former wards of the Home, and focus groups whose members reconstructed versions of life in the Home. The analysis of archival records, material, and texts provided some useful facts about the Home and its residents. It is worth adding that, if only in a vicarious sense, I was a *participant-observer* to the extent that my many memories of and familiarity with life in the Children's Home offered advantages, insights, and clues that would not be available to a more impartial researcher.

Again, my queries and conversations were not in search of facts or other forms of supposedly "hard data" that could be converted into statistical frequencies and distributions. Neither did I assume that my respondents, or even the printed records, newsletters, and the like, could give me objective truths about the Children's Home and its people. To quote the intellectual historian, Hayden White, "It is possible to tell several stories about the past, and there is no way, finally, to check them against the fact of the matter. The criterion for evaluating them is moral or poetic."[4]

Research that tracks down the facts-of-the-matter is generally tabular, serial, quantifiable. When research deals with stories, autobiographies, or other personal reports, the inquiry takes on a more metaphoric complexion: the facts-of-the-matter are often transformed into myths or sagas that lend a touch of drama, mystery, or heroism to the ordinary record of life. It is quickly apparent that, in trying to understand anyone's personal account, it can be sliced in many ways.

Shelley Taylor, for example, speaks of the illusions one must create when, above all, the event in question (like having been institutionalized) might threaten one's self-esteem and well-being.[5] Taylor maintains that the need to devise an illusion is neither a dishonest nor an unhealthy act; as illusions burnished the reminiscences of the Home's alumni, they served to strengthen feelings of self-esteem and worth. This ploy of the teller's imagination works out a soothing scheme, the invention of an account of what occurred, why, and how that explanation resolves what would otherwise remain a painful experience. Some former wards managed this search quite simply, explaining, "That's the way it was, then. Who knew different?" Others went to some length to tease out something halfway positive from the troubling past. The illusion also allows one the sense of personal control and the ability to master distress. Rarely did I come across reconstructions of the past that did not underscore the morale of surviving, of "making it"; some even spoke of personal triumph. Not the least, the illusion confirms one's goodness and merits when all the successes are sorted out and one comes to feel part of, identifies with, a fraternity "that always did good."

Often the voices of my narrators would shift in person, in time, or in place. As I mentioned earlier, the flow and meanings of the alumni's recollections would sometimes switch between *two* voices: one, the confident declarations of the elderly narrator; the other, the forlorn murmurings of the child whom the story is all about.

And yet another slice of a personal reality spreads between these illusions, voices, and other factors. As I listened closely to the tales and banter about those early years and later life, it occurred to me that the story itself would often shift in focus and purpose. To put it simply, the narrative could be *incidental*, centered on a specific, seemingly freestanding event, and/or *existential*, expressing a greater life theme. The former is not insignificant: the teller might have many purposes in recounting certain incidents—to amuse, convince, prove something, or illustrate one's talents, for example. The Friday night kugel capers, the lumpy oatmeal tactics, twenty girls in one bathroom, "when I got my first period," becoming a shoe salesman—these and numberless other episodes tell about the special events that embellish the otherwise unexceptional routines of life. In the stories we have reviewed it is evident that these episodes often weave into and provide the gist of the larger existential narrative: Bertha's life theme of never being victim is expressed by the tricks she pulled on Hollander; Joey's commitment to "doing it on my own" is seasoned with accounts of his solitary cracks at "making a buck."

That, as White said about stories of the past, "there is no way, finally, to check them against the fact of the matter," is underscored when other ambiguities are noted. There is the matter of unavoidable selectivity involved in who is telling the story and how the story is told; in gender differences; the inevitable moral overtones that can be heard; and in the role of the researcher who may interpret sometimes as an insider, other times an outsider. Just these few tensions make it apparent why a more modest investigator might prefer to count noses, frequencies, and distributions. Still, if we can be comfortable, as we are in daily life, with narrative blends of "truths" and "fictions," the ethnographic inquiry will awaken not just understanding but *verstehen*, an even deeper sense of knowing, compassion, forbearance, and, on occasion, celebration of spirit and triumph.

This text is, itself, a story—a montage of collected words, records, pictures of people and events. It is an unfinished account of hardship joined with the ironies and paradoxes of the patriarchal institution, all tempered by Yiddish wit and enthusiasm. As social research it is a story that differs in an important way from fiction. Both reflect the creativity and imagination of the human mind, but where the novelist is free to conjure up any plot or character, the social researcher is constrained in his or her interpretations by the information and observations gathered. Both fiction and ethnography deal with lives but the novelist can remain invisible, allowing the story, in a manner of speaking, to tell itself. The researcher, because he or she is the journey's guide and interpreter, must be ever "up front." Personal bias, the urge to generalize, or other dispositions cannot be shut out of inquiry that places the researcher midst the lives and affairs of real people. Therefore, over the course of this report I have tried to share with the reader my rationales and perspectives.

THE JEWISH CHILDREN'S HOME

As I have traced them, the procedures, philosophy, and standards of the Home were vestiges of child care of another day; as an image out of time, the Children's Home fits the classic outlines of the concept of an institution, orphanage, or asylum. Thus, it is useful to recall and sum up select features of the Home and its wards as a prelude to some thoughts about the role of institutions for children as redress for current social problems. Such traces of the past are instructive in suggesting a vision of institutional care that can benefit particular casualties of present social disorders.

To say it again, an institution is a social invention designed to ameliorate the intractable problem of what to do about the dependent child, the cast-off child, the hopeless child. Society's romance with foster care as a tolerable substitute for family life or as a preferable alternative to institutional care has come to grief all too often. At its best, the institution or asylum literally *saved* children, rescuing them from the streets, alleys, and their noxious families. To counteract what was considered a young life already corrupted, the asylum, in effect, set out to remoralize the child and instill a sense of self-reliance and virtue.

In creating a protective shelter, the Rochester Jewish Children's Home was founded in accord with these intentions. Unlike modern social services, the Home's birth was a simple and specific expression of the immigrant Jewish community's concern about its shattered families and dependent children. It was not an upshot of a needs survey or the result of deliberations by a centralized planning body; the elders of the local community—Rabbi Sadowsky,

A. D. Joffe, Hy Kolko, William Markin, Alfred Hart, and others—simply determined that a shelter was needed and with dedication and personal effort brought the Home into being.

Like other children's asylums grounded in a system of moral beliefs (whether secular or ecclesiastical), the Jewish Children's Home was governed by its own paternalistic principles. Bound by the enduring and rigid framework of Orthodox Judaism and based on the Halakah, the laws of the Scriptures, the Home's philosophy, program, and methods were firmly cast: at the center was the injunction for the child's respect for and obligation to parents or their surrogates. This imperative did not have to be articulated or formalized as a policy statement: it was as ingrained as the understanding that food preparation would conform to the religious dietary laws.

Since such Orthodox doctrines had already survived, unscathed, the Diaspora with its inquisitions, exiles, pogroms, and other trials, there was no question that these Talmudic principles of child care would equally resist the progressive and secular recommendations of the emerging field of child welfare. At the same time, it must be said again that the patriarchy that characterized the discipline and routines of the Home was not out of line with the rules of many families and their expectations of their children in that time and community. Recall that the Children's Home was created and sustained precisely because the community felt that the other long established Jewish children's home in Rochester had become "modern" and "strayed" from fundamental Orthodox doctrines. The Home cleaved wholly to these doctrines; there is no indication that by so doing it provoked any discord among the administration, the Board, the community, and even the officials of the state welfare system about the basic efficiency, utility, and function of the Children's Home.

And so, from the outset, the ideology, culture, and rules of this institution were durably in place. The Home's mission in providing shelter, sustenance, and education for its wards was simple and straightforward: to produce a good Jew and good citizen, self-reliant and virtuous. Such bureaucratic trimmings as committee assignments and responsibilities, delegation of tasks, policy-making structures, and other complex systems that characterize modern social services were absent: the superintendent alone was in charge. To be sure, he was responsible to a Board of Directors whose membership rarely changed. But since patriarchs, at least the men of this group, respected one another's authority, Mr. Hollander exercised his power unhindered and singlehandedly. He was, as the kids put it, The Boss. As has been amply shown, the rules, rituals, and routines that he imposed, combined with his artful talents for popping up in unexpected corners, outlived the many changes occurring in child care during his tenure. Only the price of growing older restricted a few of his habits: in later years, the superintendent was less likely to chaperon the children's march to school or other events.

These few comments allude to the *structure* of the children's institution, the physical and organizational setting that enclosed the lives of our friends: it was a basic congregate arrangement, minimally staffed, controlled by top-down authority, strictly organized, regulated, and disciplined. It fit the common stereotype of the orphanage or asylum.

If an institution were defined by its *structure* alone, that factor alone would have to be considered an *independent variable* or the only major force that modifies the lives of its inmates. This perspective is faulty and inadequate: in real life, the institution must be regarded as an organism in which its structure, like the human constitution, is one of many dynamics that are unconditionally and bilaterally linked with other lives and other systems.

To be sure, the physical structure of the Children's Home, the motley assortment of worn buildings, was what first leaped to the eye; paired with the plain, proletarian architecture of St. Bridget's Church down the street, they encroached into the arrangement of working-class residences (and occasional homely shops) lining both sides of Gorham Street. But the Home was much more than just this shell of yellow bricks in the eyes of the community, its officials, and neighbors: some were grateful when it was welcomed as a needed shelter; others lamented its presence as just an "orphanage"; it was thought of favorably when the good deeds of its wards were recognized; and it was held with suspicion by some just because it was an asylum.

For its residents, the Home held many meanings. The children were quick to spot paradoxes and inconsistencies in the way the Home was structured, especially in its autocratic climate of inflexibility, regimentation, and control. To be sure, these regulations did preserve order and routines that scarcely changed over the years. At the same time, these codes of conduct were so strict or sufficiently absurd as to invite the kids to dare to test and challenge authority. With considerable zest, they schemed, outwitted, and overcame while, for survival purposes, conforming to the rules and routines of daily life; as is so evident, very few considered themselves passive unfortunates or hapless victims while they eagerly probed limits or exploited possibilities. The more capricious escapades became part of the residents' culture and tradition and, as I will show shortly, helped mold the quality of *resilience* that made flowering and growth possible. For they were discovering within and among themselves their unique talents for improvisation that later would prove to be useful, if not necessary, for solving the enigmas that were part of becoming an adult. As I learned from our conversations, a keen touch of irreverence seasoned their slant on life.

The children learned to adapt to the disparities between the coldness of an institution managed and operated by adults and the native warmth, as many alumni recalled, of a shared world of children where "people looked after you," "picked you up," "cared." I have always been grateful that I had been allowed to partake of this generous spirit of fraternity. Some of the Home's kids must have envied my being part of a real family (Phil speaks sentimentally of "the house of tall people across the street"; for "Rolly," our home was her secret "other home" where she would linger as long as possible). Of course, I took my family for granted. But because my sister and brother were much older—to me, almost grownups—I envied the kids' ready-made brotherhood. Even now, the companionship and pleasures the Home and its kids offered me as a child contribute to how I know and define myself.

The features of the Rochester Jewish Children's Home deserve to be noted again in more prototypical terms. In itself, it had its mission, creeds, administration and structure, its internal inconsistencies and dynamics, its opportunities and shortcomings, and was immediately situated in its immigrant community. Altogether, the spirit of Yiddishkeit was the glue that joined these many forces into a vibrant folk culture. Whereas Judaism decreed the concrete laws, rules, and rituals of the setting, Yiddishkeit shaped the norms, the more generous customs bearing on how (or if) such codes of conduct were carried out. In Yiddishkeit could be found the comfortable metaphors, the comic ironies of daily life. It supplied the idioms for earthy conversation; the recipes for gustatory delights; an ingrained moral sense of proper obligation to one's comrades; the unwritten laws that allowed for playful, inventive audacity and daring as rejoinders to pompous authority; and much more in relation to the countless paradoxes of being a Jew in an otherwise secular or Christian world.

Yiddishkeit did not in itself make the institution good or bad, helpful or harmful. It represented, however, the ethos of this particular institution, the customs, manners, beliefs that sculpted the special culture of the Home. The structure of the institution, the hard husk of rules and procedures, codified its purpose and identity. But its culture, the informal ways in how life gets worked out among its members, instilled the vitality, the peculiar cadence of being, zest, humor, and healthy defiance that made life more tolerable. And these conditions, in turn, nurtured the incentives, even the provocations, for healthy choices, for strength and resilience. And so, I will argue that although these dynamics may take many other forms, depending on the particular setting, they are the energies (whether in or out of harmony with program, plans, and functions) that need to be known and understood as the forces that drive the institution itself. This understanding is especially important in thinking about institutions that can serve contemporary needs of children.

THE CHILDREN—YOUNG AND OLD

Stories, memories, reflections fill these pages and chapters, celebrating ordinary lives. Were these lives less ordinary or less fortunate the task of attempting to explain why and how these things turned out as they did would be relatively straightforward. It would be possible to select from certain conventional theories and frameworks of child development and behavior that purport to explain what went wrong.

Considering that lives gone wrong was not evident, there are perspectives that might help explain (*a*) how these youngsters not only survived institutional life but, (*b*) matured as responsible, caring citizens who (*c*) were underrepresented on any official measure of dependency, crime, or mental health, and (*d*) over time maintained stable families and raised children whose achievements are truly exceptional.

Conventional explanatory schemes are closely linked to the "illness model" of psychology. Anthony and Cohler observe that the clinical eye, since Hippocratic times, has been trained to detect even the most minuscule aspects of disease, while at the same time paying little heed to the health and well-being of those who would scarcely bring themselves to the attention of clinicians.[6] If the latter did show up at the clinic, there would be no professional schedules to record their well-being. The clinician could only shrug and retreat mumbling something unpretentiously "unprofessional" about this person as "feeling well" or "doing OK."

Fortunately, these psychological frameworks have not been our only means for making sense of the intricacies and ambiguities of becoming an honest-to-goodness human being. Great literature has always been captivated with the inexhaustible forces within and outside the protagonist, always centered on the mystique of becoming rather than on tidy notions of phases, stages, and agents that have little to say about talent and power. The bildungsroman mentioned before in relation to Isidore's chronicle often came to mind as I listened over again to stories told about the adversities and adventures of early years and the crossing into adulthood. This genre of literature, the apprenticeship novel, captures these remarkable passages, telling in charming ways about the moral, psychological, and intellectual development of its young champion.

To be sure, the graduates' narratives are not as calculated and contrived as some of the classic novels about the rite of passage into adulthood.[7] Literary judgments aside, these graduates were the qualified authors of their own lives. Their stories and the narratives of others who have endured trauma and deprivation equally acclaim their personal qualities, their strength, inventiveness, playfulness, and endurance.

RESILIENCY

Only recently has the theory of resiliency claimed a small corner of the literature of the behavioral sciences. George Vaillant defines resilience as the "self righting tendencies" of the person, "both the capacity to be bent without breaking and the capacity, once bent, to spring back."[8] Reflecting on a fifty years longitudinal study of men whose childhoods were marked by severe risk, Vaillant tells how he was struck with their ability to "spin straw into gold, laugh at themselves, display empathy . . . and worry and plan realistically," characteristics that apply equally to the alumni of the Home. Gail Sheehy carries this definition a step further in her tribute to what she calls the "victorious personality":

> One may be born with a naturally resilient temperament, but one develops a victorious personality. Those who do often come to believe they are special, perhaps

meant to serve a purpose beyond themselves [consider the disproportionate number of the Home's alumni who entered the helping professions]. Among the elements that contribute to a victorious personality are the ability to bend according to circumstance, self-trust, social ease . . . and the understanding that one's plight is not unique.[9]

It may be overstatement to grant the concept of resiliency the status of a theory; certainly it lacks the sophistication and complexity—and the abstractness—of, say, Freudian or Eriksonian models of development. Indeed, it is a rather straightforward confirmation of the fact that people do flourish and prosper despite—and in some instances, in response to—hardship and handicap. It is a means of devising answers to the unorthodox question, "What went right?" in a field somberly preoccupied with the opposite question.

And so the concept of resiliency might not strike everyone as particularly novel or enlightening or as a breakthrough in the field of psychology. It is, after all, merely a high-flown version of what our culture has always admired about both the hardiness and pliability of the human spirit. While social Darwinism has taken this standard to an extreme, in a more kindly sense, society as a whole has always assumed that, perhaps with some help and support, its members will literally stand up and be counted. Nevertheless, when Anthony and Cohler set out to edit a text on resilience, they were astonished at the sparseness of the literature on this topic: "One would have thought that the picture of children triumphing over despairing, degrading, depressing, depriving, and deficient circumstances would have caught the immediate attention of both clinicians and researchers, but the survivors and thrivers appear to pass almost unnoticed amidst the holocaust of disadvantage and the tragedies of those who succumbed to it."[10]

The idea of resilience is not far removed from dominant attitudes and expectations in the periods prior to and succeeding the founding of the Children's Home. Its assumptions about the strength and powers of the person conform with the common-sense sentiments of that time, the belief that both children and adults are obligated to choose and act. I have not been able to show that John Dewey's philosophies of human behavior directly influenced Bernstein, Reeder, and other progressive superintendents of that era whose programs encouraged and developed such forms of resilience as self-reliance, independence, pride, and competency. Still, history tells us that Dewey's ideas increasingly gained acceptance by educators and others concerned with the well-being of children. Writing in 1922, he outlined a theory of action not foreign to current ideas about resilience. Speaking of freedom, Dewey observed that it contains three important elements: "(i) efficiency in action, ability to carry out plans despite cramping and thwarting obstacles; (ii) the capacity to vary plans, to change the course of action, to experience novelties; and (iii) the power of desire and choice to be factors in events."[11]

In the same period, textbooks on child development put these ideas in normative if not moralistic terms. Phyllis Blanchard, a social psychologist, placed responsibility squarely where she considered it belonged. She wrote in 1928: "From the viewpoint of the group, human behavior is roughly divided into two kinds: that which conforms to social standards and that which deviates so far from these standards as to be unacceptable. In judging the behavior of children, adult standards are used as the norm."[12] Dr. Blanchard's commentary tends to explain the terse, critical, and judgmental entries in the ward's records that I noted earlier. "Doing well at school, but still needs discipline," "stubborn and ungovernable," "indolent and inefficient, but helpful," "sweet smile and pleasant personality," or "neat and is interested in personal appearance," are judgments that correspond with this unconditional view of children's behavior.

These standards also corresponded with one's moral duties. "Virtuous" is perhaps as appropriate as "moral" since, as the above case entries show, estimations of one's character were based on the either/or judgments about whether one's actions conformed with or deviated from accepted social standards. Other virtues could include "courageous," "honest," "dependable," "cooperative," "hardworking," "thrifty"; their antitheses were, of course, considered vices.

In speaking about this kind of moral development, John Dewey cautioned that it would be a mistake to consider morality "as a separate department of life" detached from persons' actions and their consequences. "Such notions . . . have a bad effect," he advised.[13]

It would seem that the precept that one is morally responsible for his or her choices and actions is now outmoded. Daniel Moynihan recently despaired the "normalizing" of outrageous deviant and immoral acts in everyday society.[14] Whatever now is defined as "morality" is, indeed, "a separate department," or unrelated to persons' actions. Taking its place is the search for psychological causes or sociological conditions that intend to *explain* behavior; such explanations relieve the individual of personal responsibility for misdeeds or misconduct. Examples of the amorality that trouble Moynihan not only abound but morbidly saturate all mediums of public discourse about the sordidness and malignance of prevailing problems.

One example: A television drama produced to enlighten the public about the scourge of addiction absolutely dismisses the question of guilt and responsibility. An addictions counselor scorns a young woman's stubborn feelings of guilt for addicting her fetus, abandoning the infant, lying to her parents, and then having some part in the death of her husband. "So you abandoned the child," the counselor sniffs. And, as if guilt itself were somehow immoral, she questions, "So what does that make you? What do you get out of holding onto all that guilt?" Other wrongdoers can pick from a catalog of external "causes"—social, interpersonal, developmental, familial, genetic, chemical, birth order—to "explain" why they damaged themselves or others or why they deserve to be considered victims. And if these causes don't quite fit, one might be invited to grub among or delve into "repressed" memories to ferret out the "real" source of one's miseries, to achieve smug vindication.

Contrast between the present perspectives on morality and those of the times of the Children's Home are accented by the last example. Although the graduates were not preoccupied with memories of anguish bred by abuse, ridicule, rejection, loneliness, or incalculable other experiences, neither were these memories "repressed." They were managed, as their stories show, not harbored as necessary defenses: lines discriminating between good and bad, right or wrong, were clearly drawn.

These moral rules, akin in some way to the modern idea of resiliency, were linked to "being and doing right" and served as guiding virtues and values. Morrie's words are probably excessive but still credible as far as other alumni are concerned: "Not having the discipline before I went into the Home, religion gave me the moral teaching, the moral character that has guided my life." The everyday rules of living were manifest as were the consequences for transgression. You had to learn to play the game within these rules. Irv had it right and spoke for my companions and me when he said: "If you broke a rule and got caught, then you got punished. The trick was in not getting caught; if you did, you had better improve your technique to reduce the odds for the next caper."

Resiliency. What are its origins? Some behavioral scientists attempted to sort out the characteristics of people who appear to be of the resilient mold, those who, as children, struggled with adversity without special help and eventually found their way into a rewarding adulthood.[15] There is agreement about one thing: that, as children, they were not exceptional "superkids."

These investigators focused largely on the personality characteristics of resilient children—temperament, cognitive skills, and self-esteem—and their social skills involving curiosity about people, cooperativeness, and friendliness. It is, of course, hard to know what came first: whether these personal and social attributes begot resiliency or whether resiliency itself was the outcome of some inherent powers and so generated these attributes. They also allowed that the traits of resiliency do not add up like collecting grades or varsity points. Rather, they tend to swell exponentially. When a child takes risks or survives a serious threat, new skills and greater self-confidence accrue. These gains challenge the child to dare and test his- or herself in other venues of his or her life and so the adventures of living multiply. As Ruth said so plainly, "Because of the troubles I had to cope with from the very beginning, I learned very early that I had to rely on myself. So it seems like I always knew I could cope with whatever came along."

Judith Jordan, in her recent essay on resilience, states that the roots of resilient attitudes and behavior are not entirely located within the person or his social supports. More in line with the experience of the Home's children, the sources of mastery and resilience are seen as the give-and-take and mutualities of interpersonal relationships.[16] The former kids put this explanation in homelier terms: "it was camaraderie . . . my group," "there was always someone who cared what happened," "by my rules, I never put myself first," "other kids came to me for help and advice," and "I had to be the mother and fight for my sibs."

Jordan argues that current studies of the psychology of resilience are too limited since they focus largely either on the *individual's* acculturation or the gains of social support. Concentration on personality (how one turns inward to find strength) or social support (turning outward for assistance and comfort) is a "separate self" model of development that works in one-directional ways. Jordan contends that this model is *an individualized*, even isolated, conception of what it means to be resilient. She submits (and the words of the Home's alumni confirm) that resilience is a relational dynamic nurtured by a two-way process of mutuality and empathy—a process of "sharing with" more so than "getting from."

As Bertha said, "We all took an interest in each other . . . took up for each other." This unspoken bond eased misfortune, sadness, the penalties of life in the Home. More important, these fellowships encouraged and applauded any show of talent for battling with trial and hardship, thereby rewarding even a flicker of courage and self-confidence. Although trust and caring, as I said earlier, perhaps were not substitutes for the affection and intimacy of a family, such sympathies could be depended on as proofs that someone was there, that trust among people was possible.

I do not intend for these generous accounts to create an aura of mawkish sentimentality: although many of the alums honestly recall the brotherhood and amities of life in the Home, there were, as Phil reminded me, a pecking order and lots of bloody battles. Kids stole, cheated, lied, and played mean tricks as I remember very well, having been at times on the receiving end. There were snotty-faced kids, whiners, bedwetters, complainers, blamers—the unkempt, pimply, unwashed boys. (Somehow, memories of the girls present far more pleasant portraits despite "twenty girls to a bathroom.")

But all that was good or bad or even malicious in the way life worked out in the Home was behind the scenes, part of the children's own world, not obvious to adults. Yes, over time there were a few "big people" one could turn to as a friend or model—Al the nightwatchman, Manny Hirsch and a few other camp counselors, Mrs. Wall the laundress, a matron, Mrs. Dillenbeck. But it was the odd community of boys and girls, of older and younger kids, the weaker and the strong, the slow and the quick who made up the *we, us, our, our own* that counted. How *we* made it, survived, fell on *our* faces, got up, overcame, prospered depended on *us* and how *we* were with each other. Ironic as it sounds, one could legitimately argue that the absence of the psychological or mental health supports now deemed so essential might have, in fact, strengthened the resiliency and hardiness of the kids. Where was there to turn but one's group? Psychological services, on the other hand, by definition tend to *individualize* and even isolate the child, concerned as they are with the inner world of feelings, drives, and the like. In so doing, the symbiotic bonds, the union with others that fosters resilience, might be slackened.

Although the Home's children at times shared this private world, a small community of their own, it did not follow that, like the boys of Golding's *Lord of the Flies*, they needed to create their own society with its peculiar rites and rituals. Quite the contrary, the boys and girls of the Home, from their first breaths, were already joined to and made bearers of the tradition, culture, and doctrines of Yiddishkeit. In plain terms, their ethos told them who they were, where they belonged, and how they were supposed to be. That they came to be residents of the Jewish Children's Home was itself a result of Yiddish imperatives, the rules of *tzedakah* that obligated the community to care for and protect its dependents. And, as I have shown in so many ways, the bond between this network of children—this group that formed the theme of *"not a family but a home"*—and the larger culture in which it was blended further enriched the articles of faith of Yiddishkeit.

And so, what I speak of as *resilience* as the medium for explaining the generally good, dependable, and often altruistic lives of the Home's children is not a quantity of something that one is endowed with in some measure or degree. Jordan considers resilience as a state of mind—the way one perceives her world—that does not have to remain narrowly self-conscious but can be open to others and to the joy and experience of "being with," "being part of" valued relationships. It is no wonder that after a half century, virtually every graduate could tell me something about the circumstances of other alums' lives—how they were, their health and well-being, what they were up to—although it was likely that there had been no personal contact for very long periods. And as this book evolved, I was regularly informed about who was ill, who had died. It is also no wonder that so many of the kids turned to charitable and altruistic ends, some as professionals, others as volunteers in community work. In brief, resilience is tied to *perception* and *context*, in this instance, to the outlooks and relationships of these folk, young and old. It was not the raw experience, the fact of institutional life alone that impressed itself directly on the minds of the children like a wound or a bruise; what counted was what that life meant and more so, with whom it was shared.

Clearly, life in the Home was perceived in many ways. But as their retrospection made clear, the meanings were more or less affirmative—not signifying a shrug of resignation, but a certain pliancy and willingness to make the most of the cards they were dealt. "It was something you had to accept," one said plainly. For another it was "just part of growing up, that's the way it was." Others saw the benefits, taking into account their unfortunate circumstances: "It was a mitzvah that there was a place to go"; and "We had things I couldn't have had in my home." Bertha, of course, defined it as a challenge: "You could either be a sniveling little nothing or misbehave and upset others." And, as Phil and Will's self-accounts showed, the Home could be a place to do battle or an opportunity to be exploited. In all these instances, to be a mensch was the goal.

As to *context* and people, on the very first page Will introduced with affection "the neighborhood and the women who lived there." Context, again, is not just physical setting and its temperament alone, but the meanings attributed to their surroundings by those who make up its milieu. Even if the point about the variety and richness of the children's ambience is already well made, it is still worthwhile for purposes of review to catalog a few items. First, there was the ethos of the Home itself, the three inclusive worlds inhabited by the residents: the formal, disciplined and adult-created; the informal, the residents' shared and companionable relations; and the private, made of personal meanings. There was the moral and spiritual world of Judaism and the tribal culture of Yiddishkeit. And, without exhausting the inventory there were "extended families" tendered by the Mothers Club, the Big Brothers and Sisters, and other auxiliaries; the neighborhood and community because the Home had no walls; and the kids' personal associations with friends and relatives, at school, in pool halls, and in other singular interests.

In contrast with life in the "natural family," where one can usually depend on roles and responsibilities, protection and care, the Home's children were frequently involved in learning processes of negotiation and compromise. The stable consistencies of patriarchal control, regimentation, and routine should not be undervalued as safeguards. Still, within these boundaries, the kids scouted out every crack in the patriarchal fortress. They learned early about ambiguity and, often hypocrisy. They "knew" in so many ways the many facets of their only resident parent figure, Mr. Hollander. They were graceful and grateful beneficiaries of the kindnesses of outsiders while wrestling with the stigma that some felt kept company with charity. They knew the Children's Home, inside and out.

Few of these elders who joined with me in reconsidering their lives did so with great regret; pride and dignity, in fact, were common themes. Perhaps if these various explanations for essentially good lives were blended and a more fundamental interpretation was attempted, it might come out this way: They did well because there was no other way to do it, given what they asked of themselves: "I had to make good, I had to be something."

Alternatives and choices were few, even before the Great Depression and certainly during that era. Getting your high school diploma was an imperative; after graduation you might postpone finding a job for awhile by taking something called "postgraduate" courses at the high school. College was an indulgence few beside the fortunate scholarship-winning boys and girls of the Home could enjoy. In whatever endeavor, the options were clear: whether as a pupil, "shoe dog," stenographer, social worker, or homemaker you either succeeded or you failed. Neither was there the refuge nor defense offered by the mythologies of the psychologies: there were no external loopholes where personal responsibility and accountability could be comfortably displaced. In some odd ways, not having parents to account to gave at least a few of the graduates a freedom of choice about career, mates, and other crucial preferences. Unlike children who feel obligated to parents, scarcely any of the graduates mentioned regret or guilt about letting someone down, going against someone's wishes, or not taking someone's advice.

"You had to be a mensch." And the standards of menschkeit guided both childhood and the ensuing years of work, marriage, and parenthood. In their own families, in defiance of conventional theorizing, the tradition of menschkeit became the legacy of their children.

Then there is an even simpler explanation. Michael Sharlitt, in his autobiography of his evolution from an institutionalized orphan to the moving force as director in transforming the Cleveland Jewish Orphanage into the internationally known Bellefaire Home, put it plainly: "I was the beneficiary of the Jews' desire to take care of their own."[17]

We have completed an intimate venture into a collection of stories of overcoming, often of gaining victory over the ordeals of growing up in, by present standards, a primitive institution. And so, based on these revealing narratives, it might seem bizarre to recommend at least a reappraisal of children's institutions as a necessary corrective for the drastic problems of some of today's youngsters. To be sure, there is nothing in the structure, program, or administration of this archaic asylum to be recommended: there are not even any lessons to be learned since the consequences of punitive regulations and rigid controls are commonly understood.

Still, there is much that is instructive about the benefits of institutional life in the wisdom shared by the former wards of the Children's Home—though, certainly, they are not outspoken advocates of asylums. In their own ways, they allude to the dynamics of how children live together, compete, share, and otherwise create their community. They do not leave out their gratefulness for the security and haven the Home provided in the darkest times of childhood. And they speak of the supports for resilience and self-reliance, the foundations for adulthood.

Two additional attitudes now need to be considered relative to the place of the children's institution in current child welfare. The first deals with the deceptive issues (some already noted) that arise when institutional or group care is pitted against or compared with the ideal of the family. The second addresses the safeguards needed by all too many children now caught within alarmingly harmful circumstances.

INSTITUTION VERSUS FAMILY?

How people think about and plan for the needy, the unfortunate, or other dependent members of the human community cannot help but be weighted by bias, presupposition, everlasting ideals, or, for that matter, myths. One myth assumes that we inhabit a kind of Platonic world, one in which the ideal of perfectibility is forever on our horizons: one of these ideals includes the myth of the close and loving family, unscathed by the brutishness that too often contradicts this vision. This ideal leads to this biased edict: No one, certainly no child, should have to live apart from the family and certainly not in an institution.

This myth is hard to dislodge since it is so securely anchored in traditional systems of belief. It projects a glow of warm family life that is expressed in and reinforced by religion, song, art, poetry, films, and other persuasive icons. Unlike other social institutions, the myth of the family creates unquestioned standards that allow parents and children few degrees of freedom for error and deviation. The modern family is expected to be the source of spontaneous affiliation, love, respect, and interdependence where affection and genuine regard are offered without demand or qualification. When the family fails, the foster family or extended family, it is hoped, at least might work around the edges of this ideal.

Failing the attainment of such ideals, the consequence, particularly in recent years, is the escalation of new pseudo-psychological industries, each promoting its own rendition of the "unhealthy family." Take your pick among *toxic, dysfunctional, co-dependent, abusive,* or *enmeshed* family types, to name a few. In an ironically titled article, "Are Parents Bad for Children?,"[18] Dana Mack refers to the rash of TV programs on parental cruelty, the list of almost 100 popular books on child abuse, and the do-it-yourself "de-repressioning of early abuses" that question whether children can indeed be entrusted to the care of their parents.

Such myths about ideal family life do little to enhance the respectability of group care for children. By comparison, the children's institution is likely to be viewed as a second- (or lesser) rate, artificial contrivance in which empathies and affections, if they are at all present, show up only after the more practical designs such as shelter, protection, and guidance are firmly in place. More so, this argument sees the loving spirit and heart of the family as "normal"; any kindness that might be found in the institution would be deemed to be "professional," part of someone's job. The need to make this comparison in the first place has been challenged here by the theme of the institution's former occupants: "It wasn't family, *but it was Home.*"

Alfred Kadushin, prominent in the field of child welfare, also strikes at these prevailing beliefs, charging that professionals in the field of child care are "victims of our own propaganda."[19] He explains that "we are family chauvinists" who assume that there is no good substitute for the family. Kadushin adds: "The tendency is to compare institutional care with an idealized version of foster family care. It needs to be remembered that foster families are *not* highly selected . . . that there is a high rate of turnover of foster families making for discontinuity of care. It needs to be remembered, also, that a structurally intact, but emotionally broken family may be more pathogenic than institutional placement."[20]

A similar, but perhaps more metaphoric position is taken by Martin Wolins, who reports on field studies of successful group care of children in Israel, the

Soviet Union, and Austria. He contends that "group care for young children and infants especially was, like eating garlic in public, just not right in a self-respecting society."[21] What is overlooked, he adds, is that at one time the adulation of motherhood and familiness was characteristic of the higher classes who employed nannies or had their children reared in boarding schools. The poor had access only to the orphanage. Against this background, Wolins notes, it was not surprising that many writers, such as Bowlby and Goldfarb, exploited this "evidence" to support the successes of families and the failure of the asylum. Children's institutions, Wolins asserts, like the stable family, can claim responsibility for the moral learning of their members, for the acquisition and knowledge of role performance, for teaching a member "to be a somebody rather than remain a something."[22]

The lives of Will and Phil and the other children in this study are surely consonant with Wolins' argument as are the judgments about institutions made by others who survived the experience. Dr. Aring's reflections on his early years in an orphanage, reported in chapter 2, emphasize the importance of the "extended family," the prominent advantage and support of life in the institution. He encourages broadening this concept to make the institution intergenerational. And Hyman Bogen, in his memoirs and history of life in the Hebrew Orphan Asylum of New York, recommends: "Group homes . . . are needed as backup for the foster home system to ensure that all needy children receive some form of consistent care. They offer stability, security, structure, values that should not be minimized at a time when the foster home system has become a huge revolving door."[23]

As a postscript, Bogen quotes the opinion of nationally known Art Buchwald who, like Mr. Bogen, is an alumnus of the Hebrew Orphan Asylum: "It is probably one of the most successful organizations in existence because it glues together people who have experienced a unique childhood—not necessarily good and not necessarily bad—but unique."[24]

Unique, to be sure. But the children's institution and its variations can only be, even under the best of circumstances, an imperfect answer to the problems of an imperfect society. And in the face of fading ideals and blistering imperfections, the institution, for a growing number of children, offers, as Joyce Ladner was cited in chapter 3, "a safer, better refuge than the current alternatives—foster care or a return to the biological family."[25]

Our Will, as both veteran and director of institutional life, said it simply in the previous chapter: "I tried to get my staff to understand that people are not crates. If it has to be an institution at least make the 'i' a small one."

TODAY'S CHILDREN: TODAY'S TROUBLES

Ladner joins a number of other leaders in the field of child welfare in rethinking the possible benefits of institutions and orphanages (among an array of other services) in response to the dire and mounting problems of today's youngsters. Cynthia Mayer, in a recent article,[26] cites a legislator, a judge, a social work educator, and Child Welfare League official who recommend the orphanage as a solution to the doubling of the number of abused and neglected children in the past decade. By the end of the next decade, according to the Orphan Project of New York City, more than 80,000 otherwise healthy children in the United States will have lost their mothers to AIDS.[27]

Although these growing numbers should put us on guard about the weight and spread of the problem, they cannot be added up to the sum of their appalling meanings and significance. Caught in our daily routines, most of us rarely come face to face with the actual conditions suffered by these children. News clips give us a glimpse of one horror of childhood or another and then quickly move on to yet another kind of catastrophe. These conditions pose more lasting threats to society that will outstrip the emergencies of these immediate problems.

Over the years required to complete this study of children of an earlier era, I became increasingly beset by the growing and unrelenting assault of daily news stories about the children of these times—those involved in grade school shootings, street gang warfare, prostitution, and the like. These conditions, dreadful enough, began to take on even more deadly shades as the perpetrators, through some peculiar psychological reasoning, were themselves transformed into victims, helpless and even innocent casualties of their circumstances. Comparing the worlds of then and now, it seemed as if an almost surreal progression had occurred in which the virtues, the standards, the culture that defined an earlier moral reality had become lost or twisted. If moral language hadn't changed much, its standards and expectations for civility had, along with a bland acceptance of amoral tendencies. In his article previously cited,[28] Moynihan deplores the fact that crime and homelessness and abandonment and abuse and other horrors have now been *normalized*. He adds that violence in all forms, the "unrestrained lashing out at the whole social structure is not only expected; it is very near inevitable."

When it comes to moral issues, sometimes small, commonplace events can offer sharper contrasts than large sets of comparative statistics or sociological analyses. To illustrate the inching decay of moral values let us recall Israel's story described in the previous chapter. It is not the moral virtue of his wartime heroics that we should consider, but the melodrama of the smuggled *condom* that earned that sixteen-year-old both inquisition and punishment: possession of a condom then aroused fears of depravity, shame, and vice. Certainly the costs of this forbidding Victorianism can be argued. But the argument fades somewhat in the light of the present where condoms are freely distributed to youth even younger than was Israel. With sexual activity no longer subject to moral restraint, all that can be hoped is that their use might at least abate the frequency of disease and pregnancy.

This decay also dilutes our hopes and expectations about how far we can go to reclaim troubled children. Traditional means of identifying and defining the problems of children and adolescents seem to have given way to more clumsy, gross, and inclusive categories. To be sure, diagnostic and statistical manuals have not been discarded and the controversial medical-diagnostic program itself still claims its authority. Nonetheless, it has become more common to talk about the abused, homeless, "crack," throwaway, dropout, latchkey, streetwise, and other rough categories. But these labels tell us less about the anguish of the special child than they do about the might of crushing social problems in which these clumps of children are entangled. They have even less to suggest about the healing, learning, and understanding the young people require.

True, these are observations of a veteran of a safer past, of the legendary, nostalgic days of unlocked front doors, goodwill, and one's share of guilt when certain morals were violated. At its best, group care served as a moralizing influence. I propose that the institution can again—and now, in many settings actually does—serve the same purposes, given the way moral values have caved in so egregiously. Already desperation has created "boot camps," military-like stockades, as an alternative to the harsher penal institution and as a means for resocializing and remoralizing school dropouts and first offenders. The evolution of such measures is a belated reaction to the multitudes of floundering young people who lack internal controls and dependable values that, for whatever reasons, neither family, community, church, schools, nor society could provide. Perhaps such hard discipline and retraining would not be necessary if secure havens were available to them at an earlier age. Ladner[29] pleads that these children deserve more in the form of permanency in what she chooses to call "the orphanage," a small-scale, caring institution that can offer children a place they can count on for nurture. Ladner grieves that "it is hard for people of liberal instinct—myself included—to prescribe a remedy for other people's children that we would not choose for our own. But no one would prescribe the current set of destructive alternatives to which so many children are being consigned. We need to get our priorities straight. Whose rights come first? The parents'? The 'system's'? Or the child's?"

There is something to be noted in the growing debate on the institution or orphanage as a solution to these grievous problems. The pros and cons of the debate are largely the positions of adult theorists and specialists. Ira Schwartz, for example, takes the affirmative side of the question, Does institutional care do more harm than good?,[30] maintaining there is no scientific (i.e., quantitative-empirical) evidence of their value. These positions, however, give little attention to the critical matter of the child's rights and the child's thoughts about the value of institutional life.

The themes of this study—derived from the heartfelt, real-life experiences of people who have endured institutional life—and the thoughts of other former inmates cited in these pages (Charles Aring, Hyman Bogen, Michael Sharlitt, for example), consider the orphanage not as intrinsically "good," "desirable," or "flawless," but necessary, restorative, and effective, especially in the absence of "normal" survival needs. And perhaps the last is the essential point.

What needs to be asked is what the institution, a home, means to the essential authority—the child who lacks a home, parents, guidance—the necessities for survival. "It was a mitzvah there was a place to go," as one of the elders put it.

Therefore, I was not surprised to hear similar thoughts spoken by young people, modern counterparts of the subjects of this study. I sought out the dozen recent graduates of an institution, Good Will-Hinckley (Hinckley, Maine), where the "Good Will Idea of Religion, Home, Education, Discipline, Industry, and Recreation" is not far removed from the mission of the Rochester Home. There is at least one important distinction, however: where the Home's wards were casualties of what were then called "acts of God" (and the occasional desertion), the present graduates were bruised by the irresponsible, abusive, forsaking dispositions of their caretakers. As well, they were harmed by their own flagrant behavior or, as Andrea put it, by "goofing off and ruining my life. . . . My parents were never home . . . I was home alone, seven or eight years old with no one to talk to. I would do things at school just to get the adults mad so they would call my house and I could have someone to talk to. Here, at Good Will, there is always an adult who will listen."

Scott's life after graduation is still a bit out of focus, but far more in his control than it was prior to his entry into the institution: "Before I got here, I was a little punk . . . figured I'd end up in prison like the rest of my family. Here they've given me a family, they've taught self respect and self esteem . . . I'll be the first person in my family to go to college. To tell the truth I'll be the first person in my family to graduate from high school!"

Gentle and poised Jen abhors any suggestion of being a victim. Her account of her younger years is closed, over. Her new life is involved with her studies at a small private women's college that granted her a scholarship: "When I was in elementary school, all this abuse was happening to me, but nobody noticed. You always think eventually it'll end but it never does. Everything from the time I was little until I came here was all downhill. I thought everything was my fault. Coming here was the biggest right decision in my life."

These are, to be sure, the kinds of "success stories" that find their way onto the pages of fund-raising appeals by social service organizations. It would be foolish to assume that all present-day wards fare that well, given the enormous odds that have piled up in their short lives—the consequences of their own confusion and wrongdoing; their psychological or psychiatric classifications; their caste as wards of state, social, or correctional agencies; the absence or instability of their families; separation from communities; and stigma, to name an odd few. Still, if we can forsake the myopia of a "cost-benefit" mentality or the demand for quantifiable "proofs" according to some arbitrary measure (e.g., rates of psychiatric admissions, welfare applications), we might consider the more inexact and qualitative benefits these children might acquire—learning about one's worth, obligations, hopes, for example—as members of the community of what now are called "Homes" or "Schools" or "Centers." It is not just that some of the boys and girls "do good," it is that they and others can now "think good." Whether, when, or how they are able to reconstruct their lives, they are perhaps more equipped to reconsider their lives, the consequences of their plans and actions, and what might fortify their resilience and ability to master the odds they face. Under the best of circumstances, they might learn to discover their own strengths instead of remaining a *problem*, a case needing cure, treatment, or management.

RECOMMENDATIONS

So far, the argument is rhetorical, but, I hope, coherent and reasonable. If institutions do serve a special function for these troubled children, one deserves to ask: how would it take shape in terms of mission, philosophy, policy, and program? Because of the number of unique variables that express, among countless other factors, the locale and community, the specific problems of children needing care, the attitudes of citizenry, funding and support (private or public), resources, staff, whether religious or secular, and so on, an all-embracing prescription for a specific institution would be about as beneficial as were the cure-all elixirs of former days.

I can, however, underscore certain principles that lend themselves as guides to the structural and operational design and plan of a special program. The fundamental postulate, derived from and securely rooted in this study of the Children's Home, is this: a "bottom-up," "inside-out" or what is now known as a "social systems" orientation should balance or, even better, inform the structural and programmatic scaffolding that gives form to the institution.

More plainly, the preceding pages bear ample evidence that what made the Children's Home "work"—serve as a source of growth for its members—was not the imposed regulations, routines, and programs alone. It was the deep-rooted culture and creative enterprise shared by the children that enveloped the bare bones of the asylum with life and meaning.

Mastery comes from within the child or from what can be shared among the group. One cannot be "empowered," that is, invested with mastery, by some one or some thing for, if that's how it works, one could equally be "disempowered" by the greater power. As we have witnessed in the accounts of the Home's children, resiliency, innate or acquired, allows for survival and strength. It is not gained or learned like a cool set of lessons; more likely resiliency is fortified by the hard times, the struggle with conflicting conditions—paradox or consistency, hypocrisy or reliability, cynicism or trust, freedom or oppression, and so on—that are bound to arise at one time or another in any congregation of people.

A "bottom-up" or "systems" perspective[31] also requires that managers and staff of the institution do not just plan *for*, provide *for*, and oversee their wards; rather, and this is the critical point, planning *with*, deciding *with*, and doing *with* are what make the difference, as Dr. Bernstein proved at the turn of the century. To the extent possible, considering the amount of control a structure requires, goals are shared rather than imposed; trust, caring, respect, and the preservation of one's dignity are sincerely demonstrated; and flexibility and regard for the prevailing culture, patterns, and dynamics of the group that make up the ordinary routines of daily life take precedence over protocol.

Nowadays, the buzzword "empowerment," overused and often misapplied, sidesteps the central issue that most clearly marks the institution: the concentration of power. It is safe to say that the unfashionable *patriarchy* of the past has been replaced with the modern, utilitarian bureaucracy—well meaning, but still "top-down" in control and governance.

Along with Martin Wolins' recommendations drawn from his study of international child-care settings,[32] I want to add the axioms that follow from the "bottom-up" principle and circumstances of group care.

EXPECTATIONS. Wolins speaks of expectations as "ironically obvious" in group care and, as the epigraph introducing chapter 3 shows, they were certainly apparent to the community of children of the Rochester Home. Children who might profit from group or institutional care frequently have been confused by the incoherent expectations imposed on them or bewildered by their absence. Clearly stated and consistent sets of expectations endow the child with something comparable to the detailed maps provided by travel services: not only do they show how to get from here to there, but what one might encounter along the way and find on arrival. As a motive for building resilience, Wolins found that more successful settings do not concede the idea of failure: from the outset, the youngster is helped to anticipate and take part in rewarding outcomes.

INDIVIDUAL HELP. Positive expectations alone are not sufficient when it comes to helping children suffering grief, fear, or the consequences of behavior problems. When social or psychological services are called for, the child should be seen as an individual but, at the same time, a vital member of his or her community of peers. The individual helping process will be enhanced by awareness of the influences, resources, relationships, and values of his or her milieu.

PEER INFLUENCES. Many of our elderly alumni speak in almost tribal terms of their early affiliations and identifications with their fellow wards; vestiges of these significant relations still remain. In terms of personal development, resilience depends on and draws from peer relations. The peer group in group care must be understood as an organism in its own right with its own life, ethos, stages, rules, and moral imperatives. Thus, at any one time, it might, for any one member, be enriching or defeating; it can enhance personhood or, just as likely, neutralize or diminish it. The intent to understand the individual child will fall short without reference to the unfolding drama within the groups wherein the youngster lives out a certain role.

SOCIAL LEARNING. The significance of peer groups and the dynamics of institutional life together affirm that an ongoing process of social learning is the genesis of effective growth and resilience. Including socialization, but more than just the learning of social norms and rules, social learning is a deliberate process of gaining knowledge and experience that exploits, makes the most of, the social and interpersonal characteristics of the particular setting.[33] Social learning involves goal setting, value learning, the acquisition of necessary problem-solving skills, and the encouragement and development of creative talents.

CONTINUITY. Placement in an institution has what some might consider troubling overtones of permanency and unconditionality. Almost paradoxically, as Wolins says, the sense of permanency is more constructive than open-endedness or unpredictability. To the children of the Home, 27 Gorham Street was, hard and fast, *their home,* the place where they lived and belonged, where they could learn, where rules were known. As case-hardened as it was, the Home was the source of their identity and sense of stability. This sense of stability would be undermined by the kind of misplaced solicitude for the child that tells him or her, "Just put up with it for awhile—it's only for the time being."

SOCIAL INTEGRATION. There is a crucial need for the institution as a community to be integrated within its larger community and society. It was the recognition of this dynamic, the immeasurable meaning and influence that the Jewish community and its people held for the children, that compelled me to broaden the scope of this study beyond the immediate boundaries of the children's lives. Such connections and involvements are not as probable nowadays because of zoning restrictions or the inflexible reluctance of neighborhoods to accept even a small group-care facility in their environs. Still, to avoid the futility of work with children within the unnatural, sequestered institution, even artificial links with real-life communities need to be devised. The residents as well as community-wise staff can be depended on as consultants for planning how these bridges might be built.

ACTIVE LEARNING. Reminiscent of the turn-of-the-century programs of Drs. Reeder and Bernstein (chapter 2), Wolins recommends the importance of socially constructive work that will strengthen confidence and a sense of ownership of one's talents. A more recent study of Israeli programs in fact recommends that *education* and not just care be the organizing concept in residential programs.[34] Such plans cannot be superimposed; the talents, interests, and aspirations of the residents, singularly and in concert, must be taken into account as they are matched with available resources and opportunities.

ADULT ROLE MODELS. If the importance of adult role models is not self-evident, recall the great influence of the unstinting interests of Alfred Hart and other Board and auxiliary members on the children's lives. Too often in the present, adults committed to the work of a particular institution seem to keep their distance. In dining halls, administrators and staff often draw together at their separate table; board members dutifully appear at scheduled meetings but, without a nod to the children whose well-being is their interest, perform their duties and vanish. Such remoteness can only reinforce residents' sense of alienation or their distrust of grownups.

IDEOLOGIES, CREEDS, RITUALS, AND RITES. The melodies of the articles of faith of Judaism and Yiddishkeit ring through this account of institutional life. It would be redundant to say much more about the displaced and aimless child's need for spiritual or credal beliefs: they serve as moral anchors, as value foundations, as a basis for identity and belonging, something worthwhile to believe in for now. Indigenous rituals, ceremonies, and special rites foster the internalization of beliefs and customs.

FOLLOW-UP AND TRANSITION. It is apparent that long- or short-term group care for children should not be used as an exodus from ordinary social living, as a period of social quarantine, followed by a perfunctory return to the community. Nor would this scheme be bettered by a follow-up program that merely checks on the graduate from time to time. The process of transition from care to community begins at the moment the youngster is admitted to the institution; in whatever way programs and policies foster security, learning, self-esteem, and growth *within* the setting, what really counts it is how they augment the child's sense of worth and the strength and ability to deal with the demands of living *outside* the institution, in the community. Although the Children's Home had no official discharge plan (other than at age sixteen you left), transition was eased quite naturally by the Home's sense of community: membership in the Alumni Association and the monthly newsletter allowed for continuity and contact. As well, graduates were encouraged to return to partake of religious services and holiday and other programs. Board members provided employment. And, as some admit perhaps grudgingly, Mr. Hollander was always available to help when problems arose in the years after leaving.

A transition curriculum should shape the orientation of the institution's general mission and program rather than be a separate resource called on when graduation is imminent. Such a scheme provides obvious advantages: it assures graduates that they deserve the same natural rights that are afforded those who depart their families—such as affection and continuity of rich relationships, an ongoing sense of belonging, and, of course, proper access to needed resources.

When a well-working transitional program creates an open-ended exchange between the institution and its graduates, important benefits accrue for all. If the setting has not become a closed system wherein policy, methods, and program are catechized, much can be learned from the alumni's experiences "out there" that can affect what we are doing "in here." Considering that the ultimate purpose of group care is not perpetuating its own existence but preparing youngsters to leave and return to a life of some quality, value, and purpose, the measure of how they are doing on the outside can serve as a yardstick of the program's effectiveness and as a guide to what might need to be modified or strengthened on the inside in response to the changing demands of a turbulent society.

From the perspective of a "bottom-up" understanding of group care, the values of these principles are summed up in the following:

THE NARRATIVE. The last word about effective care is not contained in the abstract realms of professional theorizing, planning, and method. It does not come out of the scientific methods of research that quantifies, surveys, or does internal or external audits. It is not the product of the ruminations of committees, panels, or task forces that authoritatively determine what is good, right, correct, or therapeutically proper for other people. To be sure, words and ideas that are instructive, insightful, and most of all, helpful can be found in all these well-intentioned deliberations.

The last word is the story people create and how that story defines their lives and aspirations. I recorded my first insight into the nuclear importance of the narrative in the opening chapter: "The stories, the autobiographies, that the graduates of the Home shared with me so willingly destroy the psychological myth that we are destined to go on ever harvesting the fruits of seeds planted in our earlier lives . . . we will be witness to the varied and extraordinary ways people were and are able to interpret their histories and weave their distinctively personal stories in a manner that preserves dignity and integrity . . . that creates a sense of mastery and worth."

One of the former wards said, "I had to make it. I had to be somebody." Another said it straight out: "You have to be a mensch." And that, after all, captures the main and central purpose of group care for children: to make possible personhood, civility, citizenship, membership—menschkeit.

IN MEMORIAM

In 1978 Barbara Myerhoff, an anthropologist, published her remarkable and touching study of elderly Jews, survivors, who frequented the Senior Citizens' Center in Venice, California. For me, the book held many poignant meanings. One, my father, David, played pinochle every Tuesday at the Center with cronies who were part of Myerhoff's study; the memory remains of the time, years ago, when it was my burden to have to greet him at the Center one day with the telling of the sudden death of his daughter, my older sister. Myerhoff's book serves as an inspiration and standard of excellence for this study of the Children's Home. My aim was to translate this experience, as Myerhoff did with her own, into a style that would be accessible to most readers. Barbara Myerhoff's death was most untimely.

Whether this Myerhoff story is apocryphal is not important. It seems that she was having a difficult time launching her study because of her questions (and what had been my questions, as well) about research with people whose lives and histories held such intimate connections with her own. The director of the Center finally approached her, cautioning that if she didn't get started soon, the population in which she was interested would soon die off. This warning was an ever-present and urgent force in my work with my elderly companions. But over the years of this inquiry, it was inevitable that some of my respondents and old friends would pass on. And so this special tribute and expression of gratitude for their wise and thoughtful observations, for allowing me to share their sentiments and memories of bygone years.

Joseph Avnet	1988
Ruth Clifton Edmonds	1993
Stanley Goldblatt	1989
Sue Rolick Handlin	1993

Finally, the circle would not be completed without special remembrance of a small group of kids, my first friends. Together, we raised pigeons, white rats, and turtles. Together, we solved a few carnal mysteries, sharing more imagination than facts about girls and the forbidden thing called "s-x." Together, a few of us skipped a good part of a semester's classes; there were certain curricular penalties but some mighty good extracurricular delights. Together we hiked and played games that no one today would recognize. Together, we more than survived our adolescence. Individually, we each tasted the successes of adulthood. But sadly, as I discovered when I returned to Rochester, not only

In Memoriam

Gorham Street was gone but their lives all too prematurely had come to an end.
I thank them for great and lasting memories that inspired this book.

Arnold Barzman
Haskell Hollander
Michael Joffe
Louis Maroz
Manny Zeitler

NOTES

1. HOME AND COMMUNITY

1. S. E. Rosenberg, *The Jewish Community in Rochester, 1883–1925* (New York: Columbia University Press, 1954), 52.

2. N. M. Cowan and R. S. Cowan, *Our Parents' Lives* (New York: Basic Books, 1989), 211.

3. Ibid., 211.

4. Ibid., 216.

5. Rosenberg, *The Jewish Community in Rochester*, 166.

6. Letter from Ruth Kolko Lebovics, May 1990, about life on Joseph Avenue.

7. D. Hartman, *A Living Covenant: The Innovative Spirit in Traditional Judaism* (New York: The Free Press, 1988).

2. ORPHANAGES: ORIGINS

1. See, for example, S. W. Downes and M. W. Sherraden, "The Orphan Asylum in the Nineteenth Century," *Social Service Review* 57, no. 2 (June 1983): 272–90; and D. J. Rothman, *The Discovery of the Asylum: Social Order and Disorder in the New Republic* (Boston: Little, Brown, 1971).

2. C. E. Silberman, *A Certain People: American Jews and Their Lives Today* (New York: Summit Books, 1985), 138.

3. W. Manchester, "The Diary of H. L. Mencken," *The New York Times Book Review* (4 February 1990), 33.

4. J. Boswell, *The Kindness of Strangers* (New York: Pantheon Books, 1988).

5. See E. Simpson, *Orphans: Real and Imaginary* (New York: Weidenfeld & Nicolson, 1987) for a discussion of the symbolism of orphanhood in literature, autobiography, and myth.

6. David Guralnik of Cleveland, Ohio, a noted expert on the Yiddish language, generously provided these definitions of the term "orphan."

7. "Honor thy father and thy mother, that thy days may be long upon the land which the Lord thy God giveth thee" (Exodus 20:12). "Cursed be he that dishonoreth his father or his mother" (Deuteronomy 27:16).

8. Boswell, *The Kindness of Strangers*.

9. R. A. Greenberg and W. P. Piper, *The Writings of Jonathan Swift* (New York: W. W. Norton, 1973), 504–06.

10. Simpson, *Orphans*, 136.

11. M. J. Morton, "Homes for Poverty's Children," *Ohio History* 98 (1989): 5–22.

12. Henry W. Thurston's book, *The Dependent Child*, published in 1931 by the New York (now Columbia) School of Social Work, a classic for its time, is the background for the discussion of child care in America. Sections of Thurston's book were based on

the significant monograph, *The Care of Destitute, Neglected, and Delinquent Children* (New York: Arno Press, 1971), originally written in 1900 by Homer Folks, then Secretary of the New York State Charities Association. Sections of Folks' monograph are included.

13. D. D. Jackson, "It Took Trains to Put Street Kids on the Right Track Out of the Slums," *Smithsonian* 17, no. 5 (August 1986): 94–104; and L. Wheeler, "The Orphan Trains," *American History Illustrated* (December 1983), 10–24.

14. M. B. Jones, "Crisis of American Orphanages, 1931–1940," *Social Service Review* 53, no. 4 (1989): 613–29.

15. N. F. Cott, ed., *Roots of Bitterness* (New York: E. P. Dutton, 1972), 141.

16. Thurston, *The Dependent Child*, 42.

17. Ibid., 45.

18. M. Grossberg, *Governing the Hearth: Law and the Family in Nineteenth-Century America* (Chapel Hill: University of North Carolina Press, 1985), 267.

19. Thurston, *The Dependent Child*, 50.

20. Ibid., 73–74.

21. J. Bernard, *The Children You Gave Us: A History of 150 Years Service to Children* (New York: Jewish Child Care Association of New York, 1973). For a detailed account of the founding of Hebrew Orphan Asylum, see H. Bogen, *The Luckiest Orphans* (Champaign: University of Illinois Press, 1992).

22. Bernard, *The Children You Gave Us*, 7.

23. Ibid., 10.

24. Thurston, *The Dependent Child*, 66–68.

25. Ibid., 69.

26. Bernard, *The Children You Gave Us*, 17.

27. M. Sharlitt, *As I Remember* (privately published, 1959).

28. Ibid., 17–18.

29. Ibid., 32.

30. Ibid., 32–33.

31. L. Ashby, *Saving the Waifs: Reformers and Dependent Children, 1890–1917* (Philadelphia: Temple University Press, 1984), 7.

32. Ibid., 4.

33. W. J. Doherty, *A Study of the Results of Institutional Care* (New York: Department of Child-Helping of the Russell Sage Foundation, 1915).

34. Ibid., 5.

35. Obituary, *New York Times*, 14 October 1934.

36. R. R. Reeder, *How Two Hundred Children Live and Learn* (New York: Charities Publication Committee, 1910), 75–76.

37. L. B. Bernstein, "Some Modern Tendencies in Jewish Orphan Asylum Work," *American Hebrew* 84 (1908): 149–51.

38. Sharlitt, *As I Remember*, 37–39.

39. Bernstein, "Some Modern Tendencies," 150.

40. R. N. Bellah, R. Madsen, R. Sullivan, A. Swidler, and S. Tipton, *Habits of the Heart* (Berkeley: University of California Press, 1985). See also A. MacIntyre, *After Virtue* (Notre Dame: University of Notre Dame Press, 1981).

41. *Fifty-sixth Annual Report of the New York Juvenile Asylum to the Legislature of the State and the Board of Aldermen of the City of New York for the Year 1907*, 17.

42. Interview with Dr. Leonard Mayo, 18 June 1990.

43. H. H. Hart, *Cottage and Congregate Institutions for Children* (New York: Russell Sage Foundation, 1910).

44. J. Ladner, "A Way Out—Orphanages for Children in Crisis," *The Cleveland Plain Dealer,* 18 November 1989, 1D.

45. C. D. Aring, "In Defense of Orphanages," *The American Scholar* (Autumn 1991), 575–79.

3. THE HOME: ORIGINS AND MEANINGS

1. See, for example, Cowan and Cowan, *Our Parents' Lives,* and S. S. Weinberg, *The World of Our Mothers* (Chapel Hill: University of North Carolina Press, 1988).

2. Garson Rockoff, *Gersha of Grosovo* (privately published, 1938).

3. I. Howe, *World of Our Fathers* (New York: Harcourt Brace Jovanovich, 1976), 71.

4. Rosenberg, *The Jewish Community in Rochester.*

5. Based on Ida Klein Richardson, "A Study of Institutional and Foster Care for Dependent Children" (unpublished master's thesis, University of Rochester, 1938). Richardson was an employee of the Jewish Orphan Asylum of Western New York.

6. Ibid., 16.

7. Ibid., 19–20.

8. Ralph Waldo Emerson, "Self Reliance," in *Essays: First Series* (Washington: National Home Library Foundation, 1932).

9. *The American Hebrew,* 28 May 1909, 101.

10. Ibid., 30 July 1909, 335.

11. *Annual Report of Jewish Orphan Asylum Association of Western New York* (1917 and 1918).

12. *Rochester Democrat and Chronicle,* 21 July 1928, 13.

13. *Report of the Jewish Children's Bureau of Rochester,* 1933, 6.

14. *The Story of Our Home,* Brochure of Rochester Jewish Children's Home, 1921.

15. Mrs. Stathe, a secretary long employed by Jewish Family Service of Rochester, recalled that the records were lodged in a back corner of the agency. I am indebted to her and the unknown individual who gave time and effort to organize these records in separate folders.

16. A. Hart, *Higher Ideals* (privately published, 1934).

4. FACTS AND FIGURES

1. Weinberg, *The World of Our Mothers,* 138.

2. Howe, *The World of Our Fathers,* 177–78.

3. *The Rochester Jewish Ledger,* 18 June 1987.

4. Biographical information excerpted from *Bulletin of the Rochester Museum of Arts and Sciences,* September 1938, 153.

5. Ibid.

6. *Home Review,* August 1943.

7. Letter from Mort Kolko, October 1992.

8. See for example G. M. Gottfried, "Qualitative Analysis of Child-Caring Experience of Religious Sisters" (Ph.D. diss., Case Western Reserve University, 1992).

5. "IT WASN'T FAMILY BUT IT WAS HOME"

1. From ongoing correspondence with Hannah Hastman, 1990.
2. Rosenberg, *The Jewish Community in Rochester*, 208–09.
3. This observation corresponds with Carol Gilligan's interpretation in *In Another Voice* (Cambridge: Harvard University Press, 1982).

6. LIFE IN THE HOME: VIEWS FROM THE INSIDE

1. H. Harlow, *Learning to Love: Selected Papers* (New York: Praeger, 1986); R. Spitz, *The First Year of Life* (New York: International Universities Press, 1965); and J. Bowlby, *Separation* (New York: Basic Books, 1973).
2. See for example A. Hertzberg, *The Jews in America* (New York: Simon & Schuster, 1989); Cowan and Cowan, *Our Parents' Lives;* Howe, *The World of Our Fathers;* and Weinberg, *The World of our Mothers.*
3. Hartman, *A Living Covenant.*
4. L. Rosten, *Treasury of Jewish Quotations* (New York: McGraw-Hill, 1972), 252–53.
5. E. Erikson, "Play and Actuality," in *A Way of Looking at Things: Selected Papers of Erik Erikson from 1930 to 1980*, ed. S. Schlein (New York: W. W. Norton, 1987), 311–38.

7. LIVES AND MEANINGS

1. L. K. Cass and C. B. Thomas, *Childhood Pathology and Later Adjustment* (New York: John Wiley & Sons, 1979).
2. G. Sorin, *A Time for Building; The Third Migration, 1880–1920*, vol. 3 of the series *The Jewish People in America* (Baltimore: The Johns Hopkins University Press, 1992), 14.
3. Pen name of Sholom Rabinowitz, whose best-known character is Tevye the Milkman in the musical *Fiddler on the Roof*, derived from Aleichem's short story.
4. Among the increasing number of works on the narrative as a medium for understanding lives, patterns, and cultures are E. Sherman, *Reminiscences of Self in Old Age* (New York: Springer-Verlag, 1991); D. E. Polkinghorne, *Narrative Knowing in the Human Sciences* (Albany: State University of New York Press, 1988); and J. Bruner, "Life as Narrative," *Social Research* 54 (1987): 11–32.
5. The Civilian Conservation Corps (CCC), created as part of the New Deal during the Great Depression, drew unmarried men to military-like camps where they worked in forest preservation, built flood barriers, and so forth. They received a monthly stipend of $30 along with board and medical care. The program ended in 1942.
6. J. Bowlby, *Loss: Sadness and Depression* (New York: Basic Books, 1980).
7. W. Goldfarb, "Effects of Psychological Deprivation in Infancy and Subsequent Stimulation," *American Journal of Psychiatry*, 102 (1945): 18–33.
8. Silberman, *A Certain People: American Jews and their Lives Today*, 139–41.

8. CLOSINGS

1. Rosenberg, *The Jewish Community in Rochester*, 210–11.
2. See C. McGovern, *Services to Children in Institutions* (Washington: National Conference on Catholic Charities, 1948), and C. G. Petr and R. N. Spano, "Evolution of Social Services for Children with Emotional Disorders," *Social Work* 35, no. 3 (1990): 228–34.

3. C. Geertz, *Local Knowledge* (New York: Basic Books, 1983).

4. Cited in F. Randall, "Why Scholars become Storytellers," *New York Times Book Review,* 29 January 1984, 31.

5. S. E. Taylor, "Adjustment to Threatening Events: A Theory of Cognitive Adaptation," *American Psychologist* 38, no. 11 (1983): 1161–73.

6. E. J. Anthony and B. J. Cohler, eds., *The Invulnerable Child* (New York: Guilford Press, 1987), x. See also S. Hauser, M. B. Vieyra, A. M. Jacobson, and D. Wertleib, "Family Aspects of Vulnerability and Resilience in Adolescence," in *The Children in Our Times: Studies in the Development of Resiliency,* ed. T. F. Dugan and R. Coles (New York: Brunner/Mazel, 1989), 109–12.

7. See for example William Golding, *Lord of the Flies* (New York: Coward-McCann, 1962); Henry Roth, *Call it Sleep* (Paterson, N.J.: Pageant Books, 1960); J. D. Salinger, *Catcher in the Rye* (Boston: Little, Brown, 1951); and the early prototype, Horatio Alger, *Strive to Succeed* (New York: Holt Rinehart & Winston, 1967).

8. G. E. Vaillant, *The Wisdom of the Ego* (Cambridge: Harvard University Press, 1993), 284–87.

9. G. Sheehy, "The Victorious Personality," *New York Times Magazine,* 20 April 1986, 26.

10. Anthony and Cohler, *The Invulnerable Child.*

11. John Dewey, *Human Nature and Conduct* (New York: Henry Holt & Co., 1922), 278–79.

12. P. Blanchard, *The Child and Society* (New York: Longmans Green & Co., 1928), 267.

13. Dewey, *Human Nature and Conduct,* 258.

14. D. P. Moynihan, "Defining Deviancy Down," *American Scholar* (Winter 1993), 17–30.

15. See for example M. Rutter, "Psychosocial Resilience and Protective Mechanisms," *American Journal of Orthopsychiatry* 57, no. 3 (1987): 316–31; and N. Garmezy, "Stress Resistant Children: The Search for Protective Factors," in *Recent Research in Developmental Psychology,* ed. J. Stevenson (Oxford: Pergamon Press, 1985).

16. J. V. Jackson, "Relational Resilience," (paper presented in Stone Center Colloquium Series, Wellesley College, Wellesley, Mass., April 1992).

17. Sharlitt, *As I Remember.*

18. D. Mack, "Are Parents Bad for Children," *Commentary* (March 1994), 30–35.

19. A. Kadushin, "Institutions for Dependent and Neglected Children," in *Child Caring: Social Policy and the Institution,* ed. D. M. Pappenfort, D. H. Kilpatrick, and R. W. Roberts (Chicago: Aldine, 1973), 145–76.

20. Ibid., 171.

21. M. Wolins, "Some Theoretical Observations on Group Care," in *Successful Group Care,* ed. M. Wolins (Chicago: Aldine, 1974), 7–35.

22. Ibid., 8.

23. Bogen, *The Luckiest Orphans,* 225.

24. Ibid., 248.

25. Ladner, "A Way Out."

26. C. Mayer, "Some Child Advocates Urge Orphanages' Return," *Boston Globe* 15 March 1994.

27. *Time,* 11 April 1994, 22.

28. Moynihan, "Defining Deviancy Down," 26–27.

29. Ladner, "A Way Out."

30. I. M. Schwartz, "Does Institutional Care Do More Harm Than Good? Yes," in *Controversial Issues in Child Welfare,* ed. E. Gambrill and T. J. Stein (Boston: Allyn and Bacon, 1994), 276–78.

31. See for example H. Goldstein, *Social Work Practice: A Unitary Approach* (Columbia: University of South Carolina Press, 1973), 185–275.

32. Wolins, "Some Theoretical Observations," 288–89.

33. H. Goldstein, *Social Learning and Change* (Columbia: University of South Carolina Press, 1981). See also M. Goldstein, "LINK: A Campus Based Transition Program for Non-College Bound Youth with Mild Disabilities," *Career Development for Exceptional Children* 16, no. 1 (1993): 75–85, for an example of use of social learning with problem adolescents.

34. J. Beker and D. Magnuson, *Residential Education as an Option for At-Risk Youth,* a special issue of *Residential Treatment for Children and Youth* 13, no. 3 (1995).

SELECTED BIBLIOGRAPHY

CHILD CARE AND ORPHANAGES: HISTORY

Ashby, L. *Saving the Waifs: Reformers and Dependent Children, 1890–1917.* Philadelphia: Temple University Press, 1984.

Bernard, J. *The Children You Gave Us: A History of 150 Years Service to Children.* New York: Jewish Child Care Association of New York, 1973.

Bernstein, L. B. "Some Modern Tendencies in Jewish Orphan Asylum Work." *American Hebrew* 84 (1908): 149–51.

Blanchard, P. *The Child and Society.* New York: Longmans Green & Co., 1928.

Bogen, H. *The Luckiest Orphans.* Champaign: University of Illinois Press, 1992.

Boswell, J. *The Kindness of Strangers.* New York: Pantheon Books, 1988.

Cott, N. F., ed. *Roots of Bitterness.* New York: E. P. Dutton, 1972.

Dewey, J. *Human Nature and Conduct.* New York: Henry Holt & Co., 1922.

Doherty, W. J. *A Study of the Results of Institutional Care.* New York: Department of Child-Helping of the Russell Sage Foundation, 1915.

Downes, S. W., and M. W. Sherraden. "The Orphan Asylum in the Nineteenth Century." *Social Service Review* 57, no. 2 (June 1983): 272–90.

Folks, H. *The Care of Destitute, Neglected, and Delinquent Children, 1909.* New York: Arno Press, 1971.

Friedman, Reena Sigman. *These Are Our Children: Jewish Orphanages in the United States, 1880–1925.* Brandeis Series in American Jewish History, Culture, and Life. Hanover: University Press of New England, Brandeis University Press, 1994.

Goldfarb, W. "Effects of Psychological Deprivation in Infancy and Subsequent Stimulation." *American Journal of Psychiatry* 102 (1945): 18–33.

Gottfried, G. M. "Qualitative Analysis of Child-Caring Experience of Religious Sisters." Ph.D. diss., Case Western Reserve University, 1992.

Grossberg, M. *Governing the Hearth: Law and the Family in Nineteenth-Century America.* Chapel Hill: University of North Carolina Press, 1985.

Hart, H. H. *Cottage and Congregate Institutions for Children.* New York: Russell Sage Foundation, 1910.

Jackson, D. D. "It Took Trains to Put Street Kids on the Right Track Out of the Slums." *Smithsonian* 17, no. 5 (August 1986): 94–104.

Jones, M. B. "Crisis of American Orphanages, 1931–1940." *Social Service Review* 53, no. 4 (1989): 613–29.

McGovern, C. *Services to Children in Institutions.* Washington: National Conference on Catholic Charities, 1948.

Morton, M. J. "Homes for Poverty's Children." *Ohio History* 98 (1989): 5–22.

Petr, C. G., and R. N. Spano. "Evolution of Social Services for Children with Emotional Disorders." *Social Work* 35, no. 3 (1990): 228–34.

Reeder, R. R. *How Two Hundred Children Live and Learn.* New York: Charities Publication Committee, 1910.

Richardson, Ida Klein. "A Study of Institutional and Foster Care for Dependent Children." Unpublished master's thesis, University of Rochester, 1938.

Rothman, D. J. *The Discovery of the Asylum: Social Order and Disorder in the New Republic.* Boston: Little, Brown, 1971.

Sharlitt, M. *As I Remember.* Privately published, 1959.

Simpson, E.. *Orphans: Real and Imaginary.* New York: Weidenfeld & Nicolson, 1987.

Thurston, H. W. *The Dependent Child.* New York: New York School of Social Work, 1931.

Wheeler, L. "The Orphan Trains." *American History Illustrated* (December 1983), 10–24.

Zmora, Nurith. *Orphanages Reconsidered: Child Care Institutions in Progressive Era Baltimore.* Philadelphia: Temple University Press, 1994.

GROUP CARE: CURRENT ISSUES

Aring, C. D. "In Defense of Orphanages." *The American Scholar* (Autumn 1991), 575–79.

Beker, J., and D. Magnuson. *Residential Education as an Option for At-Risk Youth.* A special issue of *Residential Treatment for Children and Youth* 13, no. 3 (1995).

Bellah, R. N., R. Madsen, R. Sullivan, A. Swidler, and S. Tipton. *Habits of the Heart.* Berkeley: University of California Press, 1985.

Bowlby, J. *Separation.* New York: Basic Books, 1973.

———. *Loss: Sadness and Depression.* New York: Basic Books, 1980.

Cass, L. K., and C. B. Thomas. *Childhood Pathology and Later Adjustment.* New York: John Wiley & Sons, 1979.

Kadushin, A. "Institutions for Dependent and Neglected Children." In *Child Caring: Social Policy and the Institution,* edited by D. M. Pappenfort, D. H. Kilpatrick, and R. W. Roberts. Chicago: Aldine, 1973, 145–76.

Ladner, J. "A Way Out—Orphanages for Children in Crisis." *The Cleveland Plain Dealer,* 18 November 1989, 1D.

Mayer, C. "Some Child Advocates Urge Orphanages' Return." *Boston Globe,* 15 March 1994.

Moynihan, D. P. "Defining Deviancy Down." *American Scholar* (Winter 1993), 17–30.

Schwartz, I. M. "Does Institutional Care Do More Harm than Good? Yes." In *Controversial Issues in Child Welfare,* edited by E. Gambrill and T. J. Stein. Boston: Allyn and Bacon, 1994, 276–78.

Spitz, R. *The First Year of Life.* New York: International Universities Press, 1965.

Wolins, M. "Some Theoretical Observations on Group Care." In *Successful Group Care,* edited by M. Wolins. Chicago: Aldine, 1974, 7–35.

JEWS IN AMERICA

Cowan, N. M., and R. S. Cowan. *Our Parents' Lives.* New York: Basic Books, 1989.

Hartman, D. *A Living Covenant: The Innovative Spirit in Traditional Judaism.* New York: The Free Press, 1988.

Hertzberg, A. *The Jews in America.* New York: Simon & Schuster, 1989.

Howe, I. *World of Our Fathers.* New York: Harcourt Brace Jovanovich, 1976.

Rosenberg, S. E. *The Jewish Community in Rochester, 1883–1925.* New York: Columbia University Press, 1954.

Silberman, C. *A Certain People: American Jews and Their Lives Today.* New York: Summit Books, 1985.

Sorin, G. *A Time for Building: The Third Migration, 1880–1920.* Vol. 3 of the series *The Jewish People in America.* Baltimore: The Johns Hopkins University Press, 1992.

Weinberg, S. S. *The World of Our Mothers.* Chapel Hill: University of North Carolina Press, 1988.

NARRATIVE MEANINGS

Bruner, J. "Life as Narrative." *Social Research* 54 (1987): 11–32.

Geertz, C. *Local Knowledge.* New York: Basic Books, 1983.

Polkinghorne, D. E. *Narrative Knowing in the Human Sciences.* Albany: State University of New York Press, 1988.

Randall, F. "Why Scholars become Storytellers." *New York Times Book Review* 29 January 1984, 31.

Sherman, E. *Reminiscences of Self in Old Age.* New York: Springer-Verlag, 1991.

RESILIENCE AND SOCIAL LEARNING

Anthony, E. J., and B. J. Cohler, eds. *The Invulnerable Child.* New York: Guilford Press, 1987.

Erikson, E. "Play and Actuality." In *A Way of Looking at Things: Selected Papers of Erik Erikson from 1930 to 1980,* edited by S. Schlein. New York: W. W. Norton, 1987, 311–38.

Garmezy, N. "Stress Resistant Children: The Search for Protective Factors." In *Recent Research in Developmental Psychology,* edited by J. Stevenson. Oxford: Pergamon Press, 1985.

Goldstein, H. *Social Work Practice: A Unitary Approach.* Columbia: University of South Carolina Press, 1973.

———. *Social Learning and Change.* Columbia: University of South Carolina Press, 1981.

Goldstein, M. "LINK: A Campus Based Transition Program for Non-College Bound Youth with Mild Disabilities." *Career Development for Exceptional Children* 16, no. 1 (1993): 75–85.

Hauser, S., M. B. Vieyra, A. M. Jacobson, and D. Wertleib. "Family Aspects of Vulnerability and Resilience in Adolescence." In *The Children in Our Times: Studies in the Development of Resiliency,* edited by T. F. Dugan and R. Coles. New York: Brunner/Mazel, 1989, 109–12.

Jackson, J. V. "Relational Resilience." Paper presented in Stone Center Colloquium Series, Wellesley College, Wellesley, Mass., April 1992.

Rutter, M. "Psychosocial Resilience and Protective Mechanisms." *American Journal of Orthopsychiatry* 57, no. 3 (1987): 316–31.

Sheehy, G. "The Victorious Personality." *New York Times Magazine,* 20 April 1986, 26.

Taylor, S. E. "Adjustment to Threatening Events: A Theory of Cognitive Adaptation." *American Psychologist* 38, no. 11 (1983): 1161–73.

Vaillant, G. E. *The Wisdom of the Ego.* Cambridge: Harvard University Press, 1993.

Index

Howard Goldstein is Professor
Emeritus, Case Western Reserve
University, Cleveland. He received
his master's and doctorate of social
work degrees from the University of
Southern California. In addition to
many articles and essays, his publications include *Social Work Practice:
A Unitary Approach* (1973), *Social
Learning and Change* (1981), *Creative
Change* (1984), and *Il Modelo Cogni-
tivo Umanistico nel Servizio Sociale*
(1988).